From Paradise
to the
Promised Land

Other Books by T. Desmond Alexander

Abraham in the Negev: A Source-Critical Investigation of Genesis 20:1–22:19

From Paradise to the Promised Land

An Introduction to the Main Themes of the Pentateuch

T. Desmond Alexander

Baker Books

A Division of Baker Book House Co
Grand Rapids, Michigan 49516

© 1995 by T. Desmond Alexander

Published in 1998 by Baker Books
a division of Baker Book House Company
P.O. Box 6287, Grand Rapids, MI 49516-6287
UNITED STATES

Second printing, August 2000

First published in 1995 by
Paternoster Press
P.O. Box 300
Carlisle, CA3 0QS
UNITED KINGDOM

Printed in the United States of America

Library of Congress Cataloging-in-Publication Data

Alexander, T. Desmond.
    From paradise to the promised land: an introduction to the main themes of the Pentateuch/T. Desmond Alexander.
        p. cm.
    Originally published: Carlisle, U.K. : Paternoster Press, 1995.
    Includes bibliographical references and index.
    ISBN 0-8010-2174-X (paper)
    1. Bible. O.T. Pentateuch–Criticism, interpretation, etc.
I. Title.
BS1225.A542   1998
222'.1061–dc21   97-44915

For information about academic books, resources for Christian leaders, and all new releases available from Baker Book House, visit our web site:
http://www.bakerbooks.com

TO
MARGARET
BOB AND JANET

Contents

Abbreviations

AB	Anchor Bible
ABD	Anchor Bible Dictionary
ABR	*Australian Biblical Review*
AJBI	*Annual of the Japanese Biblical Institute*
AOAT	*Alter Orient und Altes Testament*
AUSS	*Andrews University Seminary Studies*
BA	*Biblical Archaeologist*
BARev	*Biblical Archaeology Review*
BASOR	*Bulletin of the American Schools of Oriental Research*
Bib	*Biblica*
BibBh	*Bible Bhashyam*
BJRL	*Bulletin of the John Rylands Library*
BR	*Biblical Research*
BRev	*Bible Review*
BS	*Bibliotheca Sacra*
BSC	Bible Student's Commentary
BT	*The Bible Translator*
BTB	*Biblical Theology Bulletin*
BZ	*Biblische Zeitschrift*
BZAW	Beihefte zur Zeitschrift für die alttestamentliche Wissenschaft
CBC	Cambridge Bible Commentaries on the New English Bible
CBQ	*Catholic Biblical Quarterly*
CTJ	*Calvin Theological Journal*
CTM	*Concordia Theological Monthly*
CTQ	*Concordia Theological Quarterly*
CurTM	*Currents in Theology and Mission*
DSB	The Daily Study Bible
EgT	*Eglise et Théologie*
Enc	*Encounter*
ETL	*Ephemerides Theologicae Lovanienses*
EvQ	*The Evangelical Quarterly*
ExpTim	*The Expository Times*
FOTL	Forms of Old Testament Literature
GTJ	*Grace Theological Journal*
HS	*Hebrew Studies*

HTR	*Harvard Theological Review*
HUCA	*Hebrew Union College Annual*
IBS	*Irish Biblical Studies*
ICC	International Critical Commentary
Imm	*Immanuel*
Int	*Interpretation*
ITC	International Theological Commentary
ITS	*Indian Theological Studies*
JAAR	*Journal of the American Academy of Religion*
JANES	*The Journal of the Ancient Near Eastern Society*
JANESCU	*The Journal of the Ancient Near Eastern Society of Columbia University*
JAOS	*Journal of the American Oriental Society*
JBL	*Journal of Biblical Literature*
JETS	*Journal of the Evangelical Theological Society*
JJS	*Journal of Jewish Studies*
JNES	*Journal of Near Eastern Studies*
JNSL	*Journal of Northwest Semitic Languages*
JRT	*Journal of Religious Thought*
JSOT	*Journal for the Study of the Old Testament*
JSOTSS	Journal for the Study of the Old Testament Supplement Series
JSS	*Journal of Semitic Studies*
JTS	*Journal of Theological Studies*
JTSoA	*Journal of Theology for Southern Africa*
LB	*Linguistica Biblica*
LTJ	*Lutheran Theological Journal*
MT	Masoretic Text
NCB	New Century Bible
NETR	*The Near East School of Theology Theological Review*
NICOT	New International Commentary on the Old Testament
NIV	New International Version
NT	New Testament
Or	*Orientalia*
OT	Old Testament
OTL	Old Testament Library
OTM	Old Testament Message
OTS	*Oudtestamentische Studiën*
PIBA	*Proceedings of the Irish Biblical Association*
PSTJ	*The Perkins Journal*
RB	*Revue biblique*
Rel	*Religion*
ResQ	*Restoration Quarterly*
SBLMS	Society of Biblical Literature Monograph Series
SJT	*Scottish Journal of Theology*
StudBT	*Studia Biblica et Theologica*
SVT	Supplements to Vetus Testamentum
SwJT	*Southwest Journal of Theology*
TB	*Tyndale Bulletin*
TD	*Theology Digest*

TDOT	Theological Dictionary of the Old Testament
Them	*Themelios*
TI	Text and Interpretation
TJ	*Trinity Journal*
TNB	*The New Blackfriars*
TOTC	Tyndale Old Testament Commentaries
VR	*Vox Reformata*
VT	*Vetus Testamentum*
WBC	Word Biblical Commentaries
WEC	Wycliffe Exegetical Commentary
WTJ	*The Westminster Theological Journal*
ZAW	*Zeitschrift für die alttestamentliche Wissenschaft*

Preface

The idea of writing an introductory guide to the first five books of the Bible arose following a brief period of teaching Asian theological students in Singapore in 1990. My experience there confirmed what had already been evident to me in Ireland: first-year students of theology and religious studies have a very limited understanding of the basic contents of the Pentateuch. While most are vaguely familiar with the better known stories of Genesis and Exodus, few could claim to have a clear understanding of the Pentateuch as a whole. What was lacking was a book suited to the needs of such students which could provide a good introduction to the actual text.

While introductory books on the Pentateuch exist, they are generally too concerned with issues of authorship and sources, too outdated in their approach to the interpretation of the text, or too technical in their presentation. Consequently, the intention of the present volume is to (a) focus on the actual content of the Pentateuch as it has been received, rather than on hypothetical sources, (b) draw on the best insights of recent research into Hebrew narrative techniques regarding the meaning of the text, and (c) be as straightforward as possible in presentation, without being non-academic in substance.

To these a further aim has been added which strictly speaking is not required in an introduction to the Pentateuch. I have sought to outline briefly the many ways in which the Pentateuchal material is taken up and used in the New Testament. Two factors have encouraged me to do this. First, many students of theology and religious studies approach the Pentateuch from a Christian perspective and are naturally interested in how this material relates to the beliefs and practices of the NT church. Secondly, and perhaps more importantly from a purely academic perspective, the New Testament documents reveal how the Pentateuchal texts were understood in a period and culture much closer to that of the Pentateuch than our own. It is interesting, therefore, to compare the NT understanding of the Pentateuch with that of twentieth-century readers. To what extent is there agreement on the meaning of the text?

Having stated the general aims of this study, some further comments may help clarify the approach adopted here. Although this volume seeks to explain the contents of the Pentateuch, it is not a verse-by-verse commentary on the text. Many good commentaries already exist. Yet, while they are especially helpful in explaining shorter units of material — for example, individual verses or chapters — they tend by their very nature to atomise the text into small units. Consequently, they may fail to highlight themes which are spread across entire books, especially when such themes do not appear to be of particular importance in any single passage. Studying the biblical texts by means of commentaries can be compared to looking at the separate pieces of a jigsaw puzzle. While we may find something of interest in each piece, it is only when all the pieces are put together that we get the complete picture. It is this larger picture which we wish to pursue in this study of the Pentateuch.

Not only may commentaries fail to give a complete picture, but they may even unintentionally give a distorted picture. By atomising the text and considering each unit independently there is ever present the danger of misinterpreting these shorter passages. This may be illustrated using the jigsaw puzzle again. Examined on its own a single piece may appear to show one thing, yet when placed alongside its matching pieces it may reveal something quite different. Obviously a knowledge of the wider context is vital for understanding the individual components of something larger. Unfortunately, scholars have not always appreciated adequately the dangers which exist in interpreting a biblical book unit by unit without taking into account sufficiently the broader context.

Alongside these shortcomings must be placed a further and much more fundamental problem. For the past two centuries the academic study of the Pentateuch has been dominated by methods which seek primarily to elucidate how the present text came into being. Encouraged by the hope of uncovering the pre-history, both literary and oral, of the received text, scholars have expended an inordinate amount of time and energy on developing the methodologies of source and form criticism. Several consequences of this should be noted. First, these methods have resulted in the text being dissected in a variety of ways. No longer is the Pentateuch generally considered to be a literary unity — which, regardless of how it was composed, it now is. Rather it is commonly viewed as a collection of literary documents and/or oral accounts linked together by editorial (or redactional) additions. Significantly, most scholarly research on the Pentateuch has sought to (a) elucidate the existence of these hypothetical sources, (b) explain the process by which they were combined to form the present text, and (c) relate the existence of these earlier sources to the history and religious development of the Israelites prior to the final composition of the Pentateuch in the exilic or post-exilic period. While scholarly endeavours to address these issues have not been wanting, the past two decades have witnessed a substantial rejection of results which for several preceding generations of scholars seemed assured. At the present time much uncertainty exists regarding how and when the Pentateuch was composed. It could even be asked, given our present knowledge, if it is actually possible to determine with any confidence the process by which the Pentateuch was composed.[1]

A second consequence of biblical scholarship focusing its resources on the pre-history of the text has been a failure to elucidate clearly the meaning of the Pentateuch in its received form. Relatively little has been said about the final form of the Pentateuch. Most studies have focused on the sources underlying the present text. Three factors have possibly contributed to this lack of interest in the Pentateuch as received. (a) In the past source critical studies have generally portrayed the earliest stages in the composition of the Pentateuch as the most interesting and important. In marked contrast the contribution of the final editor was considered to be insignificant. Consequently, there was little incentive to examine in detail his work. Moreover, when scholars did consider it they generally looked only at the material assigned specifically to him. It was believed to be inappropriate or unnecessary to consider the entire Pentateuch in order to establish an understanding of the final redactor. (b) Many scholars appear to have assumed that a detailed explanation of the pre-history of the Pentateuch reveals all that needs to be known about the text as received. However, as R. Polzin has rightly observed:

> Traditional biblical scholarship has spent most of its efforts in disassembling the works of a complicated watch before our amazed eyes without apparently realising that similar efforts by and large have not succeeded in putting the parts back together again in a significant or meaningful way.[2]

We need to recognise that the Pentateuch as we now have it is much more than the sum of its component parts. (c) Scholars have tended to consider the study of the Pentateuch in its final form as less demanding, and, therefore, of less academic value, than the investigation of its hypothetical sources. Such reasoning is fallacious, however. The value of the final form of the Pentateuch should not be judged on the basis of the ease or otherwise of studying it. Rather, such study should be undertaken because of the inherent importance of the text as we have received it. While some still fail to take seriously the study of the Pentateuch in its final form, it is encouraging to see that many more scholars now recognise the importance of doing so.

Even if one grants the importance of source and form criticism, there are various arguments which strongly favour an approach that gives prominence to the final form of the Pentateuch. First, this is the form in which the text has been received. Whatever the process by which it was composed, it is now a unified literary work.[3] Even if, as seems very likely, various sources were used in its composition, it must be recognised that the final editor, whoever he (or she?) may have been, appropriated all the source material as his own and used it to compose the present narrative which begins in Genesis and continues through to the end of Deuteronomy. It is, therefore, essential to view the entire Pentateuch as reflecting the outlook of the final editor, not merely those portions which are normally assigned to the last editorial stage. Second, a detailed and comprehensive study of the Pentateuch in its final form must have priority in sequence over the approaches of source and form criticism. It is methodologically unsound to explore the pre-history of the text without having established a clear understanding of how the present text is constructed as a literary work. To do otherwise is to set the cart before the horse. Similarly, on pedagogical grounds, it is surely improper to expect students to appreciate and apply critical methods before they have understood the content and literary structure of the received text. Unfortunately, it is frequently the case that students are introduced to scholarly opinions regarding the process by which the text was composed, without knowing what the text itself is saying. Third, new literary approaches to the study of Hebrew narrative provide fresh insights into the meaning of many Pentateuchal passages. Frequently, these insights offer new ways of approaching problems which in the past were resolved by resorting to source or form critical solutions. Scholars in general are now more confident about taking seriously the present integrity of the text. Fourth, a clear understanding of the final form of the Pentateuch is important if we are to appreciate how it influenced later writers. The writers (and earliest readers) of the NT were all pre-critical in their understanding of the Pentateuch; they did not think in terms of different literary and/or oral sources underlying the text, each reflecting different theologies. For them the Pentateuch was a single entity; this was how they understood and interpreted it. All of these reasons argue for an approach which treats with respect the received text of the Pentateuch.

From the preceding comments it will be evident that the position adopted in this book differs markedly from that often followed by others. The object of our study is the final form of the Pentateuch as it has been handed down to us in the Hebrew text. Little attention will be given to possible sources or the process of composition; much has been written on this elsewhere. Rather it is our aim to map out the terrain of the Pentateuch as it now stands by drawing attention to its main features; in a work of this kind it is not possible to comment on every detail. To enable the reader to assimilate the contents of the Pentateuch more easily the material has usually been approached book by book. Sometimes attention is focused on major themes running throughout entire books. Elsewhere shorter blocks of material which deal with specific subjects are examined. The intention has been to allow the text to determine the approach which seems most appropriate. For example, the themes of 'seed', blessing and land run throughout the book of Genesis.[4] On the other hand, the account of the building of the tabernacle dominates most of the final third of the book of Exodus. When blocks of material are examined I have tried to follow the natural divisions of the text.

Although the text locates the events described in particular periods of history, it does not specify any date for the final composition of the material. Because of continued uncertainty about the actual date of the final redaction, and to make the work as broadly acceptable as possible, no attempt has been made to date the composition of the Pentateuch or to interpret it against a specific historical background.

References to the rest of the OT have been kept to a minimum. To have included all the relevant material would have added considerably to each chapter and shifted the focus of the book from the Pentateuch to the OT as a whole.

To provide an up-to-date introduction to the Pentateuch I have sought to include within this work the best insights of contemporary studies. However, to keep the presentation as straightforward as possible I have deliberately avoided engaging in detailed critique of the views of other scholars. Three factors have persuaded me to adopt this approach. First, to interact meaningfully with all that has been said would have increased dramatically the size of this present volume and have taken it far beyond an introductory guide. Second, since many writers discuss the Pentateuchal material from the perspectives of source and/or form criticism, it has to be recognised that they are addressing very different issues from those being examined here. While this does not automatically exclude the possibility of meaningful interaction, it does make it much more difficult to achieve. Moreover, it would require a detailed discussion of past and contemporary views on the process by which the Pentateuch was composed; something which would have added considerably to the length of this volume. Third, the primary purpose of this study is to focus the reader's attention on the text of the Pentateuch itself, rather than on the writings of contemporary scholars. For those interested in following up individual topics I have included suggestions for further reading at the end of the book.

Acknowledgements

A number of chapters have appeared in print elsewhere; these have been modified to varying degrees to conform to the overall pattern of presentation adopted in this volume. Chapter 2 appeared as 'Genealogies, Seed and the Compositional Unity of Genesis', *Tyndale Bulletin* 44.2 (1993) 255–270. Chapter 5 was first published as 'Abraham Re-assessed Theologically: The Abraham Narrative and the New Testament Understanding of Justification by Faith' in R.S. Hess, P.E. Satterthwaite and G.J. Wenham (eds.) *He Swore an Oath: Biblical Themes from Genesis 12–50* (Cambridge; Tyndale House, 1993) 7–28.[5] Much of the material in chapters 6–10 was first published in 1994 in the *New Bible Commentary (21st Century Edition)* and I am grateful to the publishers, IVP, for permission to reproduce this in a modified form.

Except where otherwise indicated, biblical quotations are from the NIV, and all biblical references follow the English rather than the Hebrew scheme of numeration. All Hebrew words have been transliterated according to standard practice; however, where for the ordinary reader the transliteration does not reflect the actual pronunciation of a Hebrew word I have added this in parenthesis.

For providing me with helpful observations on sections of this study I am grateful to Claude-Bernard Costecalde, Ian Hart and Albert Ong. For reading the manuscript in its entirety and suggesting many improvements I am especially grateful to John Brew, James McKeown and Alan Millard. Needless to say they can in no way be held responsible for any shortcomings which remain. I wish also to express my thanks to the staff of

The Paternoster Press for their valuable assistance in the final stages of the production of this book. Finally, words cannot express the debt I owe to my wife Anne for her interest and encouragement in all my labours.

SOLI DEO GLORIA

NOTES

1. It is enlightening to consider the ongoing debate regarding the composition of the Synoptic Gospels. Even when NT scholars have the opportunity of comparing three similar and closely related texts, major and minor differences of opinion still exist as to how these texts were composed. If such is the case when we have a number of texts to compare, what would the situation be like if only one text were extant? Would, for example, NT scholars using only Matthew's Gospel have arrived at a solution similar to that proposed by proponents of Markan priority? Probably not. If doubts continue to exist over the composition of the gospels, how can OT scholars with any confidence delineate correctly the sources underlying the books of the Pentateuch? Surely the time has arrived (a) to acknowledge seriously the limitations of source and form criticism and (b) to avoid the construction of theories regarding the development of Israelite history and religion which rest primarily on the supposed sources of the Pentateuch.

2. R. Polzin, ' "The Ancestress of Israel in Danger" in Danger', Semeia 3 (1975) 82–83.

3. By this I mean that the books of Genesis to Deuteronomy are linked together in such a way that, while they may be viewed as separate entities, it is clear that they have been made dependent upon one another with the later books presupposing a knowledge of the earlier ones and the earlier books being incomplete without the addition of the later ones. In this connection it should also be noted that on this basis the Pentateuch itself is incomplete and is linked in a special way to the material in Joshua to 2 Kings.

4. While I have tended to restrict the study of particular themes to individual books, it should be noted that certain themes cannot be restricted in this way (e.g., land, descendants, blessing). While such themes tend to be dominant in one book, they may, however, be picked up elsewhere in the Pentateuch as important motifs echoing earlier material. As such they are important indicators to the overall unity of the Pentateuch in its received form.

5. 2nd edition, Grand Rapids/Carlisle: Baker/Paternoster, 1994.

MAPS
AND
DIAGRAMS

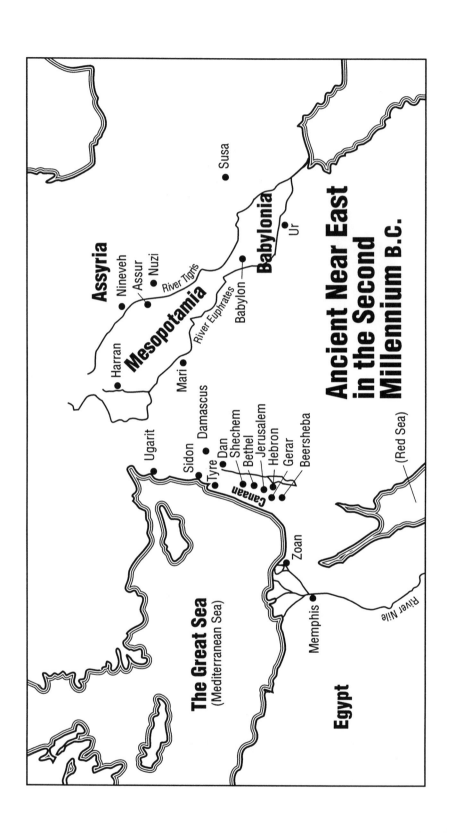

Ancient Near East in the Second Millennium B.C.

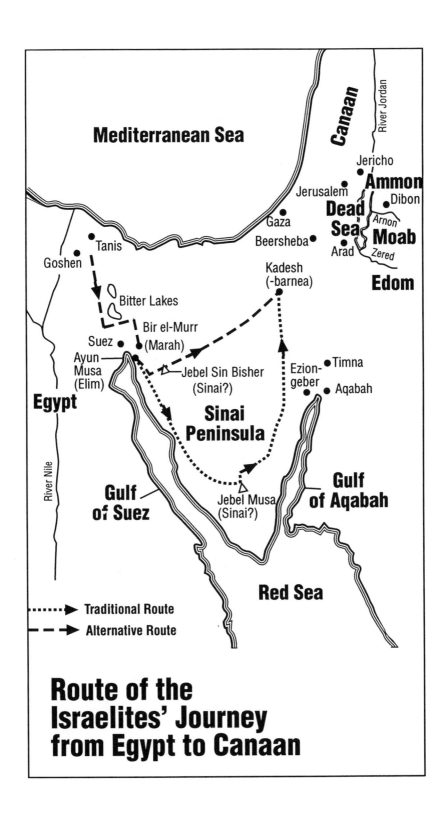

Mediterranean Sea

Canaan

River Jordan

Jericho

Ammon

Jerusalem

Dibon

Gaza

Dead
Sea

Arnon

Beersheba

Moab

Arad

Zered

Tanis

Goshen

Kadesh
(-barnea)

Edom

Bitter Lakes

Bir el-Murr
(Marah)

Suez

Ayun
Musa
(Elim)

Jebel Sin Bisher
(Sinai?)

Ezion-
geber

Timna

Aqabah

Egypt

Sinai
Peninsula

River Nile

Gulf
of Suez

Jebel Musa
(Sinai?)

Gulf
of Aqabah

Red Sea

······▶ Traditional Route

– – ▶ Alternative Route

Route of the
Israelites' Journey
from Egypt to Canaan

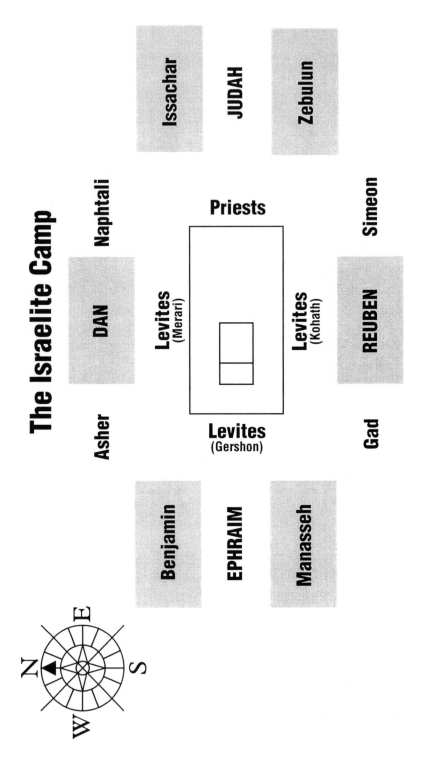

The Israelite Camp

Schematic floor plan
of the Tabernacle

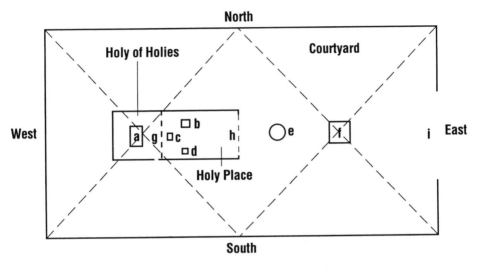

North

Holy of Holies   Courtyard

West   East

Holy Place

South

a. Ark of the Covenant b. Table for the loaves c. Altar for incense
d. Lampstand e. Basin f. Altar for offerings g. Curtain h. Screen i. Entrance

Cut-away diagram of the Tabernacle

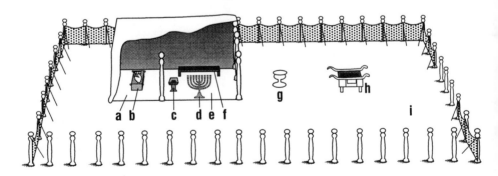

a. Holy of Holies b. Ark of the Covenant c. Altar for incense d. Lampstand
e. Holy Place f. Table for the loaves g. Basin h. Altar for offerings i. Courtyard

[1]

A Brief Survey of the Pentateuch

The first five books of the Bible (Genesis, Exodus, Leviticus, Numbers, Deuteronomy) have played an important role in the formation of the religious outlook of Jews, Christians, and, perhaps to a lesser extent, Moslems. Although contemporary scholars differ as to the identity of their author(s) and their date(s) of composition, it is clear that they were already important religious texts by the 4th century BC. Thus, for a period of at least two thousand four hundred years, these books, often referred to as the Pentateuch or Torah, have exercised a profound influence, both knowingly and unknowingly, on countless millions of human beings. For this reason, if for no other, they deserve close and careful scrutiny.

Yet in spite of their influence many people have but a casual acquaintance with the contents of the Pentateuch, being familiar with only the better known episodes which comprise but a small part of the whole. This present volume seeks to guide the reader through the Pentateuch, outlining its contents and main themes, and exploring the significance of the ideas and concepts found within it.

Before embarking on a fuller study of the individual books which compose the Pentateuch, it may be helpful to provide a brief overview of the whole, highlighting in the process those themes which will be examined in more detail in subsequent chapters.

As presently constituted the Pentateuch consists of five books which have been composed in the light of each other to form a single unit. Various factors reveal the interdependence of the individual books. Primary among these is the plot which begins in Genesis and flows logically through to the end of Deuteronomy. Certain threads run through this plot uniting the different books. For example, Genesis introduces the idea that the land of Canaan is promised to the descendants of Abraham, Isaac and Jacob. The fulfilment of this promise sets the agenda for the books of Exodus to Deuteronomy, and beyond. The deliverance of the Israelites from Egypt is recorded in the first half of Exodus. Their subsequent journey through the wilderness towards Canaan is narrated in Exodus, Leviticus and Numbers. The account of this journey ends in Deuteronomy with the people located on the plains of Moab east of the Jordan. Similarly, much of the Pentateuch is united by the figure of Moses, with the opening chapters of Exodus describing his birth and the final chapter of Deuteronomy recording his death.[1]

Apart from threads which run through a number of books, adjacent books are normally linked closely together. For example, Genesis concludes with Joseph making the sons of Jacob swear that they will carry his bones up from Egypt (Gen 50:25). The exact fulfilment of this request is picked up later in Exod 13:19. Whereas instructions for the setting apart of priests are given in Exodus 29, the account of their appointment comes later in Leviticus 9. While Num 20:12 anticipates the death of Moses outside the promised land, the account of this happening comes in Deuteronomy 34.

Even Genesis, which is generally viewed as being quite different in character from the remaining books of the Pentateuch, is clearly integrated into the overall plot. Apart from the promises to the patriarchs which are very significant, the whole of the Joseph story provides an essential link between the stories of Abraham, Isaac and Jacob living in Canaan and the account of their descendants being divinely rescued from Egypt.

In the light of these observations it is important not to dismiss lightly the present unity of the Pentateuch. Although the books of Genesis to Deuteronomy are made up of very diverse components, which may superficially give the impression of disunity, someone has skilfully brought them together to form a narrative plot which exhibits considerable unity. In its present form the Pentateuch is clearly a unified work.

The basic plot of the Pentateuch may be outlined as follows. At the outset human beings are created in order to enjoy a special relationship with God and to exercise authority on his behalf over the earth. However, the disobedience of Adam and Eve alienates them from God, and as a result they are punished by divine curses and expelled from Eden. While the early chapters of Genesis concentrate mainly on the terrible consequences of these initial developments, the rest of Genesis, from chapter 12 onwards, moves forward with the hope that humanity may yet be reconciled to God.

Central to this hope of reconciliation are the divine promises made to Abraham. The importance of these should not be underestimated; they set the agenda for all that follows in the rest of the Pentateuch and beyond. From a careful study of the Abraham narrative it is clear that there are two main promises. First, there is the promise that through the 'seed' of Abraham 'all nations on earth will be blessed' (Gen 22:18). Although of primary importance for reversing the consequences of what took place in the Garden of Eden, this promise remains unfulfilled by the conclusion of the Pentateuch. Significantly, within Genesis this promise is specifically linked to a future royal lineage which will be descended from Abraham through his great-grandson Judah.[2]

Other divine promises to Abraham centre on the establishment of a great nation. These promises generally emphasise two aspects of this: descendants and land. Significantly, God guarantees to Abraham through a special covenant that his descendants will be given the land of Canaan some four centuries later. For this promise of nationhood to be fulfilled various developments must occur and these are recorded in the rest of the Pentateuch. Interestingly, however, the promise of nationhood, like the promise of blessing for the nations of the earth, remains unrealised by the end of Deuteronomy.

The two promises of blessing and nationhood are closely linked. The blessing of the nations can occur only after the promise of nationhood has been fulfilled. This explains why the Pentateuch concentrates on the establishment of Abraham's descendants as a nation in the land of Canaan. Indeed, because so much attention is given in the Pentateuch to this latter promise, it tends to overshadow the promise of blessing. It is clear, however, that the establishment of Israel as a nation is part of the process by which the nations of the earth will be blessed. This is apparent from the fact that God expects Israel to be 'a kingdom of priests and a holy nation' (Exod 19:6). At the heart of this is the idea that Israel will exercise a mediatorial role between God and other peoples.

Much of the Pentateuch is devoted to the setting apart of Israel as a nation distinct from all others. The primary purpose behind this is that Israel should be an example of how true communion with the LORD may be achieved. Consequently, the Pentateuch anticipates in part a return to the kind of divine/human relationship enjoyed in Eden, with the Israelites living in harmony with the LORD on land blessed by him. Yet, although God comes to dwell in the midst of Israel, the people still do not experience the same intimate communion with him that Adam and Eve originally enjoyed. While the making of the Sinai covenant and the building of the tabernacle brought about an important advance in God's relationship with one section of humanity, this did not give the Israelites immediate and unhindered access to the divine presence. Barriers still existed between God and the people. Only Moses enjoyed what might be described as intimate contact with God. Thus, God's relationship with Israel as a people merely anticipated that which was yet to come in conjunction with the blessing of the nations of the earth.

Another aspect of Israel's mediatorial role was that she should exemplify the kind of righteousness required by God. To this end she was to be a holy nation governed by God's decrees and laws. The importance of this is highlighted in the covenant obligations given first at Sinai and repeated later on the plains of Moab. Israel as a nation was expected to reflect God's holy and perfect nature to the other nations of the earth.

Although the Pentateuch emphasises that the Israelites were especially privileged by the fact that the LORD had revealed himself to them through signs and wonders in Egypt and then later through verbal communication at Sinai, it also highlights their waywardness in failing to trust and obey God completely. In spite of all that he did for them, their shortcomings are a recurring feature of the narrative in Exodus to Numbers. Moreover, even as they stood poised to possess the promised land, the LORD reminded them that, although they would initially enjoy his blessing, they would eventually be unfaithful. As a result they would be exiled from the land and no longer know God's presence in their midst.

This latter observation highlights another important idea within the Pentateuch. The enjoyment of the benefits of the divine promises is linked to a trust in God's ability to fulfil them. Faith in God marked by obedience is highlighted in a variety of ways, both positively and negatively. The absence of faith was responsible for the disobedience of Adam and Eve in the Garden of Eden. Faith was central to the life of Abraham, who is presented as a model for others to follow. Similarly, it was important in the experience of the Israelites in the wilderness. Here, however, it was their frequent lack of faith that is highlighted. Later, in Deuteronomy, Moses encouraged the people to trust and obey the LORD in order that they might take possession of the promised land. While the benefits of the divine promises may be forfeited due to human failure, the promises will ultimately be realised because they originated with God.

Although the Pentateuch gives a very distinctive history of the world from its creation to the arrival of the Israelites on the borders of Canaan, it is much more than a history of what has taken place. The divine promises of nationhood and blessing, which are so important to the development of the plot, remain unfulfilled by the end of Deuteronomy. As a result, the Pentateuch is orientated towards the future. What will become of these promises? To answer this we must look beyond the concluding chapters of Deuteronomy.[3] As it stands, the Pentateuch is an unfinished story.

NOTES

1. In the light of the importance of Moses it is hardly surprising that an early and enduring title for the Pentateuch has been 'The Books of Moses'.
2. This is discussed more fully in chapter 2.
3. In the light of this observation it is important to note that the books of Joshua to 2 Kings provide a vital sequel to the Pentateuch.

[2]

The Royal Lineage in Genesis

SUMMARY

The book of Genesis has been carefully composed to focus on a unique family line, starting with Adam and continuing down to the twelve sons of Jacob. This line of 'seed' includes various individuals who all enjoyed a very special relationship with God: Enoch, Noah, Abraham, Isaac, Jacob, Joseph and Judah. Significantly, Genesis anticipates (a) that the descendants of this line will become very numerous and (b) that a royal dynasty will arise from the descendants of Judah.

INTRODUCTION

For many readers Genesis is a collection of unconnected stories interrupted here and there by apparently irrelevant genealogies. Yet the present text has been carefully shaped to highlight the importance of a family lineage which begins with Adam and is traced through to the sons of Jacob. To appreciate this we shall consider first the overall structure of the book and the function of the various genealogies found within it. Next, we shall examine briefly the concept of 'seed' and observe how Genesis deliberately traces a single line of descendants. Finally, we shall draw some conclusions about the nature of this special lineage before briefly observing how it is understood in the New Testament.

THE STRUCTURE OF GENESIS

A quick survey reveals that Genesis consists of narrative sections which are linked together by genealogies. Significantly, many of these narrative sections and genealogies are introduced by similar headings. These occur in 2:4; 5:1; 6:9; 10:1; 11:10,27; 25:12,19; 36:1,9; 37:2.[1] The common element in

6

all of these headings is the Hebrew word *tôlĕdot* which is translated in the NIV as 'account'. The word itself is associated with 'giving birth' and when linked to a person or object refers to what that person or object produces. For example, the initial words of 11:27 could be translated, 'And these were born of Terah'; the NIV has 'This is the account of Terah'.

The *tôlĕdot* headings serve two functions. Firstly, they are like chapter headings in modern books. Some of them introduce major narrative sections, indicating a new stage in the development of the plot. These major sections deal mainly with the lives of Adam, Noah, Abraham, Jacob and Joseph, and they are introduced by the headings in 2:4, 6:9, 11:27, 25:19 and 37:2 respectively. The other *tôlĕdot* headings introduce either linear genealogies (see Diagram A) which list descendants who belong to the central family line (5:1; 11:10), or segmented genealogies (see Diagram B) which provide details about the family members of some of the minor participants in Genesis (10:1; 25:12; 36:1,9). To ensure that the main line of descent is clearly established, segmented genealogies are never used; only linear genealogies are employed (5:1–32; 11:10–26).

DIAGRAM A

A linear genealogy

M gave birth to N	M
	|
N gave birth to O	N
	|
O gave birth to P	O
	|
	P

Secondly, the *tôlĕdot* headings function like a zoom-lens on a camera. They focus the reader's attention on a particular individual and his immediate children. This enables the author of Genesis to trace the fortunes of the main family line without having to follow in detail the lives of all other relatives. In this way Genesis highlights the importance of the lineage which, beginning with Adam, is traced through Adam's youngest son Seth to Noah, the father of Shem, Ham and Japheth. The next stage of the line takes us from Shem to Terah, the father of Abraham, Nahor and Haran. We then move from Abraham to Isaac, from Isaac to Jacob, and, finally, to Jacob's twelve sons.

DIAGRAM B

A segmented genealogy
A gave birth to B,C,D
B gave birth to E,F,G
C gave birth to H,I,J
D gave birth to K,L,M

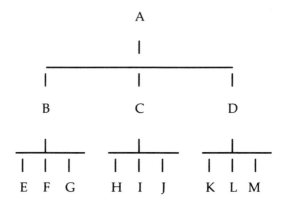

THE CHOSEN 'SEED'

Closely linked to the genealogical structure of Genesis is the frequent use of the Hebrew word *zeraʿ* which is perhaps best translated as 'seed'. Unfortunately, the NIV translates *zeraʿ* using a variety of terms — the most common being 'descendants', 'offspring', 'seed', 'children', 'family', 'grain', 'semen', 'line', 'people'. For this reason the importance of the concept of 'seed' in Genesis is easily missed. *zeraʿ* is a keyword, however, occurring 59 times in Genesis compared to 172 times in the rest of the Old Testament.[2]

Several factors are worth noting briefly about the use of the term 'seed' in Genesis. (a) The Hebrew word *zeraʿ* , like the English word 'sheep', can be either singular or plural; it may denote a single seed or many seeds. An example of the former comes in 21:13 where Ishmael is described as Abraham's 'seed'. On the other hand, in 28:14 *zeraʿ* refers to the descendants of Jacob 'who will be like the dust of the earth'. (b) 'Seed' normally denotes an individual's natural child or children. When Eve gives birth to Seth she comments, 'God has granted me another child (seed) in place of Abel, since Cain killed him' (4:25). In 15:3 Abraham laments the fact that although his heir is Eliezer of Damascus, he is not of his own seed; this reflects the fact that as yet Abraham and Sarah have no child of their own. (c) The Hebrew word *zeraʿ* conveys the idea that there is a close resemblance between the 'seed' and that which has produced it. We see this underlying the comment that plants and trees are to produce seeds 'according to their various kinds' (1:11–12).

THE LINEAGE OF ADAM

When Genesis is viewed as a whole it is very apparent that the genealogical structure and the concept of 'seed' are closely linked in order to highlight a single, distinctive, family lineage (see Diagram C). Moreover, although Genesis concludes by noting that the total seed of Jacob was reckoned as numbering seventy (46:6–27), within this group of seventy special attention is focused on the status given to the descendants of two of Jacob's sons, Joseph and Judah. As we shall observe below, although Joseph's younger son Ephraim receives the blessing of the first-born from his grandfather Jacob (48:1–22), it is to Judah and his descendants that the promise of kingship is given (49:8–12).

When we examine the nature of the main family lineage in Genesis various features are noteworthy. First, the lineage is always traced through male descendants, and all are clearly named.[3] Yet, while it might be expected that the line of 'seed' would always be traced through the eldest son, this is not so. In a number of instances a younger son is given priority over an older brother, and, interestingly, on each occasion the text of Genesis suggests why this occurs. For killing his brother Abel, Cain, the first-born, is passed over in favour of Seth, the third-born (4:1–25). Although Ishmael is Abraham's first-born son, he is excluded from the line of 'seed' because he is the son of Sarah's Egyptian maidservant Hagar (16:1–16; 17:18–21; 21:9–20). Thus, as the divinely intended 'seed' of Abraham, Isaac enjoys priority over Ishmael. While Esau is born before Jacob his secondary position to Jacob is divinely predicted prior to the birth of the twin boys (25:23). Furthermore, the narrator appears to justify this choice by highlighting Esau's attitude towards his birthright, which he sells to Jacob for a pot of red stew (25:29–34), and by the fact that he displeases his parents by marrying two Hittite women (26:34–35).

A more complex situation exists regarding the twelve sons of Jacob, where both Judah, the fourth-born, and Joseph, the eleventh-born son, are privileged before older brothers. On the one hand, the blessing of the first-born is passed on by Jacob to Joseph's family when he blesses his two sons Manasseh and Ephraim (48:1–22). Remarkably, once again the younger son,

DIAGRAM C

The Main Family Lineage in Genesis

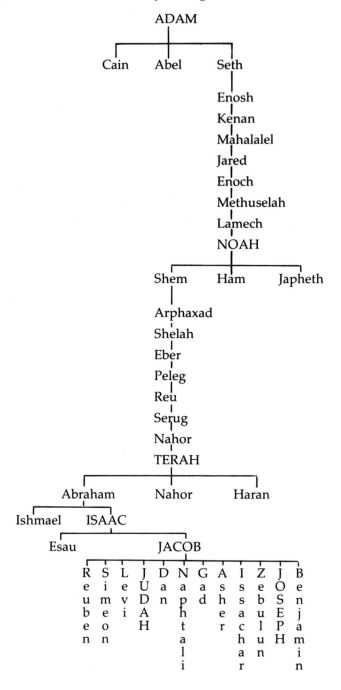

Ephraim, receives the superior blessing. On the other hand, Jacob indicates that the royal line is to be traced through Judah (49:8–12; cf. 1 Chr 5:1–2).[4] Once again the Genesis narrative reveals that the eldest brothers, Reuben, Simeon and Levi, are excluded from enjoying their father's foremost blessing due to certain unseemly actions (35:22; 34:25–30).

Second, it is noteworthy that the central family line exists due to the gracious activity of God. At the outset Eve recognises this following the birth of Seth: 'She named him Seth, saying, "God has granted me another child (seed) in place of Abel, since Cain killed him" ' (4:25). It is, however, in the lives of Abraham, Isaac and Jacob that we see most clearly God's role in sustaining the family line. In the account of Abraham's life one of the first details recorded is that 'Sarai was barren; she had no children' (11:30). As the Abraham story unfolds, God reiterates on various occasions that Sarah will indeed give birth to a son (17:16–21; 18:10–14), and this in spite of the fact that both Abraham and Sarah are well beyond the natural age of having children; Abraham is one-hundred years old (17:17; 21:5) and Sarah ninety (17:17). When at last Sarah gives birth to Isaac, the text specifically states that this is due to divine intervention: 'Now the LORD was gracious to Sarah as he had said, and the LORD did for Sarah what he had promised' (21:1). A similar situation is recorded very briefly in 25:21 regarding Isaac and Rebekah: 'Isaac prayed to the LORD on behalf of his wife, because she was barren. The LORD answered his prayer, and his wife Rebekah became pregnant.' Remarkably, history repeats itself yet again in the case of Jacob, for we learn that his wife Rachel was also barren (29:31). When Rachel eventually gives birth to a child of her own, once again the narrative affirms God's part in this:

> Then God remembered Rachel; he listened to her and opened her womb. She became pregnant and gave birth to a son and said, 'God has taken away my disgrace'. She named him Joseph, and said, 'May the LORD add to me another son' (30:22–24).

All of these examples highlight that God is actively responsible for the continuation of the family line.

Third, the Genesis narrative emphasises the existence of a special relationship between God and individual members of the main family line. We see this in a variety of ways. Sometimes it is highlighted in the briefest of comments. For example, we read that 'Enoch walked with God; then he was no more, because God took him away' (5:24). The *tôlĕdot* heading of Noah is immediately followed by the statement, 'Noah was a righteous man, blameless among the people of his time, and he walked with God' (6:9).[5] Elsewhere the presence of a special relationship is revealed in considerably more detail. This is so in the longer accounts concerning Noah, Abraham, Isaac, Jacob and Joseph. In the cases of Noah and Abraham, God not only reveals future plans but also establishes eternal covenants through both of them. Isaac and Jacob also receive revelations from God confirming, in particular, promises which were previously made to Abraham. Although God never reveals himself directly to Joseph, he enables him to discern future events by interpreting dreams. Furthermore, the account of Joseph's time in Egypt highlights God's providential care of him.

While the members of the main family line enjoy God's favour and blessing, their faults and failures are never disguised. We see Noah becoming drunk (9:20–21), Abraham being less than fully truthful concerning his marriage to Sarah (12:10–13), and Jacob wilfully deceiving his father (27:1–40), to mention the more obvious short-comings. Nevertheless, in spite of such faults, the members of the family line are viewed as more righteous than others. This is perhaps most evident in the case of Noah, who is introduced as 'a righteous man, blameless among the people of his time' (6:9) and who, with his family, is not condemned to destruction by the flood like all other human beings. Abraham's righteousness is highlighted in various ways. It is first mentioned specifically in 15:6 where the narrator comments that 'Abram believed the LORD, and he credited it to him as righteousness'. Later, the extent of Abraham's righteousness is revealed by his willingness to obey God and sacrifice his much loved son Isaac (22:1–19). Although, in comparison to the other patriarchs, relatively little information is given about Isaac the fact that he clearly enjoyed God's favour suggests that he too was viewed as righteous (cf. 26:12–13,23–24). Jacob's relationship with God develops over a long period of time, and although Genesis focuses initially on his deceptive behaviour (27:1–29), we see him eventually taking active steps to rid his household of foreign gods (35:1–5). Like Abraham and Isaac, Jacob too knows God's blessing. Furthermore, all three patriarchs actively worship God by building altars and offering sacrifices (12:7–8; 13:18; 22:9; 26:25; 35:1–7).

Fourth, as noted above, the concept of 'seed' implies a resemblance between the 'seed' and the one who has produced it. In the context of Genesis this suggests that sons will resemble their fathers. The most obvious example of this comes in the record of Isaac's stay in the region of Gerar (26:1–35). Here Isaac's behaviour mirrors closely that of his father. Like

Abraham he pretends that his wife is his sister (26:1–11; cf. 12:10–20; 20:1–18), is involved in a dispute with the inhabitants of Gerar over the ownership of certain wells (26:17–25; cf. 21:22–34), and enters into a covenant with Abimelech (26:26–31; cf. 21:22–34). In a different way, Jacob's sons resemble him in that they too knowingly deceive their father (27:1–29; 37:12–35). Significantly, those elder sons who are overlooked in favour of younger brothers, generally exhibit behaviour which is not in keeping with that expected of the line of seed. For example, Reuben's affair with his father's concubine Bilhah (35:22; cf. 49:3–4) and the murderous actions of Simeon and Levi prevent them from receiving the blessing of the first-born from their father Jacob (34:1–31; cf. 49:5–7).

Members of the main family line are not the only ones in Genesis to share common features; the same is true of others. Cain's murderous actions are repeated by his descendant Lamech (4:19–24). Similarly, among the descendants of Ham, who sinned against his father Noah, we find listed the Canaanites (who include the inhabitants of Sodom and Gomorrah) and the Amorites (10:15–19), all of whom are viewed worthy of divine punishment (cf. 13:13; 15:16; 19:1–29).

Fifth, the 'seed' of the main family lineage is frequently mentioned in the divine promises which are an important feature of the patriarchal stories. Three aspects of these promises deserve special notice. (a) God promises the land of Canaan to the 'seed' of Abraham. This is mentioned specifically when Abraham first arrives in Canaan, 'To your seed I will give this land' (12:7), and repeated on various occasions to Abraham, Isaac and Jacob (13:15; 15:18; 17:8; 22:17; 26:3; 28:13; 35:12; cf. 24:7; 24:60; 28:4; 48:4). On the significance of these promises concerning land, see chapter six. (b) It is frequently stressed that the 'seed' of Abraham will be very numerous.[6] Three images are used to highlight the extent of the 'seed': the dust of the earth (13:16; 28:14), the stars of the heavens (15:5: 22:17; 26:4) and the sand of the seashore (22:17; 32:12). The fulfilment of the promise of numerous descendants, like that of land, clearly lies beyond the book of Genesis, indicating that Genesis merely records the beginning of something which will only be completed later. (c) It is emphasised that through the 'seed' all nations on earth will be blessed (22:18; 26:4; 28:14). This and the promise of numerous descendants will be examined more fully in the next chapter when we consider the theme of blessing in Genesis.

Sixth, there are strong grounds for believing that the main line of descent in Genesis is viewed as a royal lineage. This possibility is implied by the divine promise made to Abraham that 'kings will come from you' (17:6), echoed in a similar statement concerning Sarah that 'kings of peoples will come from her'(17:16). Moreover, although Abraham is never directly designated a king, he is sometimes portrayed as enjoying the status of a king. We see this in his defeat of the eastern kings in chapter 14, in the desire of Abimelech, king of Gerar, to make a covenant with him (21:22–34), and, finally, in the title 'mighty prince' (literally, 'a prince of God') given to him by the Hittite inhabitants of Hebron (23:6).

While there are only a few allusions to kingship in chapters 25–36, these are nevertheless noteworthy. Isaac's importance is reflected in Abimelech's wish to enter into a treaty with him (26:26–31), as he had previously done with Abraham. In a divine promise which echoes chapter 17, Jacob is promised that 'kings will come from your body' (35:11). Finally, the brief comment in 36:31, 'These were the kings who reigned in Edom before any Israelite king reigned', indicates that whoever wrote this either anticipated or already knew of a royal dynasty within Israel.

The subject of kingship is prominent in the Joseph story. At the outset his brothers interpreted Joseph's first dream as implying that he will be a king: 'Do you intend to reign over us? Will you actually rule us?' (37:8). His second dream reinforces this idea (37:9–11), and later we witness the fulfilment when Joseph rises from the obscurity of an Egyptian prison to hold the office of governor of Egypt, second only to Pharaoh (41:39–43).

Although Joseph enjoys the spotlight in chapters 37–50, it is noteworthy that of the other sons of Jacob most attention is focused on Judah.[7] This is particularly so in chapter 38 where we have one of the more unusual episodes in the book of Genesis. The inclusion of this story in Genesis can best be accounted for by noting that it focuses on Judah's reluctance, following the deaths of his sons Er and Onan, to allow Er's wife Tamar to marry Judah's third son Shelah in order to produce 'seed' and so maintain the family line. When Tamar eventually becomes pregnant by deceiving Judah, he is forced to acknowledge the righteousness of her actions (38:26). Significantly, the account concludes by recording the birth of Perez (and his twin brother Zerah) from whom the royal line of David is descended.[8]

Judah's importance is further indicated by the special blessing which he receives from his father in 49:8–12. Without considering every aspect of this blessing, the following points are worth noting. (a) When compared with the other blessings pronounced by Jacob upon his sons, the length and content of

Judah's blessing clearly suggests that he enjoyed a special relationship with his father. Only Joseph receives a comparable blessing. (b) Jacob states that Judah and his descendants will exercise leadership over his other brothers and their descendants (49:8). We see this especially in the comment that 'Your father's sons will bow down to you' (49:8) and in the reference to the sceptre and ruler's staff not departing from Judah (49:10). (c) Jacob anticipates that eventually there shall come in the royal line of Judah one to whom the nations will submit in obedience (49:10) and whose reign will be marked by prosperity and abundance (49:11). Such comments would clearly have been very important for the royal line of David, justifying their claim to rule over the rest of Israel.[9]

CONCLUSION

The entire book of Genesis is clearly composed around a special family line. On the one hand, we are informed that the 'seed' of this lineage will become very numerous and possess the land of Canaan, and, on the other hand, our attention is drawn to one particular line of 'seed' which will become a royal dynasty. Thus, Genesis focuses on both the birth of the nation of Israel and the early ancestry of the Davidic monarchy. In that the nation and the king are of the 'seed' of Abraham, they share a common origin, and, as recipients of the divine promises, a common destiny.

NEW TESTAMENT CONNECTIONS

In the New Testament various passages relate directly or indirectly to the family lineage which we have noted in Genesis. By far the most important connection is that this special line of seed finds its fulfilment in Jesus Christ. Since Genesis anticipates a royal line of seed descended from Judah, it is easy to understand how Jesus, 'the son of David' (cf. Rom 1:3; 2 Tim 2:8), is linked to the 'seed' of Abraham. This is explicitly stated by Paul in his Galatian letter: 'The promises were spoken to Abraham and to his seed. The Scripture does not say "and to seeds", meaning many people, but "and to your seed", meaning one person, who is Christ' (Gal 3:16). The same idea probably underlies other New Testament passages which associate Abraham with David. For example, Matthew's genealogy of Jesus begins with Abraham and is traced downwards through David to Joseph (Matt 1:1–17).[10] In Zechariah's song of praise the arrival of a saviour from the house of David is viewed as the fulfilment of the oath which God swore to Abraham (Luke 1:68–75). In a slightly less obvious way the same link is found in Peter's speech in Acts 3:12–26. Here Peter explains that Jesus as the suffering Messiah fulfils God's promise to Abraham that through his 'seed' all peoples on earth will be blessed (cf. Acts 3:25–26).

Although the New Testament writers view Jesus as belonging to the line of Abraham/David, they reveal that he is much greater than either Abraham or David. Thus John 8:52–58 and Matthew 22:41–46 record Jesus' own assessment that he is superior to Abraham and David respectively. A similar claim is also recorded regarding Jesus and Solomon in Matthew 12:42 (cf. Luke 11:31). Further links between Jesus and the 'seed' of Abraham will be noted in chapters five and six.

The special lineage in Genesis also appears in Paul's letters to the Romans and Galatians. In Romans 9 and Galatians 4 he draws an important distinction between 'natural children' and 'children of promise'. Using the Genesis stories concerning Ishmael/Isaac and Esau/Jacob he argues that 'not all who are descended from Israel are Israel. Nor because they are his descendants are they all Abraham's children' (Rom 9:6–7). Paul is concerned to show that natural descent from Abraham is no guarantee of salvation. Thus, he demonstrates from Genesis that although Ishmael and Esau are both descendants of Abraham, they are not part of the chosen line of 'seed'.

Another element of Paul's discussion in Romans and Galatians is that the seed of Abraham should resemble him. We see this clearly in his comments in Gal 3:6–7:

> Consider Abraham: 'He believed God, and it was credited to him as righteousness.' Understand, then, that those who believe are children of Abraham.

The same point underlies Paul's words in Rom 4:16–17:

> Therefore, the promise comes by faith, so that it may be by grace and may be guaranteed to all Abraham's offspring — not only to those who are of the law but also to those who are of the faith of Abraham. He is the father of us all. As it is written: 'I have made you a father of many nations.' He is our father in the sight of God, in whom he believed — the God who gives life to the dead and calls things that are not as though they were' (Rom 4:16–17).

In both these passages Paul argues that the true children of Abraham are those who, like Abraham, exercise faith. Consequently, descent from Abraham counts for nothing unless his natural descendants resemble him by being made righteous through faith. On this, we shall have more to say in chapter 5.

NOTES

1. In Genesis the term *tôlĕdot* is used elsewhere only in 10:32 and 25:13.

2. These statistics exclude the one occurrence of the Aramaic word *zeraʿ* in Daniel 2:43. In Genesis *zeraʿ* comes in 1:11(x2),12(x2), 29(x2); 3:15(x2); 4:25; 7:3; 8:22; 9:9; 12:7; 13:15,16(x2); 15:3,5,13,18; 16:10; 17:7(x2),8,9,10,12,19; 19:32,34; 21:12,13; 22:17(x2),18; 24:7,60; 26:3,4(x3); 28:4,13,14(x2); 32:12; 35:12; 38:8,9(x2); 46:6,7; 47:19,23,24; 48:4,11,19.

3. This does not necessarily imply that every generation is included in the record. R.R. Wilson, *Genealogy and History in the Biblical World* (Yale Near Eastern Researches 7; New Haven: Yale University Press, 1977) 133–134, notes that even in written genealogies there is a tendency to limit the maximum length of the lineage to ten generations, such as we have in Genesis chs. 5 and 11. Consequently, it is not uncommon to find Near Eastern genealogies being modified by the addition and omission of names. Examples of this process of 'telescoping' are also to be found in the biblical texts (e.g. compare 1 Chr 6:3–14 and Ezra 7:1–5; cf. W.H. Green, 'Primeval Chronology', *Bibliotheca Sacra* 47 [1890] 285–303).

4. In Num 2:3 and 10:14 the tribe of Judah comes first in lists involving all the tribes (cf. Josh 15:1). The pre-eminence of the tribe of Judah may also be observed in the layout of the Israelite camp during the wilderness period. Judah was located on the east side, nearest to the entrance into the tabernacle.

5. The Hebrew original of the comments in 5:22,24 and 6:9 that Enoch and Noah 'walked with God' uses a distinctive form of the verb 'to walk' — the *hitpaʿel* form. The same form occurs elsewhere in Genesis in 3:8; 13:17; 17:1; 24:40; 48:15. Apart from 3:8, where God is the subject of the verb, and with the possible exception of 13:17, on all of these occasions the verb 'walk' denotes a special relationship with God. N.M. Sarna comments, 'this expression seems originally to have been a technical term for absolute loyalty to a king' (*Genesis* [The JPS Torah Commentary; Philadelphia/New York/Jerusalem: Jewish Publication Society, 1989] 123).

6. This is clearly linked to the divine promise to Abraham in 12:2 that 'I will make you into a great nation'. The nature of this nation — holy and righteous — becomes a prominent theme in Exodus, Leviticus and Deuteronomy.

7. See 43:8–9; 44:16; 44:18–34; 46:28.

8. There are interesting parallels between chapter 38 and the book of Ruth which concludes by giving the genealogy of king David beginning with Perez the son of Tamar (Ruth 4:18–22). Although Tamar and Ruth are non-Israelites, they both play an active role in continuing the royal line. It is also interesting to observe that David names one of his daughters Tamar (2 Sam 13:1).

9. In passing it is noteworthy that Gen 1:28 indicates that human beings were created by God to rule over the earth. This being so, Adam is to be viewed as the first member of this royal line. However,

not only was Adam a king, but he was also a priest (see chapter 3). In the light of this, the concept of priest-king takes on a special significance. In Genesis we encounter this unusual status in the figure of Melchizedek. Clearly, it is implied that anyone who enjoys this particular status resembled Adam before he was expelled from the Garden of Eden. Later, the Israelites are called by the LORD to be a royal priesthood (Exod 19:6).

10. Although the genealogy ends with Joseph, Matthew nowhere claims that Joseph is the natural father of Jesus; he merely observed that Joseph was married to Mary the mother of Jesus (Matt 1:16). In keeping with this, the immediately following account is concerned to show that Joseph adopts Jesus as his son (Matt 1:18–25).

[3]

Paradise Lost

SUMMARY

The motif of 'land' is important in Genesis due to the special relationship which God establishes between the first man and the ground; a relationship reflected in their respective names *'ādām* and *'ădāmâ*. At harmony with God, each is dependent upon the other. However, when the first human couple disobeyed the LORD God and ate of the forbidden fruit, two important consequences followed. First, their relationship with the ground was severely affected; no longer did the earth give willingly of its bounty to satisfy their needs. Secondly, they were expelled from Eden and so deprived of a unique environment in which to commune with God. With every subsequent unrighteous act humankind was further alienated from the earth. The accounts of Cain killing Abel, Noah and the flood, and the tower of Babel all reveal the increasing tension which existed between humanity and the earth. In each episode divine judgement comes in the form of exile and alienation from the earth. Against this background the divine gift of land to Abraham is significant. It is indicative of Abraham's positive relationship with the LORD and anticipates the divine presence in the midst of the nation of Israel.

INTRODUCTION

A careful reading of Genesis reveals that the concept of land figures prominently in the thinking of the author. From the initial creation of the dry land through to Joseph's desire that his bones be buried in the land promised by God to Abraham, Isaac and Jacob, there is hardly an episode in the entire book which does not in one way or another mention land. While not all references to land are to be viewed as equally important, it is

19

clear that the relationship between human beings and the earth is of major interest to the author.

Before looking at the theme of land in Genesis it may be helpful to observe briefly that in the Hebrew text three different terms are used for 'land'. By far the most common is the word *'ereṣ* (*'erets*) which comes 312 times in Genesis. Usually *'ereṣ* (*'erets*) denotes either the earth as a whole (e.g. 1:1,10,26) or a particular country (e.g. 12:1,5). The term *'ădāmâ* occurs 43 times and normally means 'ground' or 'soil' (e.g. 2:5,7,19). The third term is *śādēh*, which comes approximately 50 times in Genesis and usually refers to wide open spaces; it is often translated 'field' (e.g. 2:19,20). Although it is possible to view each term as having distinctive aspects, they may on occasions be used to denote the same thing.[1]

THE CREATION OF THE EARTH

The opening chapter of Genesis establishes the nature of the earth's relationship to both God and humanity. Of fundamental importance is the belief that the earth is created by God; by merely speaking he brings order to that which is 'formless and empty' (1:2). With the creation of the dry land, God establishes three distinct realms: 'sky', 'land' and 'seas' (1:6–10). Of these the most important is the land. Unlike the sky and the seas, the land plays an active role in God's creative activity. It is divinely commanded to produce both vegetation (1:11–12) and living creatures (1:24). Having created the earth, God delegates authority to human beings to govern it and its creatures (cf. 1:28).

Complementing Genesis 1, the account in 2:4–25 develops more fully the close relationship which exists between the man and the ground. Two factors highlight this close relationship. First, the man is actually made from the ground: 'the LORD God formed the man from the dust of the ground and breathed into his nostrils the breath of life, and the man became a living being' (2:7). Second, in the Hebrew original the terms for 'man' and 'ground' are very similar; they are respectively *'ādām* and *'ădāmâ*. This unique relationship between the first man and the ground is further emphasised when the LORD God places him in the Garden of Eden with responsibility 'to work it and take care of it' (2:15). Here the man is portrayed as a tenant placed in charge of his master's garden, and, with one exception, permitted to enjoy freely all of its produce (2:16–17). Thus, Genesis 1–2 highlights the special relationship which exists between God, humanity and the land/ground. Human beings are charged by God to exercise authority over the earth, and the earth is divinely empowered to produce food in abundance for humankind. Dependent upon each other humanity and the earth are both accountable to God.

THE GARDEN OF EDEN AS SANCTUARY

In Genesis 2–3 the Garden of Eden functions as the meeting place between the LORD God and the first human couple. Interesting parallels exist between Eden and the later sanctuaries, in particular the tabernacle and Jerusalem temple.[2] (1) The LORD God walks in Eden as he later does in the tabernacle (3:8; cf. Lev 26:12; Deut 23:15; 2 Sam 7:6–7). (2) Eden and the later sanctuaries are entered from the east and guarded by cherubim (3:24; Exod 25:18–22; 26:31; 1 Kgs 6:23–29). (3) The tabernacle menorah (or lampstand) possibly symbolises the tree of life (2:9; 3:22; cf. Exod 25:31–35). (4) The pair of Hebrew verbs in God's command to the man 'to work it (the garden) and take care of it'(2:15) are only used in combination elsewhere in the Pentateuch of the duties of the Levites in the sanctuary (cf. Num 3:7–8; 8:26; 18:5–6).[3] (5) The river flowing from Eden (2:10) is reminiscent of Ezek 47:1–12 which envisages a river flowing from a future Jerusalem temple and bringing life to the Dead Sea. Finally, gold and onyx which are mentioned in 2:11–12 are used extensively to decorate the later sanctuaries and priestly garments (e.g. Exod 25:7,11,17,31).[4] Gold in particular is associated with the divine presence.

Since Eden is a paradise where divinity and humanity enjoy each other's presence, it is hardly surprising that it becomes a prototype for later sanctuaries. Although human beings enjoy close fellowship with God within the tabernacle and Jerusalem temple, direct access into God's immediate presence is limited to once a year and then only for the high priest.[5] However, within Eden the first man and woman have the unique privilege of being able to relate to God face to face without fear or shame. Against this background the account of their disobedience is all the more tragic.

EXPELLED FROM EDEN

The harmony of Eden ends when the man and the woman knowingly disobey God and eat from the tree of the knowledge of good and evil (3:1–13; cf. 2:16–17). Two consequences are significant regarding the subject of land. First, God curses the ground because of Adam's disobedience (3:17–19). No longer is the ground divinely empowered to produce food in abundance. Man must work by the sweat of his brow in order to eat.

Furthermore, his task is made more difficult because the ground 'will produce thorns and thistles' (3:18). No longer is the man at harmony with the ground from which he was taken and upon which he depends for food.

Second, the man and the woman are banished from the Garden of Eden (3:23). Like a landlord expelling an unsatisfactory tenant, God ousts them from Eden. The reason for their expulsion is recorded by the narrator: 'He must not be allowed to reach out his hand and take also from the tree of life and eat, and live for ever' (3:22). Separated from the tree of life, each human will experience death, the divine punishment for eating from the tree of the knowledge of good and evil (2:17). To ensure that human beings may not return to Eden, God places 'cherubim and a flaming sword flashing back and forth to guard the way to the tree of life' (3:24). Expelled from Eden, Adam and Eve will no longer enjoy the intimacy of God's presence. While this does not mark the end of God's relationship with humanity, it does indicate a dramatic change. The special relationship which was established at creation will exist only with those to whom God now makes himself known. No longer will humanity automatically have a personal knowledge of God. Thus, as a result of human disobedience the initial harmony of creation between God, humanity and the land is replaced by alienation.

CAIN — A RESTLESS WANDERER ON THE EARTH

The relationship between human beings and the ground is important in the story of Cain killing his brother Abel. Initially, Cain is described as one who 'worked the soil (ground)' (4:2). When, out of jealousy, he kills his brother, the LORD God confronts him regarding his crime. The relationship between Cain's action and the ground is highlighted in God's speech:

> What have you done? Listen! Your brother's blood cries out to me from the ground. Now you are under a curse and driven from the ground, which opened its mouth to receive you brother's blood from your hand. When you work the ground, it will no longer yield its crop for you. You will be a restless wanderer on the earth (4:10–12).

Whereas Adam's punishment resulted in the ground being difficult to toil, Cain is actually 'driven from the ground' and forced to become a restless wanderer. He must also go out from the LORD's presence (4:14,16). Alienated from both God and the ground, Cain's punishment resembles that of his parents.

Two points are worth underlining from the story of Cain killing Abel. First, the narrative highlights the continuing relationship between humanity and the ground. Cain's actions have a direct bearing upon the ground; it is stained by Abel's blood. Second, each unrighteous action increases humanity's alienation from the ground. The ground, which was to nourish humankind, is now the agent of divine punishment. The natural environment no longer automatically favours humanity as God intended; it is now hostile and the extent of this hostility is in direct proportion to the unrighteousness of human beings.

THE FLOOD NARRATIVE

The subject of land is prominent in the account of Noah's rescue from the flood. It first appears in the naming of Noah by his father Lamech.

> When Lamech had lived 182 years, he had a son. He named him Noah and said, 'He will comfort us in the labour and painful toil of our hands caused by the ground the LORD has cursed' (5:28–29).[6]

Here Noah is presented as the one who will bring relief to those already heavily burdened by the task of working the ground. Behind this comment is the hope that the ever worsening relationship between humanity and the ground will be reversed by Noah.

God's decision to send a flood which will destroy all living creatures is clearly linked to the wickedness of humankind (cf. 6:5).

> Now the earth was corrupt in God's sight and was full of violence. God saw how corrupt the earth had become, for all the people on earth had corrupted their ways. So God said to Noah, 'I am going to put an end to all people, for the earth is filled with violence because of them. I am surely going to destroy both them and the earth' (6:11–13).

Once again we see how the continual violence of humanity has a direct bearing upon the earth. Through the shedding of innocent blood the ground is polluted, reducing its fertility. Consequently, the task of tilling the ground had become almost unbearable by the time of Noah.

The flood narrative in 6:9–9:19 exhibits close parallels with Genesis 1. The description of the flood waters gradually covering the entire earth, including the highest mountains, portrays a return to the earth's original state prior to the separation of the land and seas (cf. 1:9–10). With the retreat of the flood waters and Noah's departure from the ark, we have the re-creation of the earth.[7] Consequently, those who emerge from the ark now inhabit ground which has been cleansed from the pollution caused by unrighteous behaviour. Yet, although the earth has been recreated, the same is not true of human nature, for, as God comments, 'every inclination of his (man's) heart is evil from childhood' (8:21). Nevertheless, God promises that he will never again 'curse the ground because of man' (8:21) by sending another flood.[8] This is subsequently confirmed in the covenant outlined in 9:8–17.

Prior to the flood the shedding of innocent blood polluted the ground, decreasing significantly its fertility. In 9:1–7 God issues certain instructions which are intended to prevent the earth from being contaminated in the future. These focus on the 'lifeblood' of both animal and humans which must be treated with due respect.

NOAH, A MAN OF THE SOIL

The episode following the account of the flood begins by describing Noah as a 'man of the soil (ground)' (9:20) and focuses briefly on his ability to cultivate a vineyard which produces an abundant crop. This part of the story is clearly intended to highlight the dramatic change which has occurred as a result of the flood. Whereas the ground's fertility was severely limited before the flood, now it produces abundantly. In this we see the fulfilment of Lamech's comments regarding Noah in 5:29.

THE TABLE OF NATIONS

The Table of Nations in chapter 10 outlines where the descendants of Noah gradually settle.[9] Of particular note are the details concerning Canaan and his sons; 10:15–18 provides a detailed list of the various people descended from Canaan, and 10:19 describes the borders of Canaan. These details are significant in the light of later developments in Genesis, when Abraham is promised by God possession of the land of Canaan (cf. 15:18–21).

THE TOWER OF BABEL

The incident involving the tower of Babel centres on humanity's desire to dwell together in one place and through co-operation to make a name for themselves (11:4). However, God views with displeasure their activities, especially their desire to build a city with a tower that reaches to the heavens. Consequently, he prevents them from continuing their building by 'confusing their language' and 'scattering them over the face of the whole earth' (11:9). Humanity is thus exiled by the LORD and hindered from establishing a community which might challenge his authority over the earth.

THE ABRAHAM NARRATIVE

As we have previously noted, the Abraham narrative marks an important turning point in the book of Genesis. This is certainly true as regards the subject of land. Whereas the early chapters of Genesis are dominated by accounts of human disobedience resulting in exile, one of the main themes of the story of Abraham is God's gift of land to Abraham and his descendants.

Several factors are significant regarding God's promise of the land of Canaan to Abraham. First, it is conditional upon Abraham's obedience to God. At the very outset Abraham must obey the LORD's call to leave his own land and go to a new land (12:1). Implicit in this divine command, and in the associated promise that God will make Abraham 'into a great nation' (12:2), is the idea that God will give Abraham a new land. The identity of this land is soon revealed as Canaan (12:5–7), and, in spite of the fact that it is already occupied by the Canaanites (12:6), the LORD confirms that Abraham's descendants will possess it. Later, in the account of the separation of Abraham and Lot, the promise of land is stated in more detail (cf. 13:14–17). These initial promises, however, are given added weight by the covenant which God makes with Abraham in 15:7–21.[10] This covenant is linked to Abraham being credited as righteous on account of his faith. Thus whereas the early chapters of Genesis focus on the loss of land as a result of disobedience, Abraham is portrayed as gaining the land due to obedience and trust in God.

Second, God informs Abraham that his descendants will only occupy the land of Canaan after a period of over four hundred years (15:13–14). The announcement of this delay has important implications for the rest the Pentateuch. Although Genesis records that Abraham and Isaac live within the borders of Canaan, the concluding chapters describe how Jacob and his family leave Canaan to dwell in Egypt. The remaining books of the Pentateuch focus on the future exodus of the Israelites from Egypt and various developments which occur prior to their taking possession of the promised land.

Third, although Abraham is divinely promised the land of Canaan, the land is already occupied by various peoples. This naturally raises the question, how can God give to Abraham land that is already owned by others? The author of Genesis, however, answers this question indirectly by indicating that the inhabitants of Canaan are unworthy occupants of the land. We first encounter this idea prior to the Abraham narrative itself in 9:20–29. Here attention is drawn to the unrighteous behaviour of Ham and the resulting curse upon his son Canaan. Implicit in this is the idea that the descendants of Canaan will behave like their forefather Ham. The identify of these descendants is provided in 10:15–18, along with details of the land occupied by them (10:19).

> Canaan was the father of Sidon his firstborn, and of the Hittites, Jebusites, Amorites, Girgashites, Hivites, Arkites, Sinites, Arvad-ites, Zemarites and Hamathites. Later the Canaanite clans scat-tered and the borders of Canaan reached from Sidon towards Gerar as far as Gaza, and then towards Sodom, Gomorrah, Admah, and Zeboiim, as far as Lasha (10:15–19).

Within the Abraham story itself various passages draw attention to the unrighteous nature of the descendants of Ham. In 13:13 the narrator comments, 'Now the men of Sodom were wicked and were sinning greatly against the LORD.' This negative view of the Canaanite inhabitants of Sodom is reflected in Abraham's attitude towards the king of Sodom (14:21–24), especially when compared with his reaction to Melchizedek king of Salem (14:18–20). In the light of these passages the later account of the destruction of Sodom and Gomorrah in ch. 19 is hardly surprising; indeed it is anticipated in 13:10. God's comment in 18:20–21 about the sin of Sodom and Gomorrah is confirmed by the events surrounding the visit of the two angels in ch. 19. Significantly, the sexual nature of the sin of the men of Sodom is reminiscent of the unrighteous action of their ancestor Ham. Another reference to the sin of Ham's descendants comes in 15:16. Here God indicates that Abraham's descendants will return to the land of Canaan in the fourth generation, 'for the sin of the Amorites has not yet reached its full measure'. Since the early chapters of Genesis have established the idea that unrighteous behaviour results in exile from the land, there can be little doubt that the present inhabitants of Canaan will be dispossessed due to their sin. The later conquest of the land by the Israelites is thus understood as an act of divine judgement upon those already living there.

Fourth, although Abraham is divinely promised that his descendants will take possession of the land of Canaan only several centuries later, by allowing Abraham to buy the cave of Machpelah in Ephron's field the Hittites of Hebron acknow-ledged Abraham's right to be an inhabitant of Canaan (Gen 23:1–20). Moreover, because the land was bought for the purpose of being a burial place this guaranteed Abraham's descendants a permanent right of ownership. Thus, although the divine promise of the land would only be fulfilled in the future, Abraham witnessed the beginning of the process.

THE JACOB STORY

The story of Jacob revolves around his temporary exile in the region of Paddan Aram caused by the deception of his father and the taking of his brother's blessing. Significantly, in spite of his deceitful behaviour Jacob receives various assurances regarding the land of Canaan. The first comes from his father in 28:4. Although Isaac encourages Jacob to leave Canaan in order to find a wife, he prays that God Almighty will bless him:

> May he give you and your descendants the blessing given to Abraham, so that you may take possession of the land where you now live as an alien, the land God gave to Abraham (28:4).

Next, just as Jacob is about to depart from Canaan God reassures him regarding the land through a dream at Bethel.

> I am the LORD, the God of your father Abraham and the God of Isaac. I will give you and your descendants the land on which you are lying. Your descendants will be like the dust of the earth, and you will spread out to the west and to the east, to the north and to the south. All peoples on earth will be blessed through you and your offspring. I am with you and will watch over you wherever you go, and I will bring you back to this land. I will not leave you until I have done what I have promised you (28:13-15).

Thus, although Jacob must flee from Canaan on account of Esau, the narrative anticipates his future return. Much later the divine promise of land is again repeated to Jacob (35:11-12).

The turning point in Jacob's exile in Paddan Aram comes when the LORD says to him, 'Go back to the land of your fathers and to your relatives, and I will be with you' (31:3). With this assurance Jacob prepares to return to Canaan. Significantly, whereas he had arrived in Paddan Aram alone he leaves with a large family and numerous possessions. In spite of all that the LORD has done for him in Paddan Aram Jacob is still very conscious of the reason for his exile there. Consequently, on returning to the borders of Canaan he makes preparations for his encounter with Esau (32:1-21). Interestingly, just as Jacob experienced the LORD's presence when he left Canaan (28:10-22), so once again he has a dramatic meeting with the LORD as he is about to re-enter the land (32:22-32). By locating these theophanies on the border of Canaan, the narrative draws attention to the importance of the land.

The reconciliation between Jacob and Esau not only brings to an end the conflict which had separated them for years (33:1-16) but also results in Jacob settling in the land of Canaan (33:17-20). Esau, however, eventually settles outside Canaan in the land of Seir (33:16; 36:6-8). Remarkably, this parting of the brothers echoes the earlier separation of Abraham and Lot; Jacob and Esau agree to dwell in different regions because the land is not able to support all of their livestock (36:7–8; cf. 13:5–18). As a result only Jacob is left dwelling in the land of Canaan.

THE JOSEPH STORY

The final quarter of Genesis revolves around the character of Joseph and tells of his role in bringing the descendants of Abraham out of Canaan and into Egypt. Given God's comments to Abraham that 'your descendants will be strangers in a country not their own, and they will be enslaved and ill-treated four hundred years' (15:13), the Joseph story provides an essential link between the Abraham and Jacob narratives and the later account of the exodus from Egypt. The overall plot of the Pentateuch requires a transition from Canaan to Egypt.

Several features of the Joseph story invite further comments as regards the topic of land. First, it is interesting to observe that it is a famine in Canaan that brings the brothers of Joseph back into contact with him in Egypt. Throughout Genesis famines are associated with God's curse upon the earth; they reflect the absence of divine blessing and highlight the lack of harmony which ought to exist between human beings and the ground. Significantly, but for the preparations made by Joseph, the effects of this famine would have been much more terrible.

Second, given Jacob's own experience of having been exiled from Canaan in Paddan Aram it is not surprising that he is somewhat reluctant to leave Canaan again. He goes only when the LORD intervenes and commands him to do so:

> Do not be afraid to go down to Egypt, for I will make you into a great nation there. I will go down to Egypt with you, and I will surely bring you back again. And Joseph's own hand will close your eyes (46:3–4).

Jacob's reluctance to go to Egypt should be viewed against other episodes in Genesis. Earlier during a famine in Canaan Abraham had gone down to Egypt (12:10–20). However, his experience there had placed in jeopardy the fulfilment of the divine promises. Later, when another famine occurred in the land of Canaan, Isaac was specifically commanded by God not to go down into Egypt (26:1–2). In the light of these events Jacob may have felt strongly inclined to remain in Canaan.

Third, although the movement in the Joseph story is from Canaan to Egypt, there are various indications that this was not to be a permanent move. This is reflected, for example, in

God's words to Jacob: 'I will surely bring you back again' (46:4). The Israelite's attachment to Canaan is also reflected in the events surrounding the death of Jacob. After his death, Jacob's embalmed body is transported back to Canaan to be buried in the cave at Machpelah alongside the bodies of Abraham and Isaac (49:29–50:14). Later, Joseph makes a similar request that his bones should be carried up from Egypt to Canaan (50:24–25). Significantly, Joseph does not expect this to happen immediately after his death, as with his father, but thinks in terms of this being done when God comes to the aid of the Israelites (cf. Exod 13:19). Thus, although Genesis ends with the account of Joseph's death, there is an expectation of things yet to come; the Israelites shall one day return to the promised land.

CONCLUSION

Genesis emphasises throughout the close relationship which human beings have with the ground. The basis for this interdependence is explained in the account of creation where the first man, Adam (*'ādām*), is created from the dust of the ground (*'ădāmâ*). Unfortunately, although God initially blesses the relationship between humanity and the earth, the disobedience of Adam and Eve in the Garden of Eden leads to a dramatic reversal of this situation. Moreover, Adam and Eve are exiled from Eden ending the intimate relationship which they enjoyed there with the LORD. Later, through the promises given to Abraham, the restoration of divine blessing becomes a possibility. This, however, will only be fully achieved when all the families of the ground are blessed. In the meantime Abraham is assured that, as part of the process by which the nations shall be blessed, his descendants will possess the land of Canaan. For them Canaan will resemble in part the Garden of Eden; there the people will enjoy a special communion with God surrounded by all the signs of God's blessing upon the land.

NEW TESTAMENT CONNECTIONS

The NT develops the concept of land in ways that are both similar and dissimilar to those found in Genesis. In order to appreciate the reason for this it is important to note that in Genesis the theme of land comes in two different contexts. Firstly, it is used in the context of humanity as a whole. All human beings must daily confront the reality that nature is under God's curse due to humanity's disobedience of him from

Adam and Eve onwards. The New Testament makes clear that nature, like all believers, awaits redemption from the bondage of decay (Rom 8:19–25). For Paul, the reconciliation of all things to God is achieved by Jesus Christ 'through his blood, shed on the cross' (Col 1:20; cf. 2 Cor 5:17–21; Eph 1:7–10). Significantly, Paul views Christ not only as the one responsible for the restoration of harmony within the cosmos, but as the creator of all things in the first instance (Col 1:15–17; cf. 1 Cor 8:6).

The climax of the re-creation process is the appearance of a new heaven and a new earth where God and human beings live together in harmony (Rev 21:1). Although this is portrayed in Rev 21:1–22:5 in terms of 'the Holy City, the new Jerusalem, coming down out of heaven from God' (Rev 21:2), it is also viewed as a return to Eden. Various factors suggest this, the most significant being the reference to the 'tree of life' (Rev 22:2; cf. Gen 2:9; 3:22,24) and the comment that 'no longer will there be any curse' (Rev 22:3).

For the author of Hebrews the goal of God's redemptive activity for humanity is expressed in terms of rest (Heb 4:1–11). Two related ideas are developed. First, this rest resembles that which God enjoyed following the creation of the heavens and the earth (Gen 2:2–3) and which humanity lost as a result of the disruption of creation following the disobedience of Adam and Eve. Second, the ancient Israelites due to their disobedience failed to obtain such rest when they took possession of the land of Canaan. However, the opportunity to enter into God's rest still exists for those who believe the gospel.

The second context in which land is used in an important way in Genesis has to do with the establishment of Abraham's descendants as a nation in the land of Canaan. Significantly, with the introduction of a new covenant embracing all nations it is hardly surprising that the NT plays down the importance of Israel as a nation. Israel's role in God's purposes has now dramatically changed and, as a consequence, it is no longer important that Israel should possess the land of Canaan. Whereas the Sinai Covenant centred on one nation, the New Covenant is international in its scope. Thus, although the promise of land to Abraham in Genesis is generally stated in terms of the land of Canaan (Gen 12:7; 13:14–17; 15:18–21; 17:8), there are indications that for the nations to be blessed, Abraham's 'seed' would exercise authority over the entire earth (49:10; cf. 22:17; Ps 2:8; Micah 5:2–5). In the light of this movement from one nation, Israel, to all nations, it is hardly surprising that there is a similar shift from thinking in terms of one land to the whole world. This, for example, is reflected in Paul's treatment of the fifth commandment, to honour your father and mother, in Eph 6:2–3. Whereas in the original context of Exod 19:12 and Deut 5:16 the commandment includes the promise of long life as regards possession of the land of Canaan, in Ephesians Paul expands this to include the whole earth.

NOTES

1. An interesting example of this comes in the Abraham narrative. The expression 'all peoples on earth' (lit. 'families of the ground') in Gen 12:3 is later replaced by the expression 'all nations on earth' (18:18; 22:18). No essential difference in meaning is meant. However, in 12:3 the emphasis is upon the oneness of all human beings in that they have a common origin, the dust of the ground. The expression in 18:18 and 22:18 highlights the idea that the earth consists of different nations. The switch from the former expression to the latter may be due to the fact that the fulfilment of the divine promise that the nations will be blessed is linked to the creation of Israel as a nation.

2. These parallels are set out by G.J. Wenham in his article, 'Sanctuary Symbolism in the Garden of Eden Story', *Proceedings of the World Congress of Jewish Studies* 9 (1986) 19–25.

3. *'ābad* (*'āvad*) 'to serve', 'to till'; *šāmar* (*shāmar*) 'to keep', 'to observe'.

4. There are about one hundred references to gold and seven to onyx in the Exodus account of the building of the tabernacle.

5. See chapter 9.

6. Although the name Noah is probably linked etymologically to the Hebrew verb *nûaḥ* (*nûakh*) meaning 'to rest', it also sounds like the Hebrew verb *niḥām* (*nikham*) 'to comfort'.

7. According to G.V. Smith, the flood narrative echoes the initial account of creation in the following ways:

> When Genesis 1 and 2 are compared with 8 and 9, one begins to perceive the extent to which the author uses repeated phrases and ideas to build the structural relationships within the units. The following relationships are found: (a) Since man could not live on the earth when it was covered with water in chaps. 1 and 8, a subsiding of the water and separation of the land from the water took place, allowing the dry land to appear (1:9–10; 8:1–13); (b) 'birds and animals and every creeping thing that creeps on the earth' are brought forth to 'swarm upon the earth' in 1:20–21,24–25 and 8:17–19; (c) God establishes the days and seasons in 1:14–18 and 8:22; (d) God's blessing rests upon the animals as he commands them to 'be fruitful and multiply on the earth' in both 1:22 and 8:17; (e) man is brought forth and he receives the blessing of God: 'Be fruitful and multiply and fill the earth' in 1:28 and 9:1,7; (f) Man is given dominion over the animal kingdom in 1:28 and 9:2; (g) God provides food for man in 1:29–30 and 9:3 (this latter regulation makes a direct reference back to the previous passage when it includes the statement, 'As I have

given the green plant'); and (h) in 9:6 the writer quotes from 1:26–27 concerning the image of God in man. The author repeatedly emphasises the fact that the world is beginning again with a fresh start. But Noah does not return to the paradise of Adam, for the significant difference is that 'the intent of man's heart is evil' (Gen 8:21) ('Structure and Purpose in Genesis 1–11,' *JETS* 20 [1977] 310–311).

8. As we shall note in chapter 4, this refers to the flood.

9. Because it indicates that the descendants of Noah were divided into different clan and nations, each with it own language, the material in chapter 10 ought to come after the account of the tower of Babel (11:1–9); 10:25 probably alludes to the creation of different nations, speaking different languages. The writer of Genesis may have felt it inappropriate to place the Table of Nations between 11:1–9 and 11:10–26, since this would bring into immediate proximity two quite different types of genealogy, both concerning the descendants of Shem.

10. Although further references to the land occur in the Abraham narrative (e.g. 17:8; 22:17), the covenant in chapter 15 marks a climax.

[4]

The Blessing of the Nations

SUMMARY

Although the first chapter of Genesis affirms that human beings were created in the divine image and blessed by God, the subsequent disobedience of Adam and Eve in the Garden of Eden resulted in a series of divine curses which radically affected human existence. The tragic events which resulted from the broken relationship between God and humankind are highlighted in Genesis 4–11. After the division of humanity into different peoples and nations, Abraham is introduced as the one through whom God's blessing will once again extend to human beings. Genesis looks forward to all families and nations being blessed through Abraham and his 'seed'.

INTRODUCTION

Blessing and cursing are important concepts in the book of Genesis. This is reflected by the fact that the Hebrew verbs for 'blessing', *bārēk*, and 'cursing', *'ārar*, occur 73 and 9 times respectively. Normally, in Genesis, blessing is associated with God's favour and cursing with his disfavour. In order to be blessed the recipient must be at harmony with the donor. Consequently, God's blessing extends only to those who seek to be righteous; the wicked are under his curse.

Genesis presents a picture of changing human fortunes. When God created the first generation of human beings they enjoyed his favour and were blessed by him (1:28). Soon this situation was disrupted by events which took place in the Garden of Eden. For disobeying God's command not to eat from the tree of the knowledge of good and evil, Adam and Eve were divinely punished through various curses. Some of the immediate consequences are described in chapters 4–11. Here we observe the total destruction of the human race, apart from

Noah and his family, and, later, the division of human beings into different nations. Whereas the accounts of the flood and of the tower of Babel highlight the disastrous consequences of evoking God's displeasure, with the call of Abraham in chapter 12 the way begins to open up for human beings to once more enjoy God's favour. Significantly, as illustrated in the record of the lives of Jacob and Joseph, God's blessing is mediated through the 'seed' of Abraham.

CREATOR AND CREATION IN HARMONY

The opening section of the book of Genesis describes how God created the heavens and the earth. It stresses the ease by which everything was made, and that nothing happened by chance; everything was made according to design. By merely speaking, God created time in the form of 'day' and 'night' (1:3–5). Next he made three distinctive regions, the sky (1:6–8), the land and the seas (1:9–11), and placed in each as appropriate plants (1:11–13), stars and planets (1:14–19), fish and birds (1:20–23), living creatures (1:24–26) and human beings (1:27–31). God's final verdict that everything 'was very good' (1:31) echoes a common refrain in the chapter, 'God said that (it) was good' (1:4,10,12,18,21,25). With remarkable brevity and skill the narrator conveys a picture of total harmony between God, the creator, and the world, his creation.

The creation of human beings comes as the climax to God's creative activity: 'So God created man in his own image, in the image of God he created him, male and female he created them' (1:27) Significantly, this comment is immediately followed by the remark that 'God blessed them and said to them, "Be fruitful and increase in number; fill the earth and subdue it. Rule over the fish of the sea and the birds of the air and over every living creature that moves on the ground" ' (1:28). Unlike all other creatures human beings alone enjoyed the privilege of being made in the divine image and having a special relationship with God. Moreover, blessed by God they were to increase numerically and rule over the earth as his representatives.

Although God's creative activity ends on the sixth day, the account of creation concludes by focusing on the seventh day in which God rested from all work (2:1–3). Of significance is the comment, 'God blessed the seventh day and made it holy, because on it he rested from all the work of creating that he had done' (2:3). The seventh day is set apart from all the other days of the week because rest is viewed as the climax of the work pattern established by God. As reflected in God's own experience, the opportunity to rest, having completed one's work, is a sacred blessing.

IN THE GARDEN OF EDEN

The account of creation in 1:1–2:3 is followed by a second in 2:4–25. Whereas the first account gives a cosmic picture of God's activity, the second is much more down to earth, portraying God as the one who personally moulds the man from clay and breathes life into him (2:7). The narrative also reveals that God provides the right environment for the man (2:8–17) and a suitable companion (2:18–25). Although the two accounts of humanity's creation differ in style, they complement each other, both emphasising the special relationship which existed between the LORD God and the first man and woman.

Unfortunately, the harmony of creation was soon broken by the serpent, who persuaded the woman, and, through her, the man, to disobey God's command by eating 'from the tree of the knowledge of good and evil' (2:17). Although few details are given, the narrative makes clear that the man and the woman were radically changed by eating from this tree. When the LORD God next visited the garden, the man and the woman were unable to hide what had taken place. Aware of their actions, God pronounced judgement on all the participants. No longer did God's blessing favour the man and the woman; now they had to endure the consequences of his displeasure. As a result of their broken relationship with God, Adam and Eve were expelled from Eden.

The contents of God's pronouncements against the serpent, the woman and the man are significant. Regarding the serpent he states,

> Because you have done this, 'Cursed are you above all the livestock and all the wild animals! You will crawl on your belly and you will eat dust all the days of your life. And I will put enmity between you and the woman and between your offspring (seed) and hers (her seed); he will crush your head, and you will strike his heel' (3:14–15).

Of particular interest here is the comment about the enmity which will exist between the 'seed' of the serpent and the 'seed' of the woman. Unfortunately, most commentators miss the obvious connection which exists between this reference to 'seed' and the fact that Genesis highlights a particular line of 'seed' (see chapter two). The implication is surely that the divine pronouncement against the serpent will be fulfilled through the divinely chosen family lineage.[1]

God's judgement upon the woman is directed against two important aspects of her life: her ability to produce children and her relationship to her husband.

> I will greatly increase your pains in childbearing; with pain you will give birth to children. Your desire will be for your husband, and he will rule over you (3:16).

Since in the future every birth will be accomplished only through pain, this pronouncement reverses in part God's initial blessing that human beings should be fruitful and increase in number (1:28).

The man's punishment is also designed to cause him maximum discomfort.

> Cursed is the ground because of you; through painful toil you will eat of it all the days of your life. It will produce thorns and thistles for you, and you will eat the plants of the field. By the sweat of your brow you will eat your food until you return to the ground, since from it you were taken; for dust you are and to dust you will return (3:17–19).

Whereas God had intended the man's work to be a responsibility undertaken with joy and satisfaction, it now becomes hard labour. On the basis of 2:7 it is obvious that the LORD God intended there to be a close and harmonious relationship between the man and the ground; this is evident in the Hebrew original where the words for 'man' and 'ground', 'ādām and 'ădāmā respectively, are very similar.[2] By disrupting the man's relationship with the ground God ensured that humanity was not able to enjoy, like their creator, rest from labour.

The story of the fall brings to a bitter end the harmony which was the hallmark of God's creative activity. We witness in particular a breakdown in relations between animals and human beings, between men and women, and, most importantly of all, between God and humanity. Genesis chapter 3 describes dramatic changes to the created world. Human beings no longer know God's blessing, but must now come to terms with his displeasure. The final act of judgement is the expulsion of the man and woman from Eden. Not only are they prevented from eating of the tree of life (3:22), but they are expelled from the place where they have enjoyed a close relationship with God. As we shall observe below, chapters 4–11 focus mainly on the terrible consequences of humanity's initial disobedience and provide a grim picture of what life was like without God's blessing. Only with the call of Abraham in 12:1–3 do we begin to see a brighter prospect with some human beings once again experiencing divine blessing in their lives.

OUTSIDE EDEN

After the departure of Adam and Eve from the Garden of Eden, the next episode in Genesis focuses on the murder of Abel by his brother Cain. Significantly, it was because Abel enjoyed God's favour that Cain became jealous and killed him. As punishment, Cain was cursed by God; the ground 'will no longer yield its crops' for him and he will become a 'restless wanderer on the earth' (4:11–12). This marks an extension of the curse imposed upon Cain's parents in Eden and highlights the fact that every unrighteous action alienates humankind further from the ground, making it even more difficult to cultivate food and so experience divinely intended rest.

The Genesis story reveals that God's curse upon the ground brought increased pain for humankind. This is highlighted particularly in a brief comment by Lamech concerning his son Noah. He named him Noah because, 'he will comfort us in the labour and painful toil of our hands caused by the ground the LORD has cursed' (5:29). Significantly, when the earth is recreated after the flood Noah is described as 'a man of the soil (ground)' (9:20), suggesting that he enjoyed greater harmony with the ground than his immediate forefathers.

The concept of curse underlies the entire story of the flood. God's decision to wipe humankind from the face of the earth is motivated by the fact that he 'saw how great man's wickedness on the earth had become, and that every inclination of the thoughts of his heart was only evil all the time' (6:5). However, Noah finds favour in God's eyes and, together with some of his family, is spared from destruction. Significantly, when Noah disembarks from the ark and offers sacrifices to God, the LORD remarks, 'Never again will I curse the ground because of man, even though every inclination of his heart is evil from childhood' (8:21). The curse mentioned here is not the one pronounced in the garden of Eden. Rather it refers to the flood. The continued existence of 'thorns and thistles' and the necessity for humankind to toil with sweat indicate that the original divine curse on the ground has not been cancelled.[3] Here God promises that he will never again send another flood upon the earth. Later this is confirmed in the covenant outlined in 9:8–17.

In passing we should note that the story of the flood exhibits close parallels with the initial account of creation. The rising of the waters marks a return to the chaos which existed at the beginning of creation (7:11–24; cf. 1:2). Later, the dry land emerges from the waters (8:1–14; cf. 1:9–10). Finally, God's blessing of Noah and his sons in 9:1 echoes closely 1:28: 'Be fruitful and increase in number and fill the earth.' Yet, although these parallels suggest that the flood story is meant to be understood as marking the re-creation of the earth, it is apparent that human nature was not renewed. We see this reflected in God's comments in 8:21 and 9:6 which draw attention respectively to the evil inclination of the human heart and the likelihood that murders will still occur.

The topic of blessing is prominent in 9:20–29. Here the narrative focuses on the contrasting actions of Ham and his brothers Shem and Japheth towards their father Noah. Whereas Ham looks 'upon his father's nakedness', Shem and Japheth take great care to cover it without seeing it. When Noah awakes he pronounces a curse upon Ham's son Canaan but blesses Shem and Japheth. Significantly, this is the first occasion in Genesis when a human being pronounces a blessing or a curse; previously it was always God who blessed or cursed. Yet, in cursing Canaan and blessing Shem and Japheth, Noah's words obviously carry divine authority. For the first time we meet something which is repeated later in Genesis: those within the chosen line of 'seed' are divinely empowered to bless or curse others.

Noah's speeches highlight another important motif in the book of Genesis; this concerns the descendants of Canaan and Shem. Whereas Canaan is destined to a future of servitude (9:25), Noah indicates that the line of Shem will enjoy a special relationship with God (9:26–27). Later, we see God promising to Abraham, a descendant of Shem, that he and his descendants will take possession of the land occupied by the descendants of Canaan (15:18–21).[4] Noah also predicts that Japheth will be blessed through having a close relationship with Shem.

Although blessing or cursing is not mentioned explicitly in the story of the tower of Babel, it is clear from the conclusion that the creation of different languages and the scattering of the peoples over the whole earth represents a further divine curse upon the human race. God's punishment is intended to prevent human beings working together in harmony.

The picture of human existence under God's curse in chapters 3–11 contrasts sharply with the initial account of their divine creation and blessing. The narrator, however, makes it very evident that God's displeasure is not arbitrary but is in proportion to the extent of human wickedness. Yet, although chapters 3–11 concentrate on the divine punishment of wicked human beings, the narrative reveals here and there that God still displays mercy in the face of unrighteous behaviour. We see this, for example, in the clothing of Adam and Eve (3:21), the placing of a mark on Cain (4:13–15), the saving of Noah and his family from the flood (6:8–8:19), and the making of an eternal covenant with every living creature (9:1–17). Significantly, the remaining chapters of Genesis develop further the possibility that human beings may once again know God's blessing in their lives.

ABRAHAM AND THE BLESSING OF THE NATIONS

The *tôlĕdot* heading in 11:27 introduces a new section in Genesis which concludes in 25:11. The central character of these chapters is Abraham and there is good reason to view him as the most important human participant in the whole of Genesis. After some brief preliminary details in 11:27–32, the account of his life begins with a short but highly significant divine speech which marks the beginning of a major new stage in God's relationship with human beings. At the heart of this speech is God's desire to bless humanity and so reverse the negative effects of the divine curses under which they live.

The LORD says to Abraham,

> Leave your country, your people and your father's household and go to the land I will show you, so that I may make you into a great nation and bless you and make your name great. Be a blessing, so that I may bless those who bless you, and curse the one who disdains you, and so that all the families of the ground may be blessed through you (12:1–3; my translation).[5]

A number of points are noteworthy. First, the fulfilment of the promises listed here is conditional on Abraham's obedience. He is commanded by God (a) to leave the security of his own country, people and family, and (b) to 'be a blessing'. Since the divine curses are due to human disobedience, it is hardly surprising that God expects obedience from Abraham before blessing him. Second, the promise that Abraham will become a great nation implies that he will have numerous descendants who will possess their own land. While the fulfilment of this lies in the future, it is important to observe that at the outset major barriers stand in the way: Abraham has neither children nor land. Third, the reference to 'a great name' alludes back to the story of the tower of Babel and possibly also to the 'men of renown' mentioned in 6:4. Whereas, the people of Babel tried to establish a 'name' for themselves without God's help (11:4), the LORD will make Abraham famous. Fourth, God promises that those who 'disdain' Abraham will be divinely 'cursed'. Implicit in this is a guarantee of protection for Abraham and victory over his enemies. The wording of the Hebrew original also indicates that whereas a few will disdain Abraham, a majority will bless him. Fifth, the climax of the passage comes in the concluding words that 'through you all the families of the earth will find blessing'. Here we meet for the first time an idea that is prominent in the rest of Genesis. Through Abraham and, as we shall observe below, his 'seed', God's blessing will be mediated to humanity. Sixth, underlying the fulfilment of all these promises is the establishment of a special relationship between God and Abraham on account of which Abraham will be blessed.[6] The promises will be fulfilled as a result of divine blessing.

Significantly, the theme of blessing is also prominent in the divine oath in 22:16–18 which marks the conclusion to the main part of the Abraham narrative.[7] Here the LORD declares to Abraham,

> I swear by myself, declares the LORD, that because you have done this and have not withheld your son, your only son, I will surely bless you and make your descendants (seed) as numerous as the stars in the sky and as the sand on the seashore. Your descendants (seed) will take possession of the cities (gate) of their (his) enemies, and through your offspring (seed) all nations on earth will be blessed, because you have obeyed me (22:16–18).

Although the wording here differs from that found in 12:1–3, we can discern the same basic ideas underlying both speeches. Yet, whereas 12:1–3 marks the beginning of the Abraham story, the divine oath in 22:16–18 comes at the climax and looks beyond Abraham to his 'seed'. Unfortunately, the identity of this 'seed' is not easy to determine. While the first mention of 'seed' denotes 'descendants' in the plural, the remaining references are ambiguous; they could refer either to many descendants or to a single descendant. This latter possibility, however, would be in keeping with the overall aim of Genesis to highlight a royal lineage.

All of the material in the Abraham story relates in one way or another to the promises highlighted in the opening verses of chapter 12 and so to the theme of blessing. Whereas some episodes focus on Abraham and his descendants possessing the land of Canaan (e.g., 13:1–18; 15:7–21), others are concerned with his lack of a son and the establishment of Isaac as his legitimate heir (e.g., 15:1–6; 16:1–18:15; 20:1–21:21). Interlinked with these episodes are passages which reflect the fulfilment of God's promise that those who bless Abraham will know God's favour and those who act against Abraham will experience God's displeasure. On the one hand, Pharaoh and Abimelech are divinely punished for taking Sarah (12:17; 20:18), and the eastern kings are defeated when Abraham rescues Lot (14:1–16). On the other hand, Melchizedek blesses Abraham and receives in return a tenth of everything captured from the eastern kings (14:18–20). Much later we learn that Abimelech enters into a covenant with Abraham in order to ensure his own prosperity (21:22–34). Finally, to underline that the divine promises to Abraham have indeed been fulfilled, in so far as this is possible during his lifetime, chapter 24 begins with the comment, 'The LORD had blessed him (Abraham) in every way' (24:1; cf. 24:35).

BLESSING IN THE REMAINDER OF GENESIS

The theme of blessing, which is so important in the Abraham story, continues to play a major role in the remaining chapters of Genesis. Among the different aspects of blessing introduced in the Abraham narrative, which are continued and developed, the following are the most important.

First, God's blessing is closely associated with prosperity. This figures prominently in a number of episodes in the Abraham narrative. When Abraham returns from Egypt we read of a conflict between the servants of Abraham and Lot due to the fact that both men have become very wealthy (13:2,5; cf. 12:16). Later, after rescuing Lot from the eastern kings, Abraham refuses to take anything from the king of Sodom lest he should claim to have made Abraham rich (14:21–23; cf. 15:1 which links Abraham's reward to the LORD). In chapter 24 Abraham's servant not only presents valuable gifts to Rebekah and her family (24:22,53), but also directly associates his master's prosperity with the LORD's blessing:

> The LORD has blessed my master abundantly, and he has become wealthy. He has given him sheep and cattle, silver and gold, menservants and maidservants, and camels and donkeys (24:35).

In the same context we may observe that Laban likewise links wealth with divine blessing (24:29–31).

Prosperity is also linked to blessing in the accounts concerning Isaac, Jacob and Joseph. Although it is only mentioned briefly, the narrator emphasises that Isaac's great wealth was due to God's blessing (26:12–13). While Jacob fled to Paddan Aram with few possessions, as a result of God's blessing, he returned to Canaan a very rich man (30:43; 32:3–21), and this in spite of attempts by his uncle Laban to limit his wealth (31:6–9). The story of Joseph also revolves around the idea that it is through God's blessing that he prospered in Egypt. Although he began life there as a slave (39:1–6), and later was imprisoned unjustly (39:6–23), he eventually became governor of the country second only to Pharaoh (41:39–43). Thus, throughout the patriarchal stories prosperity is closely tied to divine blessing.[8]

Second, God's blessing is also associated with fertility. We see this in Genesis ch. 1 where the first reference to God blessing the man and the woman is directly followed by the command, 'Be fruitful and increase in number' (1:28). This close association of blessing and fertility is echoed later in 9:1: 'Then God blessed Noah and his sons, saying to them, "Be fruitful and increase in number and fill the earth".' The same phrases are used when first Isaac and then God bless Jacob in 28:3 and 35:11 respectively (cf. 48:4). In the Abraham story the lack of fertility is the setting against which the LORD promises Abraham that he will become a great nation. Thereafter we have frequent reminders that the 'seed' of Abraham will be as numerous as the dust of the earth (13:16; 28:14), the stars of the heavens (15:5: 22:17; 26:4) and the sand of the seashore (22:17; 32:12). The topic of fertility is also prominent in the story of Jacob where it dominates the competitive relationship between Leah and Rachel (29:31–30:24) and, on a different level, the relationship between Jacob and Laban (30:25–43). Here also fertility is linked to divine blessing (cf. 29:32–33; 30:6,17–18,20,22–24,27–30). Clearly the ability to reproduce is viewed as a sign of divine blessing.[9]

Third, and most importantly of all, the power to mediate God's blessing to others is passed on through the chosen line of patriarchs. This is highlighted in Genesis in two different ways: (a) through God renewing his special relationship with the head of each generation, and (b) through a unique blessing which each father bestows on his 'first-born' son.

In the patriarchal stories the LORD renews his special relationship with the head of the chosen family in each generation. Thus, the promises associated with God's desire to bless Abraham in 12:1–3, and later confirmed by oath in 22:16–18, are passed on to his 'seed'. When Isaac is faced with a famine in the land of Canaan, the LORD appears to him and says,

> Do not go down to Egypt; live in the land where I tell you to live. Stay in this land for a while, so that I may be with you and bless you. For to you and your descendants I will give all these lands and will confirm the oath I swore to your father Abraham. I will make your descendants (seed) as numerous as the stars in the sky and will give them (your seed) all these lands, and through your offspring (seed) all nations on earth will be blessed, because Abraham obeyed me and kept my requirements, my commands, my decrees and my iaws (26:2–5).

Much of the speech echoes 22:16–18, highlighting Abraham's willingness to obey God and sacrifice Isaac. In this way God encourages Isaac to obey him. As in 12:1–3, God's blessing through the fulfilment of the divine promises is dependent upon Isaac obeying him and remaining in Canaan. Interestingly, chapter 26, which is the only chapter to focus exclusively on Isaac, contains three explicit references to God blessing him (26:12,24,29).

The story of Jacob also includes a divine speech containing promises regarding numerous descendants, possession of the land, and the blessing of all peoples on earth. It occurs when Jacob is fleeing to Paddan Aram in order to escape from his brother Esau. God says,

> I am the LORD, the God of your father Abraham and the God of Isaac. I will give you and your descendants (seed) the land on which you are lying. Your descendants (seed) will be like the dust of the earth, and you will spread out to the west and to the east, and to the north and to the south. All peoples on earth will be blessed through you and your offspring (seed). I am with you and will watch over you wherever you go, and I will bring you back to this land. I will not leave you until I have done what I have promised you (28:13–15).

Although it is not mentioned specifically, the contents of the speech, which resemble very closely earlier divine statements, clearly imply that God will bless Jacob. In response, Jacob vows that if God will indeed protect him and bring him back safely to his father's house, 'then the LORD will be my God and this stone that I have set up as a pillar will be God's house, and of all that you give me I will give you a tenth' (28:21–22). Significantly, when many years later Jacob returns from Paddan Aram, God appears to him again and, blessing him (35:9), states,

> I am God Almighty: be fruitful and increase in number. A nation and a community of nations will come from you, and kings will come from your body. The land I gave to Abraham and Isaac I also give to you, and I will give this land to your descendants after you (35:11–12; cf. 48:3–4).

Here God confirms Jacob as the heir to the covenant earlier established with Abraham and Isaac.

In the light of these divine speeches it is apparent that Abraham, Isaac and Jacob all enjoy the same privileged relationship with the LORD. While Abraham and Isaac have other children, they are not part of the chosen lineage and so do not have the same unique relationship with God.[10] Significantly, it is because of this special relationship that the patriarchs are able to mediate God's blessing to others. This blessing, however, is in direct proportion to how the patriarchs and their 'seed' are treated by others. Apart from the examples in the Abraham story considered above, the stories of Jacob and Joseph contain further illustrations. Laban learns by divination that the LORD has blessed him because of Jacob (30:27). Potiphar and his household prosper on account of Joseph (39:2–6), as does the prison warder (39:20–23). Later, following Joseph's appointment as governor over Egypt, not only is the entire nation enabled to survive a seven-year famine (47:13–26), but other nations also benefit from his wise leadership (41:56–57). Finally, it should also be noted that when Pharaoh offers Joseph's relatives 'the best part of the land' (47:6), Jacob blesses him (47:7–10).

The other way in which the Genesis narrative reveals that the power to bless others is granted to succeeding patriarchs is through the paternal blessing of the first-born. Clearly, it was the custom that the first-born son should receive from his father a special blessing which gave him privileges not enjoyed by other sons. This idea lies at the heart of the account of Jacob deceiving his father Isaac in order to obtain the blessing about to be given to Esau (27:1–40). So important is this blessing to Jacob that he is prepared to face both his father's displeasure, should he be found out (27:11–12), and his brother's anger at being deprived of what by custom was rightfully his (cf. 27:41). Although Isaac becomes fully aware that he has been deceived by Jacob, he subsequently blesses him again before sending him to find a wife in Paddan Aram.[11] This suggests that Isaac willingly accepts what has happened (28:1–5).[12]

The subject of paternal blessing also figures prominently in chapters 48 and 49. In the first of these we have the account of Jacob blessing Joseph's two sons, Manasseh and Ephraim. Not only does Jacob deliberately give the younger son Ephraim the superior blessing (48:17–20), but significantly, Ephraim receives the rights of the first-born which should have gone to his father's older brother Reuben (cf. 1 Chr 5:1). In chapter 49 we have a long list of pronouncements which Jacob makes regarding his twelve sons. The narrator's comment in 49:28 indicates that these are given in the context of Jacob blessing his sons, with each one receiving 'the blessing appropriate to him'; that is, the content of these blessings reflects Jacob's attitude towards each son. Without examining them in detail, it is significant that the pronouncements concerning the eldest brothers Reuben, Simeon and Levi are all negative, whereas those given to Judah and Joseph are very favourable. It is especially worth noting that when Jacob blesses Judah he comments that one of his royal descendants will have 'the obedience of the nations' (49:10). Although it is not explicitly stated that the nations will be blessed as a result, in the light of Genesis as a whole, this would seem to be implied.

By highlighting the patriarchs' special relationship with God and their ability to impart a unique blessing to one of their sons, Genesis draws attention to the privileged position of the 'seed' of the chosen lineage.

CONCLUSION

As a whole the book of Genesis records three important phases regarding the theme of divine blessing. At the outset all of creation, including especially humanity, experiences God's favour. However, as a result of the disobedience of Adam and Eve, a significant reversal occurs with human beings and the rest of creation coming under God's curse. The tragic consequences of this are noted throughout the rest of Genesis. However, at the beginning of the Abraham narrative God not only promises to bless Abraham but also through him to bless all the families of the earth. The remaining episodes of the patriarchal narratives focus on this latter promise by linking it to the 'seed' of Abraham. Genesis, however, concludes by indicating that the ultimate fulfilment of God's promise to bless all the nations of the earth through the 'seed' of Abraham still lies in the future.

NEW TESTAMENT CONNECTIONS

The most obvious allusions in the New Testament to the theme of blessing in Genesis come in Acts 3:25–26 and Gal 3:14. In the first of these passages Peter suggests that Jesus Christ is the one through whom God's blessing will come to others.

> And you are heirs of the prophets and of the covenant God made with your fathers. He said to Abraham, 'Through your offspring all peoples on earth will be blessed.' When God raised up his servant, he sent him first to you to bless you by turning each of you from your wicked ways (Acts 3:25–26).

Paul makes the very same point in Galatians: 'He redeemed us in order that the blessing given to Abraham might come to the Gentiles through Christ Jesus . . .' (Gal 3:14). In both of these contexts Jesus Christ, the 'seed' of Abraham, is the one in whom the divine promise that all peoples of earth will be blessed is fulfilled. The same idea is also prominent in Rom 15:8–12, although the concept of blessing is not mentioned specifically. With these passages one might also include Rom

4:6–9. While Paul does not specifically mention the text of Genesis in these verses, his brief comment regarding divine blessing, based on Ps 32:1–2, comes in the context of his argument that Abraham is the father of those who have faith, both Jews and Gentiles.

Other passages which may allude indirectly to the concept of blessing highlighted in Genesis include Elizabeth's reaction to Mary in Luke 1:42–45, and the beatitudes of Jesus in Matt 5:3–12 and Luke 6:20–26.

NOTES

1. The precise meaning of Gen 3:15 has been the subject of much debate and it is not possible to review here the wide variety of opinions which have been expressed. One observation, however, is worth noting. W. Wifall suggests that behind this verse one can discern a Davidic or royal background. In particular he highlights various expressions found in 'royal' Psalms which bear a close resemblance to 3:15.

> David is addressed as God's 'anointed' or 'messiah' (Ps 89:21,39; 2 Sam 22:51) whose 'seed' will endure forever under God's favor (Ps 89:5,30,37). As Yahweh has crushed the ancient serpent 'Rahab' (Ps 89:11), so now David and his sons will crush their enemies in the dust beneath their feet (Ps 89:24; 2 Sam 22:37–43) . . . In Ps 72:9, the foes of the Davidic king are described as 'bowing down before him' and 'licking the dust'. In the familiar 'messianic' Psalms, God is described as having placed 'all things under his feet' (Ps 8:6) and will make 'your enemies your footstool' (Ps 110:1) ('Gen 3:15 — A Protevangelium?' *CBQ* 36 [1974] 363).

2. See chapter 3.

3. The syntax of the Hebrew original indicates that God promises here not to add to the curse pronounced against the ground in 3:17. Furthermore, the Hebrew word for 'curse' in 8:21 comes from a different root than that used in 3:17.

4. Among the various nations listed in 15:19–21, the following are named as descendants of Canaan in 10:15–18: Hittites, Amorites, Canaanites, Girgashites and Jebusites. Furthermore, 10:19 draws attention to the fact that the borders of the Canaanite clans reached as far as Sodom and Gomorrah (cf. 14:1–24; 18:16–29).

5. Two aspects of the translation adopted here require comment. First, the imperative form *wĕhyeh* (*vĕhyeh*) 'be' in 12:2d is maintained; NIV reads 'and you will be a blessing'. Secondly, special consideration has been given to the fact that the imperatives 'go' and 'be a blessing' are both followed by cohortatives. In such contexts the cohortative normally expresses purpose or result. To highlight this syntactic arrangement, the imperatives 'go' and 'be a blessing' are followed by 'so that'.

6. Abraham is later designated the friend of God in 2 Chr 20:7; Isa 41:8.

7. The Abraham narrative falls into two sections separated by a brief genealogy in 22:20–24. The main narrative is 11:27–22:19, with 23:1–25:11 forming an appendix. The divine speeches in 12:1–3 and 22:16–18, which come at the beginning and end of the main section, form what is known technically as an 'inclusio', marking the boundaries of the narrative. Whereas the promises in 12:1–3 are conditional on Abraham obeying God, the oath in 22:16–18 comes as a reward for Abraham's obedience, confirming the fulfilment of the earlier divine promises. Significantly, the divine oath in 22:16–18 marks the ratification of the covenant of circumcision promised in 17:1–16. For a fuller discussion, see chapter 5.

8. The idea that God blesses the righteous materially is important in the Old Testament. However, it needs to be remembered that the Old Testament counterbalances this belief by teaching that the righteous may suffer (e.g., the story of Job) and that the wicked may prosper (e.g., Ps 49).

9. The reference to the rapid increase of the Israelites in Exod 1:7 provides an important link between the books of Genesis and Exodus.

10. This is highlighted, for example, in chapter 17 where God explicitly states that the covenant will be established through Isaac and not Ishmael (17:19–21). Although Ishmael is here blessed by God (17:20), he does not enjoy the same standing as Isaac.

11. Interestingly, this blessing echoes 1:22,28; 9:1,7.

12. While some readers may feel that, by deceiving his father and stealing his brother's blessing, Jacob acts immorally, various details in the narrative suggest that Jacob's actions are pardoned, at least in part, by the narrator. First, it is emphasised that Rebekah not only instigates the deception (27:5–10) but also states that she will accept full responsibility should the deception be discovered (27:13). Second, the narrator appears critical of Isaac for allowing his appetite for wild game to influence his attitude towards Esau (25:28). Thus, because of his love for Esau, Isaac seemingly ignores the implications of the divine statement made prior to the birth of the twin boys that Esau will be subservient to Jacob (25:23). Third, the concluding comments of chapter 26, that Esau's wives were a source of grief to Isaac and Rebekah (26:34–35), together with the earlier story of Esau selling his birthright for some stew (25:29–34), suggest that Esau is not worthy of the special paternal blessing. In the light of these factors, responsibility for Jacob's deception is shared by all the family members.

[5]

By Faith Abraham . . .

SUMMARY

The Abraham story (11:27–25:11) forms the heart of the book of Genesis. At the outset Abraham is the recipient of major divine promises (12:1–3). Significantly, the fulfilment of these promises is linked to Abraham's obedience to God. As the narrative develops a special attention is drawn to the fact that Abraham's faith in God is credited to him as righteousness (15:6). In response God covenants unconditionally to give Abraham's descendants the land of Canaan (15:18–21). Later God initiates a second covenant which differs from the first in two main ways: (a) in order for the covenant to be established Abraham must remain loyal and obedient to God, and (b) it guarantees that Abraham will be the father of many nations who will be blessed through him and his 'seed'. This second covenant is later established by divine oath when Abraham displays total trust in God through his willingness to sacrifice his son Isaac (22:16–18). The entire narrative highlights Abraham's faith in God as he awaits the fulfilment of the initial divine promises.

INTRODUCTION

In terms of the number of chapters given over to him Abraham is clearly the most important of all the human characters in Genesis. Moreover, his life marks an important watershed in God's relationship with human beings. Although there are in chapters 3–11 indications that divine mercy will triumph over the consequences of the fall, it is with Abraham that a clearer picture begins to emerge. The divine promises associated with his call (12:1–3) reveal that he is to play a central role in restoring humanity's broken relationship with God.

48

OVERVIEW OF THE ABRAHAM NARRATIVE

The Abraham narrative falls into two sections separated by a brief genealogy in 22:20–24; the main section consists of 11:27–22:19, with 23:1–25:11 forming an appendix. Running through the main section are the three closely intertwined themes of seed, land and blessing.

Within the Abraham narrative the theme of seed centres on the divine assurance that Abraham will have many descendants. The initial promises that Abraham will become a 'great nation' (12:2) and that his 'seed' will possess the land of Canaan (12:7) are set against the background of Sarah's inability to have children (11:30). Later, after the LORD assures Abraham that he will have a son of his own and many descendants (15:1–5), Sarah persuades him to have a child by her maidservant Hagar (16:1–4).[1] By naming him, Abraham claims Ishmael as his own (16:15). Afterwards, however, God reveals on two separate occasions that Sarah will indeed have a son who will be Abraham's true heir (17:15–21; 18:9–15). Eventually, Sarah gives birth to Isaac (21:1–7), and he is established as Abraham's heir through the divinely approved departure of Hagar and Ishmael (21:8–21). Thus, Isaac's birth marks the first step towards the fulfilment of the divine promise that Abraham will become a 'great nation' and have numerous descendants.

The second theme in the Abraham narrative concerns land. Initially, God commands Abraham to leave his own land and 'go to the land I will show you' (12:1). Although it is not mentioned specifically that Abraham will possess this land, the promise that he will become a 'great nation' (12:2) implies that his descendants will possess it; the Hebrew term *gôy* 'nation' denotes people inhabiting a specific geographical location and forming a political unit. Thus, when Abraham first arrives in Canaan, the LORD promises, 'To your offspring (seed) I will give this land' (12:7). Later, following the separation of Lot from Abraham, God repeats this promise, emphasising the extent of the land to be possessed by Abraham's descendants (13:14–17).[2] The topic of land reappears in 15:7–21 where the idea is introduced that Abraham's descendants will take possession of the land of Canaan only after a period of four hundred years during which they will be slaves in another country (15:13–14). This revelation of a delay regarding the acquisition of the land probably explains why the promise of land, which is prominent in chapters 12–15, is mentioned less frequently in the remaining chapters of the Abraham narrative (cf. 17:8; 22:17). Although later episodes highlight Abraham's acquisition of a well at Beersheba and a tomb at Hebron, these mark only the beginning of the process by which God will fulfil his promise to Abraham regarding land and nationhood.

The third main strand in the Abraham narrative is, as we have already noted in chapter five, the idea that Abraham and his 'seed' will be a source of divine blessing, or possibly cursing, for others. This is highlighted in both the initial call of Abraham and the concluding oath in 22:16–18. Although various episodes reflect in part the divine blessing or cursing of others (e.g. the visit to Egypt [12:10–20], the abduction of Lot by the eastern kings [14:1–24], the rescue of Lot from Sodom [18:16–19:29], the abduction of Sarah by Abimelech [20:1–18] and the treaty between Abimelech and Abraham [21:22–34]), it is clear that, like the promise of nationhood, the promise of God's blessing upon all the families of the earth will only be fulfilled in the future (cf. 22:18).

This brief survey of the themes of seed, land and blessing establishes their presence within Genesis 12–25. To explore further how they are developed within the Abraham narrative we shall examine in more detail the initial call of Abraham in 12:1–3, the covenants in chapters 15 and 17, and the divine oath in 22:16–18. This will enable us to have a clearer picture of how the overall narrative is structured.

THE DIVINE CALL OF ABRAHAM IN GEN 12:1–3

Within the context of the book of Genesis the divine speech in 12:1–3 is very important. It marks the beginning of a new stage in God's relationship with humanity, and sets the agenda for the entire Abraham story, and beyond, introducing those themes which will be developed in the subsequent narrative. The LORD says to Abraham,

> Leave your country, your people and your father's household and go to the land I will show you, so that I may make you into a great nation and bless you and make your name great. Be a blessing, so that I may bless those who bless you, and curse the one who disdains you, and so that all the families of the ground may be blessed through you (12:1–3; my translation).

Two features of this speech are noteworthy in the present context. First, the fulfilment of the divine promises is conditional upon Abraham's obedience. By commanding him to leave his homeland and be a blessing, God places the onus on Abraham to obey in order that the promises concerning land, descendants and the blessing of others may be fulfilled.[3] Secondly, the climax of the speech comes in the statement, 'so that all the families of the ground may be blessed through you'. The primary motive behind the call of Abraham is God's desire to bring blessing, rather than cursing, upon the nations of the earth. The promise that Abraham will become a great nation, implying both numerous seed and land, must be understood as being subservient to God's principal desire to bless all the families of the earth.[4]

Abraham's positive response to God's command is noted immediately, and his arrival in the land of Canaan is rewarded by the assurance that 'to your descendants (seed) I will give this land' (12:7). The subject of land dominates ch. 13 where, following the separation of Lot and Abraham, God confirms that Abraham's many descendants will take possession of the land of Canaan (cf. 13:14–17). The promise of land then comes to an important climax in ch. 15 with God covenanting to give Abraham's descendants the land 'from the river of Egypt to the great river, the Euphrates' (15:18).

THE UNCONDITIONAL PROMISSORY COVENANT OF GEN 15

Chapter 15 falls into two parts which have in common the subject of inheritance. Whereas verses 1–6 are concerned with Abraham's immediate and future heirs, verses 7–21 focus on what shall be inherited. Abraham is reassured by God (a) that he will have a son of his own from whom shall come numerous descendants, and (b) that after several centuries these descendants will take possession of the land of Canaan. Interestingly, the two parts of the chapter parallel each other structurally. They both begin with a divine statement (15:1; 15:7) followed by a question from Abraham (15:2: 15:8). Next we have God's response involving an appropriate sign (15:4–5; 15:9–17),[5] and finally, a concluding comment by the narrator (15:6; 15:18–21).

Two elements in the chapter deserve special attention. First, verse 6 contains the observation that 'Abram believed the LORD, and he credited it to him as righteousness'. The rarity in Genesis of such comments by the narrator makes them all the more important when they occur. Here Abraham is viewed as righteous in God's sight because he believes unreservedly that the LORD will fulfil his promise regarding a son and numerous descendants. Thus, Abraham is reckoned righteous on account of his faith in God's promise, rather than due to any deeds performed by him.

Secondly, the LORD makes a covenant with Abraham which affirms that his 'seed' will possess the land of Canaan. This marks the climax of the earlier divine promises regarding land and descendants found in 12:7 and 13:14–17. Several features of

the covenant are worth noting. (a) It guarantees unconditionally what the LORD has stated to Abraham. Nowhere is it
indicated that the fulfilment of the covenant is dependent upon
the actions of either Abraham or his descendants; God
covenants unreservedly to fulfil his promise that Abraham's
descendants will possess the land of Canaan. For this reason
it may be designated an unconditional promissory covenant.
(b) The structure of the chapter suggests that there is a link
between the making of the promissory covenant in verses 18–
21 and the comment about Abraham believing God in verse 6.
Because of the righteousness imputed to Abraham, God
blesses Abraham by guaranteeing that the divine promises
regarding descendants and land will be fulfilled. (c) The terms
of the covenant mention only descendants and possession of
the land; there is no reference to blessing being mediated to
others. This omission is significant and is one of the main ways
in which this covenant differs from that outlined in ch. 17. The
covenant in ch. 15 guarantees only some of the divine promises
mentioned in 12:1–3. For the remainder we must look ahead to
ch. 17.

THE ETERNAL COVENANT OF CIRCUMCISION IN GEN 17

The introduction of a second covenant in chapter 17 is somewhat surprising. Why should God make another covenant with
Abraham? To answer this, it is necessary to observe that the
covenant in chapter 17 differs in a number of important ways
from that given in chapter 15. First, it is a conditional covenant.
Whereas the promissory covenant of chapter 15 is unconditional, the establishment or ratification of the covenant of
circumcision is dependent upon Abraham's continuing obedience to God. This is highlighted in the introduction to the
covenant. After identifying himself as El Shaddai (God
Almighty), the LORD says to Abraham, 'Walk before me and be
blameless so that I may confirm my covenant between me and
you and increase you greatly' (17:1–2; my translation).
Unfortunately, many English translations fail to appreciate the
distinctive syntax of the Hebrew original and so miss the
important link which exists between the initial imperatives,
'Walk before me and be blameless', and the fact that these must
be obeyed before the covenant will be established. The
covenant will be ratified by the LORD only if Abraham walks
before God and is blameless. Significantly, for the actual
establishment of the covenant we must look to the divine oath
which concludes the account of the testing of Abraham in ch.
22.[6]

Secondly, the covenant of circumcision differs from the promissory covenant of chapter 15 in that it is an eternal covenant. Whereas the covenant of chapter 15 is a divine guarantee to Abraham that his descendants will possess the land of Canaan, the covenant of circumcision entails a continuing special relationship between God and Abraham's 'seed'. Although the covenant may embrace those who are not Abraham's natural children — others within his household, including foreigners, may be circumcised (17:12) — God makes it clear that his covenant is intimately linked to the chosen family line; it will be established with the promised 'seed' Isaac and not Ishmael (17:19–21).

Thirdly, whereas the emphasis in chapter 15 is solely upon descendants and land, the covenant in chapter 17 focuses primarily on Abraham as the father of many nations. God states,

> As for me, this is my covenant with you: You will be the father of many nations. No longer will you be called Abram; your name will be Abraham, for I have made you a father of many nations. I will make you very fruitful; I will make nations of you, and kings will come from you (17:4–6).

These words are echoed briefly regarding Sarah: 'I will bless her so that she will be the mother of nations; kings of peoples will come from her' (17:16). The mention of nations coming from Abraham and Sarah presents a problem if this is interpreted as referring only to those nations which are directly descended from both of them; strictly speaking, only the Israelites and Edomites come within this category.[7] However, it is likely that the concept of 'father' is not restricted here to actual physical descendants. Rather Abraham is the 'father' of all who are circumcised. Thus God instructs Abraham to circumcise not merely his own family members but every male 'including those born in your household or bought with your money from a foreigner — those who are not your offspring (seed). Whether born in your household or bought with your money, they must be circumcised' (17:12-13).[8]

By changing Abram's name to Abraham, God underlines the importance of the fact that he will be the father of many nations. This occurs not because these nations are his natural descendants but because he is for them the channel of divine blessing. This understanding of 'father' is probably reflected in the unusual comment that Joseph 'was father to Pharaoh' (45:8). Furthermore, when God blesses Jacob in 35:11, echoing an earlier blessing by Isaac upon Jacob (28:3), a distinction is drawn between 'a nation' and 'a community of nations' coming from him. The implication would seem to be that whereas many nations will be closely associated with him, only one nation will be directly descended from him.[9]

In the light of the divine promises given in 12:1–3 it is clear that the covenants in chs. 15 and 17 complement each other. Whereas ch. 15 focuses on descendants and land, the emphasis in ch. 17 is upon Abraham as the one who imparts God's blessing to others; in this capacity he is the father of many nations. This understanding of the covenant of circumcision is later reflected in the divine oath of ch. 22 which establishes the covenant with Abraham.

THE DIVINE OATH IN GEN 22:16–18

The divine speech in 22:16–18 forms a frame with Abraham's call in 12:1–3 and so brings to a conclusion the main section of the Abraham narrative. All that was promised conditionally in 12:1–3 is now guaranteed by divine oath:

> I swear by myself, declares the LORD, that because you have done this and have not withheld your son, your only son, I will surely bless you and make your descendants (seed) as numerous as the stars in the sky and as the sand on the seashore. Your descendants (seed) will take possession of the cities (gate) of their (his) enemies, and through your offspring (seed) all nations on earth will be blessed, because you have obeyed me.

This oath not only signals the end of the main section of the Abraham narrative, but also establishes the covenant of circumcision promised in ch. 17. By demonstrating his obedience to God, even to the point of being willing to sacrifice his only son, Abraham fulfils the conditions laid down in 17:1; he shows beyond doubt his willingness to walk before God and be blameless.

Evidence supporting the idea that ch. 22 should be linked to the covenant of circumcision in ch. 17 may be deduced by considering the account of the covenant with Noah in chapters 6–9.[10] An analysis of this earlier covenant reveals that it has the following structure:

(a) The promise of a covenant   6:18
(b) The obligations of the covenant   6:14–16,19–21;
                                      7:1–3
(c) The fulfilment of the obligations 6:22; 7:5
(d) The sacrifice of a burnt-offering 8:20
(e) The establishment of the covenant 9:9–17

Remarkably, the same structure emerges if chapters 17 and 22 are taken together. Chapter 17 records the promise of a covenant with Abraham, accompanied by certain obligations: Abraham is to walk before God and be blameless. While these are more general than those given to Noah, God later tests Abraham's obedience in a specific way; he demands that Abraham should offer up his only son Isaac as a burnt-offering (22:2). In spite of the terrible consequences of killing his heir, Abraham displays his willingness to fulfil even the most testing of divine commands. After God's intervention and the deliverance of Isaac, Abraham offers up as a burnt-offering a ram which has been unexpectedly provided.[11] Finally, God establishes the covenant with Abraham by swearing an oath (22:16–18).

By linking chapters 17 and 22 new light may be shed on a number of issues. First, it is possible to account for the divine testing of Abraham. Through his obedience in ch. 22 Abraham demonstrates his willingness to keep the conditions of the covenant laid out in 17:1. Secondly, the fact that the events of ch. 22 are part of a conditional covenant explains why Abraham is considered in 22:16–18 and 26:2–5 to have merited by his obedience the divine guarantee of the promises concerning seed, land and the blessing of others. Thirdly, the oath in 22:16–18 forms a very fitting conclusion to the main section of the Abraham narrative. Although many scholars view verses 15–18 as a later addition to the original account of the testing of Abraham, the structure of the covenant requires the sacrifice of a burnt-offering before God could confirm with an oath the earlier promises. Verses 15–18 are not only an integral and essential part of ch. 22 but of the entire Abraham narrative.[12]

The divine oath in 22:16–18 not only embraces the contents of the earlier promissory covenant regarding many descendants and land but also includes the additional aspect that all nations will be blessed through Abraham's 'seed'. The mention of 'seed' is significant. Unfortunately, the identify of this 'seed' is not easy to determine. While the first mention of 'seed' denotes 'descendants' in the plural, the remaining references are ambiguous; they could refer either to many descendants or to a single descendant. This latter possibility deserves special consideration for three reasons. First, the book of Genesis as a whole devotes considerable attention to tracing a line of 'seed' which, beginning with Adam and ending with Judah, forms the early ancestry of the Davidic dynasty. Unfortunately, the importance of this single line of descendants is generally overlooked by scholars. Secondly, the Jacob and Joseph stories give prominence to the blessing which the patriarchs, as members of this family line, may bestow on others. Although Esau and Jacob are both the 'seed' of Isaac, it is clear that the brother who receives the father's blessing will be favoured more than the other. Thus, it is Jacob who experiences God's blessing and is able to mediate it to others. Similarly, Joseph is undoubtedly favoured by his father Jacob who eventually imparts the blessing of the firstborn to Joseph's son Ephraim (48:1–22). Significantly, Genesis focuses on the blessing which others receive through Jacob and Joseph. They alone are presented as the ones who may impart blessing to others. Although other 'seed' exist, the Genesis narrative usually associates the power to bless with those who receive the first-born blessing. Thirdly, in announcing the covenant of circumcision to Abraham, God emphasises the unique role of Isaac; it is with Isaac that the covenant will be established and not with Ishmael (17:19,21). Given the limited interest which Genesis displays in the descendants of Ishmael, it seems logical to conclude that the 'seed' of Abraham mentioned in 22:18 does not include Ishmael and his descendants. For these reasons, the possibility exists that the final reference to 'seed' in 22:18 denotes a single descendant.

Clearly the covenants in chapters 15 and 17 differ markedly. Whereas chapter 15 records an unconditional promissory covenant which does not necessarily entail an ongoing relationship between God and the descendants of Abraham, the covenant of circumcision is both conditional and eternal. Furthermore, while it is implied in chapter 15 that Abraham's faith, credited as righteousness, is the catalyst for the making of the promissory covenant, the establishment of the covenant of circumcision rests on Abraham's obedience to God. As reflected in 26:2–5, Abraham's obedience is an important factor in the establishment of this eternal covenant.

CONCLUSION

Viewed as a whole, the Abraham narrative provides an interesting picture of the interplay between divine word and human faith and obedience. Initially, the LORD makes a series of promises, the fulfilment of which is conditional upon Abraham's obedience (12:1–3). As Abraham in faith obeys and journeys to Canaan, God declares that he shall have both land and descendants (12:7; 13:14–17). In time these statements are confirmed in a promissory covenant (15:18–21) which is linked to Abraham being credited as righteous on account of his faith (15:6). The narrative, however, does not conclude here, but goes on to highlight Abraham's continuing faith in and obedience to God, as revealed in the establishment of the eternal covenant of circumcision (17:1–27; 22:1–19), a covenant which focuses on the divine blessing that will come through Abraham and his 'seed' to all nations. Thus from beginning to end, faith expressed in obedience is the hallmark of Abraham's relationship with the LORD.

Abraham's faith, however, is all the more remarkable when the following factors are also taken into account. Firstly, it is clear that the divine promises concerning nationhood (i.e. seed and land) and the blessing of all the families of the earth will never be fulfilled in Abraham's lifetime; at the very most Abraham will only experience the firstfruits of their fulfilment. Secondly, circumstances exist or develop which militate against the fulfilment of these promises. Sarah's barrenness is a major obstacle for much of the narrative, and even when all seems assured with the birth of Isaac, God himself places the future fulfilment of the promises in jeopardy by demanding that Abraham sacrifice Isaac. Yet, in spite of these factors Abraham displays a faith in God which in the book of Genesis is matched only by that of Noah.

NEW TESTAMENT CONNECTIONS

There is little doubt that within the New Testament Epistles the most noteworthy aspect of Abraham's life is his faith. We see this very clearly in Hebrews 11 which provides a detailed list of those 'ancients' who were commended for having faith. Significantly, approximately one-third of the chapter is devoted to Abraham (Heb 11:8–19), making him by far the most important person listed.[13] Fittingly, the author of Hebrews highlights Abraham's faith as an example of 'being sure of what we hope for and certain of what we do not see' (Heb 11:1).

As regards Paul's understanding of Abraham, in Romans 4 and Galatians 3 the emphasis is clearly on the fact that, according to Genesis 15:6, Abraham was justified or made righteous by his faith and not by being circumcised and keeping the law.[14] For Paul, the sequence of events in the Abraham story is all important. Since Abraham is credited as righteous prior to being circumcised, circumcision is not necessary in order for an individual to be reckoned righteous in God's eyes. He writes,

> We have been saying that Abraham's faith was credited to him as righteousness. Under what circumstances was it credited? Was it after he was circumcised, or before? It was not after, but before! And he received the sign of circumcision, a seal of the righteousness that he had by faith while he was still uncircumcised. So then,

he is the father of all who believe but have not been circumcised, in order that righteousness might be credited to them. And he is also the father of the circumcised who not only are circumcised but who also walk in the footsteps of the faith that our father Abraham had before he was circumcised (Rom 4:9–12).

Here Paul stresses that Abraham is the father of those who have faith, whether they are his natural descendants or not (cf. Rom 9:6–8). Thus, he concludes that Jews and Gentiles can only be justified by faith.

A similar, but not identical, argument is advanced in Gal 2:5–3:29 as Paul responds to those who emphasise the necessity of circumcision in order to be children of Abraham and hence recipients of the promises made to him. He writes,

Consider Abraham: 'He believed God, and it was credited to him as righteousness.' Understand, then, that those who believe are children of Abraham (Gal 3:6–7).

By stressing the importance of faith over against circumcision Paul concludes that it is not necessary for an individual to be circumcised in order to be a child of Abraham.

Paul, however, does not conclude his argument in Galatians at this point. He focuses on three further aspects of the Abraham narrative in order to drive home his case that the Gentiles are now the recipients of God's blessing. First, he sees in the justification of the Gentiles the fulfilment of the divine promise to Abraham that all nations would be blessed through him.

The Scripture foresaw that God would justify the Gentiles by faith, and announced the gospel in advance to Abraham: 'All nations will be blessed through you.' So those who have faith are blessed along with Abraham, the man of faith (Gal 3:9).

By highlighting the importance which the Genesis narrative places on all nations being blessed through Abraham, Paul challenges the view of his opponents that God's blessing was only intended for the actual descendants of Abraham.

Secondly, Paul argues that the divine promises made to Abraham find their ultimate fulfilment in Jesus Christ. To arrive at this conclusion Paul focuses on the concept of 'seed'. He argues that the promises were given to Abraham and to his 'seed', implying one person, and that this 'seed' is Jesus Christ. Some biblical scholars conclude that while Paul adopts here a form of rabbinic exegesis which might have been practised by his Jewish contemporaries, his approach is clearly not in keeping with modern critical methods of exegesis. Unfortunately, these scholars have perhaps too readily dismissed Paul's interpretation without examining in detail how the term 'seed' in used in Genesis. As noted in chapter two, the Hebrew word *zera*ᶜ 'seed' is clearly a keyword in Genesis and while it sometimes denotes a group it may also refer to a single individual (e.g. Gen 4:25; 21:13). This latter possibility is significant, especially when we observe that the entire book of Genesis focuses on a particular line of seed which enjoyed a special relationship with God. Remarkably, Genesis devotes considerable attention, especially in the patriarchal stories, to identifying the seed of this special line. Furthermore, there are clear indications that this line of seed formed the early ancestry of the royal line of David. Apart from the reference to kings being descended from Abraham (17:6), Jacob's blessing of Judah in 49:8–12 indicates that royalty will come from the line of Judah. If Genesis as a whole focuses on a royal line of seed through which God will fulfil his promises to Abraham, then Paul's interpretation of the term *zera*ᶜ as referring to Jesus Christ is in keeping with the common NT understanding of Jesus as the Davidic Messiah. Thus, Paul affirms that it is only through faith in Jesus Christ, the 'seed' of Abraham, that Jews and Gentiles may now receive the blessing given to Abraham and become God's children.

Finally, Paul also argues in Galatians that the divine covenant made with Abraham takes precedence over the law given several centuries later at Mount Sinai. Whereas his opponents were advocating that believers must keep the law in order to be righteous, Paul responds by noting that the law, given later to fulfil a temporary role until Christ came, could never make anyone righteous since it merely indicated the righteousness required by God, not the means of achieving such righteousness. As such it underlined the necessity of becoming righteous through faith.

Since Paul uses the Abraham narrative in four distinctive ways in Galatians to challenge the view of his opponents that Gentile believers must be circumcised and obey the law of Moses in order to know God's salvation, it is apparent that his understanding of the gospel was heavily influenced by his reading of Genesis 12–25.

Abraham's faith is also discussed in Jas 2:20–24. Here, however, the context differs from that found in Romans and Galatians. Whereas Paul seeks to demonstrate the priority of faith over circumcision, James is concerned to clarify the nature of saving faith: 'What good is it, my brothers, if a man claims to have faith but has no deeds? Can such faith save him' (Jas 2:14)? At the heart of James's discussion is the desire to show that true faith in God will exhibit itself in righteous actions.

Thus, he focuses on Abraham and in particular the offering of Isaac on the altar.

> Was not our ancestor Abraham considered righteous for what he did when he offered his son Isaac on the altar? You see that his faith and his actions were working together, and his faith was made complete by what he did. And the scripture was fulfilled that says, 'Abraham believed God, and it was credited to him as righteousness', and he was called God's friend. You see that a person is justified by what he does and not by faith alone (Jas 2:21–24).

Here James reveals how faith in and obedience to God cannot be separated. While James accepts that Abraham was justified by faith, as stated in Genesis 15:6, he views the later actions of Abraham as visible expressions of his inner faith. Undoubtedly, he focuses on Genesis 22 because of the way in which Abraham is rewarded for his willingness to sacrifice Isaac. For James there can be no separation of faith and deeds. Thus, he views Abraham's actions in chapter 22 as the fulfilment or culmination of what was stated in Genesis 15:6.

Although James writes, 'that a person is justified by what he does and not by faith alone' (Jas 2:24), it is clear from the context that he does not actually contradict what Paul has to say in Romans and Galatians. Both men were addressing different situations and therefore highlighted different aspects of Abraham's faith. On the one hand, Paul concentrated on Genesis 15:6 because he was responding either directly or indirectly to those who wished to emphasise the necessity of circumcision for salvation. On the other hand, James was concerned to show that Abraham's faith, by which he was justified, produced righteous actions. Thus, he writes, 'faith without deeds is dead' (Jas 2:26). Undoubtedly, Paul and James would have agreed wholeheartedly with what the other had to say, given the different problems that confronted them.

The final New Testament passage to be considered briefly is Heb 6:13–18. It is included here not because it focuses on Abraham's faith, but because it draws attention to the oath which God gave in order to guarantee beyond doubt the fulfilment of the divine promise made to Abraham.

> Because God wanted to make the unchanging nature of his purpose very clear to the heirs of what was promised, he confirmed it with an oath. God did this so that, by two unchangeable things in which it is impossible for God to lie, we who have fled to take hold of the hope offered to us may be greatly encouraged (Heb 6:17–18).

The oath mentioned here clearly refers to Gen 22:16–18. By anticipating the coming of a royal descendant of Abraham who will impart God's blessing to the nations, this oath is an important part of the NT understanding of Jesus Christ's mission.

NOTES

1. It was a custom in the ancient Near East that the maidservant of a barren wife might act as a surrogate mother.

2. Although Abraham is mentioned as possessing the land, there is no suggestion that the present inhabitants of the land will be dispossessed during Abraham's lifetime.

3. As it stands the divine speech to Abraham falls naturally into two halves, each introduced by an imperative. Whereas the first half focuses on the promise of nationhood, the second centres on the blessing of others. As we shall observe below, this two-fold division is reflected in the two covenants found in chs. 15 and 17.

4. The importance of the theme of blessing is underlined by the five-fold repetition of the root *bārēk* 'to bless' in 12:2–3.

5. The first sign, the stars in the heavens, conveys the vast number of Abraham's descendants. The second sign is more complex. The sacrificial animals probably represent Abraham's descendants, the birds of prey are the Egyptians and 'the smoking brazier with a blazing torch' indicates God's presence. The sign thus looks forward to the release of the Israelites from slavery in Egypt and the subsequent presence of the LORD in their midst. After the exodus God's presence was indicated by the pillar of cloud by day and the pillar of fire by night (Exod 13:21; 19:18; 20:18).

6. Although the covenant of circumcision is initiated in ch. 17, it is only finally established in ch. 22. A period of time must elapse between the initiation and the establishment of the covenant due to its conditional nature. What establishes the covenant is not the act of circumcision itself, but obedience to God.

7. The Israelites and Edomites are descended from Jacob and Esau respectively. The Ishmaelites and Midianites are probably not to be included here because they are not descended from Sarah. N.M. Sarna, *Genesis* (The JPS Torah Commentary; Philadelphia/New York/Jerusalem: Jewish Publication Society, 1989), 124, observes that the phrase ' "father of many nations" has a more universal application in that a large segment of humanity looks upon Abraham as its spiritual father.'

8. Those who were circumcised enjoyed a special relationship with each other. We witness evidence of this in chapter 34 where the sons of Jacob promise Shechem and his father Hamor that if they are circumcised, 'Then we will give you our daughters and take your daughters for ourselves. We'll settle among you and become one people with you' (34:16). Against this background the killing by Simeon and Levi of all those who have just been circumcised is exceptionally repulsive to their father Jacob (34:24–31).

9. The same idea of blessing being mediated to others may underlie Noah's comments regarding the relationship between

Japheth and Shem: 'May God extend the territory of Japheth; may Japheth live in the tents of Shem . . .' (9:27).

10. Six important parallels can be observed between the two covenants.

> First, both covenants are described as eternal or everlasting covenants, *běrît 'ôlām* (9:16; 17:7,13,19). Second, these covenants are accompanied by an appropriate sign. In the case of Noah it is the rainbow (9:12–14), and in the case of Abraham it is circumcision (17:11). The rainbow is related to rain which in turn would remind the people of the flood. Circumcision relates to the procreation of descendants which is a point of emphasis in the covenant of ch. 17. Third, in both cases, the expressions used of the formation of the covenant are *hēqîm běrît* (9:9,11,17; 17:7,19,21) and *nātan běrît* (9:12; 17:2). Fourth, the covenants in chs. 9 and 17 are spoken of by God as 'between me and you' (9:12,15; 17:2,7). However, at the same time they also include the descendants of Noah and Abraham (9:9,12; 17:7,9). Fifth, the benefit which each covenant brings for those with whom it is established is that they shall not be cut off (9:11; 17:14). Sixth, the divine command in 17:1, 'Walk before me and be blameless', resembles the description of Noah in 6:9, 'Blameless in his generation; Noah walked with God'. The word 'blameless', *tāmîm*, is found only on these two occasions in the whole of Genesis. This list of similarities highlights the close parallels which exist between the two covenants (T.D. Alexander, 'Genesis 22 and the Covenant of Circumcision', *JSOT* 25 [1983] 19–20.)

11. It is noteworthy that in the whole of Genesis it is only here and in 8:20 that the term 'burnt-offering' is used to designate a sacrifice.

12. The proposal supported by various commentators that originally in vv. 1–14 the sparing of Isaac was the reward for Abraham's obedience is surely inadequate. Had Abraham disobeyed the divine command and stayed at home, the life of Isaac would never have been placed in any danger. The sparing of Isaac is hardly a suitable reward for Abraham's obedience.

13. Moses, who is next in importance, receives about half the space given to Abraham (cf. Heb 11:23–28).

14. Genesis 15:6 is quoted in Rom 4:3 and Gal 3:6.

[6]

Who is the LORD?

SUMMARY

Exodus is essentially a book about knowing God through personal experience. The plot centres on the relationship which develops between the LORD God and the Israelites, from the dramatic meeting with Moses at the burning bush (3:1–4:17) to the glory of the LORD filling the tabernacle (40:34–38). Throughout Exodus God always takes the initiative, revealing himself not only through words, but also through signs and wonders. In differing ways he reveals his most significant attributes: his sovereign majesty, his holiness, his power to perform signs and wonders, his awesome glory; his righteousness; his compassion.

AN OVERVIEW OF EXODUS

The book of Exodus continues the story of Genesis by tracing the destiny of the children of Jacob. Although Exodus itself forms a continuous account it may be divided into two parts, both focusing on the theme of knowing God. The first half of the book is dominated by the theme of coming to a personal knowledge of God. At the outset Moses encounters God at the burning bush, and in the ensuing conversation discovers much about God's nature, including his divine name, the LORD (3:1–4:17). The theme reappears when Pharaoh expresses his ignorance about the LORD: 'Who is the LORD, that I should obey him and let Israel go? I do not know the LORD and I will not let Israel go' (5:2). As the various signs and wonders unfold the Egyptians gradually come to acknowledge the LORD's sovereign power. When God finally lures the Egyptian army to its death in the Sea of Reeds it is with the expressed purpose that 'the Egyptians will know that I am the LORD' (14:4,18). In celebration of their deliverance from Egypt the Israelites worship God in a dynamic song of praise which highlights their knowledge of him: 'Who among the gods is like you, O LORD? Who is like you — majestic in holiness, awesome in glory, working wonders?' (15:11).

The second half of Exodus develops further the theme of knowing God by focusing on the establishment of a special relationship between the LORD and the Israelites. To this end the narrative concentrates on two topics which receive extensive coverage, the making of a covenant and the construction of the tabernacle. The former of these, like the signing of a contract or the taking of marriage vows, sets out the conditions under which the Israelites must live in order to enjoy an ongoing relationship with God; these conditions are recorded in the Decalogue (20:3–17) and the Book of the Covenant (21:1–23:33). The people are required to reflect God's righteous and compassionate nature if they wish to experience his continued blessing and presence. Exodus records not only the establishment of the initial covenant agreement (chs. 19–24), but also the events surrounding the making of the golden calf which almost brought the covenant relationship to an early and abrupt conclusion (chs. 32–34). The construction of the tabernacle forms a natural sequel to the making of the divine covenant. Built according to divine instruction, the tabernacle becomes the focal point of the LORD's presence in the midst of the people, and reminds them, through its materials and structure, of God's sovereign, holy nature. Following the erection of the tabernacle, the LORD takes up residence in the midst of his people (40:34–38), bringing the book of Exodus to a fitting conclusion.

THE ISRAELITES IN EGYPT

The initial two chapters of Exodus record events which span a period of several centuries and form a bridge between the detailed account of the life of Joseph in Genesis 37–50 and the report of the Israelites' release from Egypt in Exodus 3–15. Not only do chapters 1–2 presuppose that the reader is already familiar with the book of Genesis, but they also continue an important trend in Genesis regarding how God is portrayed. Whereas Genesis begins with God as the central participant in the story, a change occurs throughout the book as God gradually retreats from the centre of the stage and adopts the role of an off-stage director. We see this most clearly with Joseph, who, unlike his immediate ancestors, has no direct encounter with the LORD. Rather, God controls the destiny of both Joseph and his wider family without revealing himself directly. The opening two chapters of Exodus also convey the impression that God no longer reveals himself in person. The narrative highlights only his providential care as reflected in the case of the two midwives and inferred in the remarkable increase of the Israelites. Against this background the narrator's comments in 2:23–25 are significant. Although the Israelites may have felt that God was no longer concerned about them, such was not the case. God was well aware of their situation, and, when the time was right, he would act in a dramatic way to free them from oppression.

Special attention is also given in ch. 2 to the events surrounding the early life of Moses and his later exile in Midian. By highlighting his remarkable deliverance from death at birth and the irony of his growing up within the household of Pharaoh, the narrative anticipates the important role which Moses will play within the rest of the book. Furthermore, the nature of this role is hinted at by his actions on behalf of those who are oppressed by others. With Moses's flight to Midian, the scene is set for God to reveal himself in a most remarkable way.

THE LORD REVEALS HIMSELF TO MOSES

Although the reader is partially prepared for the encounter between God and Moses, it must have come as a surprise to Moses. Several elements of the meeting are worth noting briefly. Firstly, Moses encounters God in a burning bush. Throughout Exodus the divine presence is frequently symbolised by fire and smoke (13:21,22; 14:24; 19:18; 24:17; 40:38; cf. Lev 9:24; 10:2; Num 9:15,16; 11:1–3; 14:14; Deut 1:33; 4:11,12,15,24,33,36; 5:4,5,22–26; 9:3,10,15; 10:4; 18:16). Secondly, Moses acknowledges God's holiness by removing his sandals; God must be approached with caution. The concept of divine holiness reappears in Exodus (and Leviticus) as a major theme.[1] Thirdly, having led his father-in-law's flock through the desert to Horeb (v. 1), Moses will later lead the Israelites to the same location (cf. 3:12; 19:1–2), where they also will witness God's holy presence revealed through fire.

Although God initially introduces himself to Moses as 'the God of your father, the God of Abraham, the God of Isaac and the God of Jacob' (3:6), the issue of his identity reappears in vv. 13-15 when Moses inquires about his name. This request is important because the Israelites believed that an individual's nature was reflected in his or her name. In Genesis different aspects of God's nature are highlighted by the names used to designate him: El Elyon (God Most High; Gen 14:18–20), El Roi

(God who sees me; Gen 16:13), El Shaddai (God Almighty; Gen 17:1), El Olam (God Everlasting; Gen 21:33). Here God introduces himself using the personal name 'Yahweh', translated in most English versions as 'the LORD' (3:15).[2] The Hebrew name 'Yahweh' is closely related to the phrase in verse 14 which may be translated in a variety of ways: 'I AM WHO I AM', 'I will be who I will be', 'I will be what I was'. An abbreviated form of this phrase comes in the statement, 'I AM has sent me to you' (3:14). Unlike previous designations, the name Yahweh does not limit God's nature to any particular characteristic: he is what he is. Furthermore, his nature does not change. He is the God worshipped by earlier generations ('the God of Abraham, the God of Isaac and the God of Jacob') and generations yet to come ('this is my name for ever, the name by which I am to be remembered from generation to generation').

Apart from revealing his name, God also informed Moses that he was to return to Egypt and assemble the elders of Israel. Together they are to ask permission from Pharaoh to take the Israelites on a short three-day journey into the desert in order that they may worship their God (3:18). Pharaoh's reaction to this relatively minor demand will reveal his strong antagonism towards the Israelites. He will refuse to accommodate them, not because their request is excessive, but because of his own hardness of heart. The narrative in chs. 7–15 reinforces this initial observation. Pharaoh will not change his mind 'unless a mighty hand compels him' (3:19). The influence of God's hand upon the Egyptians will be such that they will readily give of their possessions in order to see the Israelites leave Egypt. These gifts will compensate the Israelites for the suffering they have already endured.

In spite of the assurance of God's presence, Moses raises a problem. What if the Israelites do not believe him? How will he convince them that God has indeed appeared to him? In response God provides three signs which involve miraculous transformations: Moses's staff will become a snake (4:2–4); his hand will become leprous (4:6–7); Nile water will become blood (4:9). Moses witnesses for himself the first two of these signs. The third, at this stage, must be accepted by faith. Significantly, when all three are later shown to the Israelites they are convinced that God has indeed sent Moses (4:30–31).

When Moses first encounters Pharaoh, the Egyptian king displays his contempt towards Moses, Aaron and, especially, the LORD: 'Who is the LORD, that I should obey him and let Israel go? I do not know the LORD and I will not let Israel go' (5:2).[3] Although Pharaoh has no knowledge of the LORD, this will soon change dramatically. The motif of knowing the LORD recurs frequently throughout the following chapters (cf. 6:7; 7:5,17; 8:10,22; 9:14,16,29; 10:2; 14:4,18). Having already revealed himself to Moses, Aaron and the Israelite elders, God will now reveal himself powerfully to Pharaoh and the Egyptians.

A further divine speech to Moses in 6:28–7:7 also anticipates the 'miraculous signs and wonders' which are to dominate chapters 7 to 14. Attention is drawn to the hardening of Pharaoh's heart and to the 'mighty acts of judgement' by which God will lead Israel out of Egypt. God declares that as a result 'the Egyptians will know that I am the LORD' (7:5). Thus the scene is set for the cycle of episodes which compose 7:8–14:31.

SIGNS AND WONDERS IN EGYPT

The Exodus narrative devotes considerable space to the account of the signs and wonders performed in Egypt. While they are often described as 'the ten plagues', this is not an entirely satisfactory designation. Firstly, although the biblical text refers to a few of them individually as 'plagues'[4] (9:3,14,15; 11:1; cf. 8:2), as a whole they are more frequently designated 'signs' (7:3; 8:23; 10:1,2) or 'wonders' (4:21; 7:3; 11:9,10; cf. 'miracle' in 7:9).[5] Secondly, there are in fact eleven miraculous signs recorded in chapters 7–12. The first of these, the episode of the staff becoming a snake (7:8–13), is generally not included in the list of 'plagues'. This was also the first sign which God gave Moses in order to convince the Israelites that the LORD had indeed appeared to him (4:2–5). The next sign which Moses performed before Pharaoh, turning water into blood (7:14–25), was also earlier used to demonstrate Moses's divine calling to the Israelites (4:8–9). Yet, whereas the Israelites believed Moses on account of these signs (4:30–31), Pharaoh paid no attention to them (7:13,22); his own magicians were able to perform the same wonders (7:11,22).

The individual accounts of the miraculous signs follow the same pattern, but with some variation to avoid monotony. Certain features are common to all eleven episodes. First, the report of each miraculous sign begins with the phrase, 'the LORD said to Moses' (7:8,14; 8:1,16,20; 9:1,8,13; 10:1,21; 11:1). The initiative for each sign rests with God, with every stage in the encounter between Moses and Pharaoh being divinely controlled. Secondly, each episode, echoing the predictions given in 4:21 and 7:3–4, concludes with an explicit reference to the hardening of Pharaoh's heart (7:13,22; 8:15,19,32; 9:7,12,35; 10:20,27; 11:10). The numerous references to the hardening of Pharaoh's heart underline the importance of this motif. The narrative describes this hardening in two ways. Whereas in the initial stages it is reported that Pharaoh hardened his own heart (7:13,14,22; 8:15,19,32; 9:34,35), the narrative switches from this to state that the LORD hardened Pharaoh's heart (9:12; 10:20,27; 11:10; 14:4,8,17), as predicted in 4:21 and 7:3. By describing the hardening of Pharaoh's heart in these ways, the narrative emphasises both the guilt of Pharaoh and the sovereignty of God.

The hardening of Pharaoh's heart stands in sharp contrast to other developments which occur in the narrative. Although the Egyptian magicians could initially duplicate the miraculous signs of Moses and Aaron, they soon reached the limit of their power and affirmed to Pharaoh, 'This is the finger of God' (8:19). Later, it is specifically noted that they 'could not stand before Moses because of the boils that were on them' (9:11). Similarly, Pharaoh's own officials were gradually persuaded of the LORD's power. When Moses predicted the 'worst hailstorm that has ever fallen on Egypt' (9:18), some of them took precautions against his threat (9:20). When Moses next warned of a plague of locusts, the officials urged Pharaoh to let the Israelites go (10:7; cf. 11:3).

While those around him gradually conceded to the LORD's power, Pharaoh remained stubbornly resistant. Nevertheless, even he was forced to make concessions as a result of the divine signs and wonders. Initially, he was willing to let the people go on the condition that Moses prayed for the removal of the frogs (8:8). Next, while he desired that the Israelites should stay within Egypt, he was persuaded to let them go a little way into the desert (8:25–28). Although he actually stated after the hail that the people could go (9:28), this never happened. When Moses threatened an invasion of locusts, Pharaoh was prepared to allow the Israelite men, but not the women and children, to go and offer sacrifices to the LORD (10:8–11). Finally, he conceded that men, women and children could go, but not their flocks and herds (10:24). Thus, in spite of his apparent willingness to give way to Moses and Aaron in the face of further divine signs and wonders, Pharaoh persistently refused to let the people go.

The final demonstration of God's power to Pharaoh and the Egyptians involved the death of the male first-born. At this point the narrative expands to give a detailed account of the events surrounding the night on which the Israelites were delivered from Egypt. The occasion was so significant that it received a special name, the Passover, and was commemorated in various ways.[6] As a result of the death of all the male firstborn in Egypt, Pharaoh was forced to recognise and concede to the power of the LORD. No longer could he deny any knowledge of the God who had demonstrated his existence by signs and wonders which surpassed anything the Egyptians had previously witnessed.

Although Pharaoh permitted the Israelites to leave Egypt after the death of the firstborn, there was to be one further demonstration of the LORD's power. To achieve this, God delayed the Israelites' departure for Canaan, and they remained in Egypt on the western side of the Red Sea (cf. 13:18; 15:4). When Pharaoh and his army pursued their former slaves, the Israelites, believing themselves trapped, were terrified (14:10–12). However, by stretching out his staff Moses provided a safe escape route for the people through the divided waters of the sea. When the Egyptians followed, Moses again stretched out his hand over the sea, this time with tragic consequences for Pharaoh and his soldiers: 'not one of them survived' (14:28). Through repetition, verses 4 and 18 draw attention to the LORD's prime motive in destroying the Egyptian army: 'the Egyptians will know that I am the LORD'. Earlier Pharaoh had rejected Moses's request to let the people go by stating, 'Who is the LORD, that I should obey him and let Israel go' (5:2)? To his own peril he eventually discovered why the LORD should be obeyed. Interestingly, the narrative also highlights the changing attitude of the Israelites from unbelief and fear in the face of the Egyptian threat (14:10–12) to faith and trust in the light of the LORD's deliverance (14:31).

As a fitting conclusion to the preceding account of the divine deliverance of the enslaved Israelites from Egyptian control, the Exodus narrative records how Moses and the people celebrated in song the majesty and power of the LORD (15:1–18). Significantly, the narrative switches from prose to poetry. The exalted language of the poetry conveys better than prose the thoughts and feelings of the Israelites as they worshipped the one who had taken pity upon them and rescued them from the tyrant's power. By rehearsing what has already been recorded in prose, the reader too is encouraged to participate in the celebrations of the Israelites. As the people responded in adoration and praise for what God had already done, they looked forward with confidence to the future. Thus, their song concludes by focusing on what God has yet to accomplish on their behalf (15:13–18). In the light of past events and future expectation it is hardly surprising that at the end of this section we read of Miriam and all the women playing tambourines and dancing with joy.

THE SINAI COVENANT

Following their divine rescue from Egypt the Israelites gradually proceeded to Mount Sinai in fulfilment of what God had earlier told Moses (cf. 3:12). Once there further developments occurred in their relationship with God. First, a special agreement or covenant was established between God and the Israelites, based on the principal that if the people obeyed God, then they would be his treasured possession. Secondly, instructions were given for the construction of a suitable dwelling place for the LORD which would be located in the middle of the Israelite camp. This would enable God to be visibly present among his people. As a result of these developments the people would have a more intimate knowledge of their God. No longer would he be a remote deity, but rather one to whom the people could physically draw near.

At Sinai God revealed himself in a new way to the Israelites. Three aspects of this revelation are significant. First, attention is drawn to the holiness of God's nature. We see this in the instructions given to Moses. The people must consecrate themselves, wash their clothes and abstain from sexual relations for three days (19:14–15). Furthermore, Moses must establish a boundary around the mountain in order to prevent the people from coming into direct contact with God; even the priests were subject to this constraint. As the ground near the burning bush was made holy by God's presence (3:5), so too was Mount Sinai (19:23). Secondly, God's presence, accompanied by thunder and lightning, fire and smoke, and the violent trembling of the mountain itself (19:16–19), was seen, heard and felt by all the people. Thirdly, God spoke directly to all those gathered at the foot of the mountain and declared the principal obligations to which they must adhere in order for the covenant relationship to be maintained (20:1–17). The effect of all this upon the people was such that they asked Moses to mediate with God on their behalf. Moses subsequently received further obligations concerning the covenant (21:1–23:33). Both sets of obligations reflected God's nature, especially his divine attributes of righteousness and compassion.[7]

Following the ratification of the Sinai covenant (24:3–8), Moses was summoned into God's presence in order to receive instructions for the building of a tent or tabernacle which would be God's dwelling place on earth. The special nature of this tent reflects certain aspects of God's character, in particular his sovereignty and holiness. Thus, the precious metals and bluish fabrics used in its construction are indicative of royalty, and the appointment of priests and the consecration of all the furnishings underline the holiness of God.[8]

While Moses was receiving God's instructions concerning the construction of the tabernacle, the people who remained at the foot of Sinai desired to have a symbol of the LORD's presence. This resulted ironically in the making of a golden calf. Whereas the tabernacle, with it golden furnishings, portrayed the LORD as a royal personage, the golden calf, in marked contrast, represented him as a mere beast. Although the people offered sacrifices, their worship of the calf degraded the one who had delivered them from slavery in Egypt. Worship, to be true, must be based on a right perception of God. The book of Exodus emphasises the importance of knowing God as he truly is, and not as we imagine him to be.

Following the golden calf incident Moses asked to see God's glory (33:18). From the LORD's response it is clear that God equated his glory with 'all my goodness' (33:19). To assure Moses of his identity, God would proclaim his personal name, the LORD. Interestingly, when God had previously revealed his name to Moses, 'Moses hid his face, because he was afraid to look at God' (3:6). Now he displayed a greater confidence. Yet, although Moses was granted the opportunity to see God as no one else had done, even he could not look upon the divine face with immunity (33:20).

When God revealed himself to Moses on top of the mountain, he stressed not only his mercy and compassion, 'forgiving wickedness, rebellion and sin' (34:7; cf. 33:19), but also his justice, 'he does not leave the guilty unpunished' (34:7; cf. 32:34). The revelation of these divine characteristics to Moses was so significant that this passage is echoed on seven occasions in the Old Testament (Num 14:18; Ne 9:17; Pss 86:15; 103:8; 145:8; Joel 2:13; Jonah 4:2). Thus, in this dramatic setting, we have stated verbally two of the most important characteristics of God's nature, mercy and justice, qualities which have already been revealed through his deliverance of the Israelites from Egypt.

Apart from this unique encounter with God on the mountain, Moses also communed with God on a regular basis by entering a tent which was pitched at some distance from the main encampment.[9] Given its specific function, this tent was known as the 'tent of meeting' (33:7).[10] Here Moses enjoyed a unique and personal relationship with God: 'The LORD would speak to Moses face to face, as a man speaks with his friend' (33:11). Although they were in close proximity to one another, even Moses the faithful servant was not permitted to look directly upon God; 33:9 implies that the tent curtain shielded

Moses, who was within, from the LORD, who was without. Remarkably, every time Moses met with God his face became radiant and remained so afterwards (34:29–35).[11]

When the tabernacle was finally erected a cloud covered it and the glory of the LORD filled it (40:34). God now dwelt in the midst of the people. The tabernacle became the 'Tent of Meeting' (40:35), replacing the tent used previously by Moses (cf. 33:7–11). Whereas Moses went inside the earlier tent and God remained outside (33:9), now God dwelt within the tent and Moses stayed outside (40:35). God's presence was visible to everyone through the cloud and fire which settled upon the tabernacle. From here he guided them on their journeys (40:36–38). Thus, Exodus comes to a dramatic conclusion by recording the arrival of the glorious presence of the sovereign God in the midst of his people Israel.

CONCLUSION

There can be little doubt that the most important theme running throughout the book of Exodus is that of knowing God. Not only does the text highlight the different ways in which God may reveal himself, but it also focuses on those attributes which lie at the very heart of his nature: his sovereign majesty, his holiness, his awesome glory, his power to perform wonders, his righteousness and his compassion.

NEW TESTAMENT CONNECTIONS

Many of the theological ideas highlighted in the book of Exodus are also found in the NT. Those associated with the Passover, the Sinai covenant and the tabernacle will be considered in the next three chapters respectively. The themes of testing in the wilderness and God's remarkable provision for the people are dealt with in chapter 14. Here we shall focus briefly on a number of other ways in which the Exodus story is echoed in the NT.

The NT writers generally picture God in the same way as he is revealed in Exodus. Paul highlights the sovereign majesty of God when he refers to him as 'the King eternal' (1 Tim 1:17) and 'the blessed and only Ruler, the King of kings and Lord of lords, who alone is immortal and who lives in unapproachable light, whom no-one has seen or can see' (1 Tim 6:15–16). Similarly, the author of Hebrews, quoting Deut 4:24, speaks of worshipping God 'with reverence and awe, for our "God is a consuming fire" ' (12:28–29).

John's Gospel contains a number of brief allusions to the exodus story. For example, we are probably intended to see in Jesus' statement, 'I am the light of the world; he who follows me will not walk in darkness, but will have the light of life . . .' (John 8:12), a reference to the cloud of fire which guided the Israelites in the wilderness (Exod 13:21–22; 14:19; 40:38). Elsewhere, Jesus alludes to the manna which Israel ate in the wilderness when he comments, 'I am the bread which came down from heaven' (John 6:41).[12]

With vivid description the author of Hebrew contrasts Mount Sinai with Mount Zion, the heavenly Jerusalem (cf. Heb 12:22). He writes,

> You have not come to a mountain that can be touched and that is burning with fire; to darkness, gloom and storm; to a trumpet blast or to such a voice speaking words that those who heard it begged that no further word be spoken to them, because they could not bear what was commanded: 'If even an animal touches the mountain, it must be stoned'. The sight was so terrifying that Moses said, 'I am trembling with fear'. But you have come to Mount Zion, to the heavenly Jerusalem, the city of the living God. You have come to thousands upon thousands of angels in joyful assembly, to the church of the firstborn, whose names are written in heaven. You have come to God, the judge of all men, to the spirits of righteous men made perfect, to Jesus the mediator of a new covenant, and to the sprinkled blood that speaks a better word than the blood of Abel (Heb 12:18–24).

Whereas the ancient Israelites encountered God at an earthly mountain, those embraced by the new covenant receive 'a kingdom which cannot be shaken' (Heb 12:28).

NOTES

1. See chapter 10.
2. The English translation fails to convey the idea that the Hebrew *Yahweh* is a personal name. Due to the veneration of the divine name Yahweh, it became the practice of Jews to substitute the Hebrew word *'ădonāy* 'lord' for the divine name; hence the English translation. When vowels were eventually added in the medieval period to the consonantal text of the Hebrew Bible, the vowels of *'ădonāy* were used in conjunction with the consonants YHWH. This in turn led to the name Yahweh being wrongly read as Jehovah.
3. Interestingly, the personal name of Pharaoh is never given. For the reader he is the unknown one.
4. It should, however, be noted that in the NIV 'plague' translates various Hebrew words.
5. It has been suggested that the plagues described in Exodus can be related to a series of natural phenomena which may have occurred

in ancient Egypt. For example, the turning of the Nile waters to blood was due to an unusually high inundation of the river during the months of July and August. The river became 'blood-like' due to the presence of red earth carried in suspension from the basins of the Blue Nile and Atbara. Such an explanation, however, does not account for the presence of such 'blood' in wooden buckets and stone jars everywhere in Egypt (7:19). Nor does it explain either the earlier sign which Moses performed before the Israelites (4:30), or the activities of the Egyptian magicians (7:22). The text consistently emphasises the divine provenance of these events. This is indicated, for example, by the many references to Moses or Aaron stretching out their hands or a staff in order to bring about the different signs or wonders. Although some of these may be associated with natural phenomena, their occurrence is clearly attributed to divine intervention.

6. See chapter 7.

7. For a fuller discussion of the Sinai covenant, see chapter 8.

8. For a fuller discussion of the tabernacle, see chapter 9.

9. The tenses of the Hebrew verbs in 33:7–11 and 34:33–35 indicate that these passages describe events which occurred on a regular basis.

10. This tent of meeting should not be confused with the tabernacle, also known as the 'Tent of Meeting' (e.g., 40:2,6), which was constructed only later (36:8–38) and which was pitched in the midst of the Israelite encampment (Num 1:53; 2:2,17). See chapter 9.

11. Moses' radiant face set him apart from the rest of the people as God's messenger. When he communicated God's words to the people, he spoke with his face uncovered. At all other times he covered his face with a veil. In this way the Israelites were able to know when Moses spoke with divine authority and when he spoke on his own behalf.

12. Although some writers have connected Jesus' special use of the expression 'I am' with God's use of the same words in Exod 3:14, it is much more likely that the 'I am' expressions in John's Gospel echo similar expressions in the book of Isaiah (especially 41:4; 43:10,13,25; 46:4; 48:12). However, given that the phrase 'I am' in Isaiah probably alludes back to Exod 3:14, it is not completely inappropriate to observe a link between Jesus' use of 'I am' in John's Gospel and its use as a divine designation in Exod 3:14.

[7]

The Passover

SUMMARY

The account of God's rescue of the Israelites comes to a climax in the killing of the Egyptian firstborn males. To distinguish them from the Egyptians, God instructs the Israelites to follow a special ritual involving a sacrificial meal. As a result their houses were 'passed over' when the LORD struck down all the firstborn in Egypt. Such was the importance of the occasion that later generations of Israelites were not to forget what the LORD had done in delivering their ancestors from slavery in Egypt. For the nation of Israel the Passover was the most significant redemptive event in their history.

INTRODUCTION

The account of the Passover in Exod 12:1–13:16 forms the conclusion to the cycle of episodes which, beginning in 7:8, displays God's power over Pharaoh (7:8–11:10). Considerable attention is focused on the fulfilment of the divine pronouncement that 'every firstborn son in Egypt will die' (11:5). The unique way in which the Israelite firstborn are protected from death furnishes the designation for this remarkable occasion, 'the Passover' (cf. 12:11,23,27).

The narrator not only recounts the main events of the first Passover through a skilful use of dialogue, but by the same technique he also highlights how the Passover was to be remembered by subsequent generations of Israelites. Firstly, they will celebrate for seven days annually the Feast of Unleavened Bread (12:14–20; 13:3–10). Several other references underline the close association between unleavened bread and the Passover (12:34,39). Given their swift departure from Egypt, it was not possible for the Israelites to observe this feast until the first anniversary of the exodus (cf Num 9:1–14). Secondly, in conjunction with the Feast of Unleavened Bread,

75

the Israelites were to commemorate the Passover through the eating of a year-old lamb or kid (12:24–27,42–50).[1] Celebrated on the evening of the 14th day of the first month the Passover preceded the start of the Feast of Unleavened Bread which began on the 15th day and continued until the 21st day of the month (cf. 12:18). Thirdly, to commemorate the survival of their firstborn sons, the Israelites were commanded to give the LORD all future firstborn sons and male animals (13:11–16). These various activities were an on-going testimony to the fact that the LORD had brought them out of Egypt with his mighty hand (cf. 13:3,9,16).

THE ACCOUNT OF THE PASSOVER

Exodus 12:1–28 is composed of two speeches containing instructions for the activities associated with the Passover. Although placed side by side the speeches were given days apart. The first speech (12:1–20) was delivered by God to Moses some time before the first Passover night; verse 3 records instructions concerning the selection of the Passover lamb or kid four days before the Passover was observed. In the second speech (12:21–27) Moses addressed the elders of Israel on the day of the Passover. Through these two speeches the narrator highlights the events leading up to the striking down of the Egyptian firstborn at midnight on the 14th day of the month (12:29). Interestingly, both speeches conclude with comments drawing attention to future commemorations of the Passover (12:14–20; 24–27). Moreover, the second speech complements the first, providing additional information on various aspects of the Passover celebration. Since the reader is able to reconstruct the events that took place from the content of the two speeches, the author refrains from describing the fulfilment of the instructions; he merely comments, 'the Israelites did just what the LORD commanded Moses and Aaron' (12:28).

Various predictions made in 11:1–10 are fulfilled in 12:29–36. The LORD strikes down at midnight all the Egyptian firstborn, causing the people to wail loudly (12:29–30; cf. 11:4–6).[2] After summoning Moses and Aaron for the final time, Pharaoh eventually permits the Israelites to leave unconditionally (12:31–32; cf. 11:1). As instructed in 11:2, the Israelites ask for and receive from the Egyptians 'articles of silver and gold' and 'clothing' (12:35). Because 'the LORD had made the Egyptians favourably disposed towards the people . . . they gave them what they asked for' (12:36; cf. 11:3). The plundering of Egypt is presented as retribution for the way in which the Egyptians treated the Israelites as slaves (cf. Gen 15:14).

With Pharaoh's permission the Israelites begin their journey to freedom travelling from Rameses to Succoth (12:37–41). The haste of their departure is marked by the fact that they have time only to prepare bread made without yeast or leaven (12:39; cf. 12:11). At last after 430 years the people are enabled to leave Egypt as a result of the mighty wonders performed by the LORD.[3]

The account of the departure of the Israelites is interrupted by 12:42–50 which records 'regulations for the Passover'. Clearly these regulations applied to both the first Passover and later commemorations (cf. 12:42). The section ends by noting the obedience of the Israelites, with verse 50 corresponding closely to 12:28, possibly indicating that the instructions belong there chronologically. By ordering the material as he does, the narrator brings together in 12:42–13:16 the three ways in which the Israelites' deliverance from Egypt was to be celebrated: by re-enacting the Passover (12:43–49); by keeping the feast of Unleavened Bread (13:3–10); by consecrating every firstborn male (13:11–16).

The narrative picks up in verse 51 where it left off in verse 41 by repeating various details (e.g., 'on that very day', 'divisions'; NIV obscures somewhat the similarity between the two verses in the Hebrew text). On the day following the destruction of the Egyptian firstborn God announces to Moses that the Israelites must set apart as special 'the first offspring of every womb . . . whether man or animal' (13:1). Moses in turn expands upon this directive as he conveys it to the people (13:11–16). It is preceded, however, by instructions regarding the celebration of the feast of Unleavened Bread (13:3–10). Although Moses and Aaron were divinely instructed about this feast earlier (12:14-20), it is only now that the people learn of it. Moses's speech to the people in 13:3–16 falls neatly into two halves, which parallel each other closely. Both begin with references to the people taking possession of the land of Canaan in fulfilment of God's oath to their forefathers (13:5,11). Next come instructions regarding the commemoration of the Israelites' deliverance from Egypt (13:6–7,12–13), and the explanation of these activities to the children (13:8,14–15). Finally, both halves are marked by similar endings, concluding with the comment that 'the LORD brought you out of Egypt with his mighty hand' (13:9; cf. v. 16).

THE PURPOSE OF THE PASSOVER RITUAL

At the heart of the Passover ritual is the slaying of a lamb or kid, the smearing of its blood on the door posts, and the eating of its meat (12:6–11,21–22). The details of the ritual parallel closely those relating to sacrifices and this is confirmed by the comment in 12:27, 'It is the Passover sacrifice to the LORD'. Yet, while resembling other sacrifices, the Passover ceremony is unique, reflecting its peculiar historical setting. Because it occurs prior to the establishment of the Aaronic priesthood (Lev 8:1–9:24), Moses commands 'all the elders of Israel' to slaughter the Passover victims (12:21). Similarly, there is no reference to the central sanctuary or altar which were first instituted after the exodus at Sinai (20:24–26; 24:4; 27:1–8). Whereas other sacrifices were normally offered up during daylight, the Passover is sacrificed at 'twilight' as this was the only convenient time due to the exploitation of the Israelites by the Egyptians. Finally, the timing of the Passover to the 14th day of the month coincides with the full-moon, the most suitable night in the month for undertaking the activities associated with the exodus from Egypt.

Special attention is focused on the use made of the animal's blood: it is smeared on the sides and tops of the door-frame of the house (12:7,22). Some scholars emphasise the apotropaic purpose of this action, designed to protect those within from hostile powers without (cf. 12:13,23). Others suggest that the blood was used to purify the Israelite houses, a proposal supported by the mention of hyssop (12:22) which is elsewhere associated with ritual purification (e.g., Lev 14:4,6,49,51,52; Num 19:6,18).

An equally important part of the Passover rite is the eating of the animal. Everyone in the Israelite community is to participate (12:47), and for each animal slaughtered there has to be an adequate number of people to eat all the meat. Special instructions are given concerning the cooking of the meat: the entire animal is roasted, not boiled (12:9); the meat must be eaten indoors and the animal's bones must not be broken (12:46). Any meat which remains to the morning must be burnt (12:10).

The description of the Passover meal parallels closely elements of the account of the consecration of the Aaronic priests in Exodus 29 and Leviticus 8. Here the slaughter of a ram together with the sprinkling of its blood and the eating of its meat form the main elements of a consecration ritual. Although there are differences of detail, these same elements underlie the Passover ritual. By participating in the Passover ritual the Israelites set themselves apart as holy. The sacrifice of the animal atones for the sin of the people, the blood smeared on the door-posts purifies those within, and the eating of the sacrificial meat consecrates those who consume it. By participating in the Passover ritual the people sanctify themselves as a nation holy to God (cf. 19:6).

CONCLUSION

The divine redemption of the Israelites from Egypt comes to a dramatic climax in the events associated with the Passover. Later generations were never to forget this unique event which signalled the beginning of the process by which the LORD established Israel as his holy people. The events and ideas associated with the Passover became a paradigm for later generations of God's redemptive activity.

NEW TESTAMENT CONNECTIONS

The crucifixion of Jesus, the central redemptive event in the NT, is linked to the Passover, the most important redemptive event of the OT period, in various ways. First, the Gospels all highlight the fact that the death of Jesus took place in Jerusalem when the Jews were commemorating the Passover by keeping the Feast of Unleavened Bread. Secondly, the Synoptic Gospels (Matthew, Mark and Luke) present the Last Supper as a Passover meal (Matt 26:17; Mark 14:12; Luke 22:7–8), emphasising its importance and the special significance of Jesus' words and actions. This final meal of Jesus and his closest disciples is subsequently commemorated in the Lord's Supper (1 Cor 11:23–33). Thirdly, the actual death of Jesus is linked to the offering of the Passover sacrifice. John's Gospel alludes to this by observing that because Jesus' bones are not broken his death resembles that of the Passover sacrifice (John 19:36; cf. Exod 12:46). This connection is made even more explicit in 1 Cor 5:7: 'For Christ, our Passover, has been sacrificed'. Finally, although other interpretations are possible, 1 Pet 1:18–19 probably also associates the death of Jesus with the Passover sacrifice.

One particular difficulty must be noted regarding the NT association of the death of Jesus with the Passover. In the OT the Passover sacrifice was always offered before the eating of the Passover meal. However, this pattern is reversed in the NT; the Passover meal is eaten on the evening prior to the crucifixion of Jesus. One solution has been to argue that the Last Supper was only a preparatory meal which took place on the evening before the real Passover celebration. Although this is a convenient explanation, the Synoptic Gospels emphasise to such an extent the preparations for this meal that it is difficult to imagine that it could be anything other than the Passover meal itself.

An alternative solution may lie in the observation that John does not explicitly say that Jesus was crucified at the very time when the Passover victims were being slaughtered at the temple. Perhaps John encountered no difficulty in the fact that Jesus was crucified the day after the other Passover sacrifices. What mattered to John was the manner of his death, not the timing.[4]

By linking the crucifixion of Jesus to the Passover, the NT church drew attention to the redemptive nature of Jesus' death. Like the original Passover sacrifice, his death atoned for the sin of the people, his blood purified and cleansed, and his body sanctified those who ate it at the Lord's Supper.

NOTES

1. The Hebrew word *śeh* denotes either a lamb or a goat. The mention of 'Passover lamb' in 1 Cor 5:7 is unfortunate. A more accurate translation of the verses is: 'For Christ, our Passover, has been sacrificed'.

2. The precise identity of 'the destroyer' (12:23) is not revealed in Exodus. According to Ps 78:49 this may refer to a 'band of destroying angels'.

3. Genesis 15:13 refers to the descendants of Abraham being enslaved and ill-treated for 400 years (cf. Acts 7:6). The larger figure of 430 years probably includes the period of peace which they enjoyed after their initial arrival in Egypt.

4. John may have believed that the timing of Jesus' death fulfilled accurately the OT regulations regarding the Passover sacrifice. He observes that the crucifixion took place on 'the day of Preparation of Passover Week' (19:14; cf. 19:31) and that the next day was to be a 'special Sabbath' (19:31). This special Sabbath clearly refers to the first day of the feast of Unleavened Bread. If we assume that this special Sabbath coincided with a normal Sabbath (i.e., it fell on a Saturday), then we may conclude that Jesus was crucified on the Friday preceding the beginning of the Feast of Unleavened Bread. Since in NT times the day was reckoned as beginning at sunset, the Friday evening marked the beginning of the first day of the feast of Unleavened Bread (that is, the 15th day of the month). If the Passover meal was eaten on the evening of the 14th day of the month, this would have been the Thursday evening (as implied in the Synoptic Gospels). For his part, John may have appreciated that the original instructions regarding the Passover assumed that the day began at sunrise. Consequently, the first day of Unleavened Bread commenced on the Saturday morning and not the Friday evening. This observation is based on the premise that the timing of the Passover celebration in the NT period differed from that intended in the original instructions due to an important change concerning the way in which

the start of the day was reckoned. Whereas the ot Passover regulations presupposed that the day began at sunrise, from the sixth century BC onwards the Jews followed the Babylonian system of reckoning the day as beginning at sunset. In view of this, the Passover sacrifice ought on the basis of the ot regulations to have been offered up on Friday with the meal being eaten on the Friday evening. If John adopted this interpretation of the timing of Jesus' death, we may assume that Jesus and his disciples followed the custom of their day and ate the Passover on the Thursday evening. John, however, sees in the death of Jesus on the Friday an exact fulfilment of the Exodus instruction for celebrating the Passover.

[8]

The Covenant at Sinai

SUMMARY

The divine rescue of the Israelites from Egypt is followed soon
after by a formalising of their relationship with God through a
special agreement. This agreement, or covenant, sets out how
the people must live in order to be a holy nation. Two sets of
obligations are placed before the people. The Ten Commandments, which make up the principal obligations of the
covenant, emphasise the importance of loving God and one's
neighbour. A further document, the Book of the Covenant,
contains more detailed obligations which take a number of
forms: some are laws which can be enforced by human courts;
others are moral rules which emphasise exemplary behaviour,
especially towards the weaker members of society; a further
group of obligations focuses on religious duties. The principal
and detailed obligations complement each other, setting out
how God expects his people to live. Obedience will ensure
God's blessing, disobedience will lead to punishment.

INTRODUCTION

At the heart of the Book of Exodus is the establishment of a
special covenant relationship between God and the Israelites.
The basic form of this agreement is found in 19:4–6. If Israel, in
the light of her divine deliverance from Egypt, will obey the
LORD, then she will be his 'treasured possession . . . a kingdom
of priests and a holy nation'. As regards this covenant four
factors are worth noting.

First, from beginning to end God takes the initiative in
making the covenant. He is the one who rescues the Israelites
from Egypt and leads them to Mount Sinai (cf. 19:4; 20:2).
There he instructs Moses as to how the people must prepare
themselves (19:10–13, 21–22). Following his dramatic arrival on

Mount Sinai, God announces directly to the people the main conditions of the covenant; the Israelites do not negotiate. Throughout God acts first and the people are invited to respond.

Secondly, God highlights Israel's special status: 'out of all nations you will be my treasured possession' (19:5). Furthermore, they will be 'a kingdom of priests and a holy nation' (19:6). The expression 'a kingdom of priests' can also be translated 'priestly kings', suggesting that the Israelites are to enjoy the privilege of being both priests and kings in their relationships with other peoples. This indicates the important role which Israel is to play in God's future plans. They are also to be a holy nation.[1] The implications of this are revealed in the obligations which God places before the people. In their daily lives they are to reflect God's righteous and loving nature.

Thirdly, the maintenance of the covenant relationship is conditional upon Israel's obedience to God. After throwing off the yoke of Egyptian slavery, the Israelites must now obey a new sovereign. Obedience to God lies at the heart of the covenant relationship (cf. 19:8; 24:3,7). However, obedience by itself does not create the special covenant relationship. It is rather a loving response to what God in his grace does first (cf. 20:6; 'those who love me and keep my commandments').

Fourthly, two sets of obligations are placed before the Israelites. The first set, the Ten Commandments (20:3–17), are announced directly to all the people by God. These are the main covenant obligations which the people must accept. Later, God gives through Moses further obligations which are recorded in a document known as the Book of the Covenant (21:1–23:33). The material in this document falls into different categories and consists of more specific obligations than those listed in the Ten Commandments. Both sets of obligations reveal how the Israelites must live in order to maintain their covenant relationship with God.

THE PRINCIPAL COVENANT OBLIGATIONS — THE TEN COMMANDMENTS (EXOD 20:1–17)

As the people stand in awe before Mount Sinai, they hear the very voice of God introducing himself to them: 'I am the LORD your God, who brought you out of Egypt, out of the land of slavery' (20:2; cf. Deut 4:12–13; 5:4). There then follows a list of stipulations which form the basis of Israel's covenant relationship with God (20:3–17). These are later termed 'the ten words'

(34:28; Deut 4:13; 10:4), from which we derive the designations Decalogue or Ten Commandments. Their importance is further emphasised when they are eventually inscribed by God on two stone tablets (24:12; 31:18; 34:1,28).

Strictly speaking, the Decalogue is not a collection of laws. Various factors set it apart from the other legal collections of the Pentateuch. First, it is spoken directly by God to the people; at this stage Moses does not act as an intermediary (20:1,19; cf. Deut 4:12–13; 5:4–5,22–27). Secondly, it alone is inscribed on stone tablets by the 'finger of God' (31:18; cf. 24:12; 32:15–16; 34:1,28). All other regulations and instructions are written down by Moses (24:4; 34:27–28). Thirdly, the Ten Commandments are not laws, since no punishments are listed. Although the second and fifth commandments appear to contain penalties, these are really 'motivation clauses' designed to promote the observance of the divine instructions. Finally, what human law court could begin to enforce the prohibition against coveting described in the tenth commandment?

The stipulations outlined by the LORD are to govern Israel's relationship with her God. These represent the principal requirements which God places upon the people of Israel for the establishment and maintenance of the divine/human covenant relationship. The covenant stipulations in chapter 20 are listed in order of descending priority and focus on the Israelites' relationship to first the LORD and then other people. The people are to be single-minded in their devotion to the one who delivered them from Egypt; they are to worship only the LORD (20:3). Furthermore, their social behaviour is to follow a pattern which places a high priority on the rights of the individual as regards life, marriage and possessions. They are to obey these commands out of love for God: 'who love me and keep my commands' (20:6).

First commandment 20:3. Sole allegiance to the LORD lies at the very heart of the covenant relationship. It is the foundation upon which everything else rests. The people were in practice to be monotheistic, worshipping only the LORD. As is made clear elsewhere in the Pentateuch, the worship of other deities was punishable by death (Num. 25:1–18; Deut 13:1–18).

Second commandment 20:4–6. Unlike contemporary peoples, the Israelites were not to make or worship visual representations of their God. In both Egypt and Canaan, human and animals forms played an important function in depicting the attributes of a deity. Any attempt on the part of the Israelites to represent the LORD using such images would produce a distorted picture of his true nature. The incident of the golden calf in chapter 32 reveals both the necessity of this prohibition, in the light of the people's desire to have some visual image of the LORD, and the serious consequences of disregarding this commandment.

Third commandment 20:7. Whereas the second commandment prohibits visual representations of God, the third focuses on verbal representations. As a sign of their respect for God, the people were to exercise the greatest caution when talking about God or invoking his name. They were to say nothing which might detract from a true appreciation of his nature and character.

Fourth commandment 20:8–11. The people were to refrain from work on the seventh day, the Sabbath. According to 31:12–18 the Sabbath was the sign of the covenant relationship inaugurated at Sinai; as such it functioned like the earlier covenant sign of circumcision (Gen 17:9–14). Anyone failing to observe the Sabbath showed their disdain for the special relationship established between the Lord and Israel.

Fifth commandment 20:12. The concept of honouring is usually associated with God or his representatives, prophets and kings. In all likelihood parents were envisaged as representing God to their children, the family unit being a miniature of the nation. Furthermore, in ancient Israel the extended family was important, and family heads played a significant role in communal matters. Any attempt to undermine their authority was an attack on the basic authority structure within the local community. The seriousness of this commandment is reflected in the fact that the death penalty was required for children who wilfully disrespected their parents (Exod 21:15,17). If parents, as authority figures within the family, are respected by children, then respect for authority figures within society at large will also follow.

Sixth commandment 20:13. This commandment, by prohibiting murder or manslaughter, demonstrates the high priority which God places upon human life. No human being has the right to take another's life because each person is made in God's image (cf. Gen 1:27; 9:6). In the Pentateuch the punishment for taking another's life is death itself. The commandment, however, does not include judicial executions for capital offences or legitimate deaths resulting from war, and it should also be noted that the Old Testament laws draw a careful distinction between premeditated and accidental deaths. (See below, under 21:1–22:20, the section entitled 'The sanctity of life'.)

Seventh commandment 20:14. In God's order of priority, the sanctity of human life is followed by the importance of the marriage relationship. Adultery here means sexual relations between a married woman and a man who is not her husband.

Those caught in adultery could be executed (Lev 20:10; Deut 22:22). Significantly, relations between a married man and an unmarried woman do not qualify as adultery. Polygamy is not automatically excluded by this commandment, although in practice it was rare in Old Testament times. Similarly, divorce was permitted, but not encouraged (cf. Deut 24:1). As a whole the Bible reveals that God desires the establishment of harmonious marital relationships and that neither partner should do anything to undermine this.

Eighth commandment 20:15. The next principle to govern the Israelites' relationship with God was respect for the property of others. Any individual found guilty of dispossessing another was punished in accordance with the value of what they stole and the injured party was suitably compensated. While other ancient Near Eastern cultures sometimes invoked the death penalty for theft, the Old Testament consistently rejects such a position, indicating clearly that God values human life and the marital relationship above property.

Ninth commandment 20:16. In the final two commandments we proceed from prohibitions involving actions to prohibitions involving words and thoughts respectively. This concludes the downward progression of priorities which we have observed. The ninth commandment emphasises the importance to truthfulness. While the prohibition against false testimony is primarily intended for a court of law, it may be extended to include any situation in which untrue words are used to harm another individual.

Tenth commandment 20:17. The final commandment forbids an individual to covet what belongs to another. Unlike all the other commands, it addresses specifically inner feelings and thoughts, such as envy or greed. If the Israelites were to enjoy a harmonious covenant relationship with God, every aspect of their lives must conform to his will. Outward adherence was insufficient; their inner selves had to be patterned according to the divine principles of morality found in the Ten Commandments.

THE DETAILED COVENANT OBLIGATIONS

Alongside the principal obligations of the Decalogue, God also gave through Moses other obligations which had to be observed. Later, Moses recorded everything that the LORD said in a document known appropriately as the Book of the Covenant (24:7; cf. 24:4). Possibly most, if not all, of this document is preserved in 21:1–23:33. As it stands it falls into four sections. First, there is a long list of laws dealing with various aspects of social life (21:1–22:20). The next part consists of moral rules or requirements which highlight the exemplary behaviour God expects of his people, especially towards the underprivileged (22:21–23:9). Thirdly, there are instructions regarding the observance of the Sabbath and religious festivals (23:10–19). The final section outlines how God would act on behalf of the Israelites, enabling them to take possession of the land of Canaan (23:20–33).

In a book which underlines God's passionate concern for justice through his rescue of the Israelites from Egypt, it is hardly surprising that a similar concern for justice should dominate the covenant which he established with the Israelites. This is most apparent in the legal material and moral rules which form the first two sections of the Book of the Covenant.

THE LEGAL MATERIAL OF THE COVENANT
(EXOD 21:1–22:20)

The material which comprises this section probably represents only some of the statutes which formed part of ancient Israel's law. In all likelihood many of those included here have been selected because they parallel God's actions in rescuing the Israelites from slavery in Egypt. At the very outset the principle is established that slaves have the right to be set free after a fixed period of time (21:1–4); this implies that the Egyptians acted illegally in holding the Israelites as slaves for a long period of time. In contrast, the inclusion of the statutes concerning a slave who loves his master (21:5–6) and a female servant (21:7–11) are intended to highlight various aspects of Israel's covenant relationship with the LORD; the Israelites will serve the LORD because they love him; having chosen Israel God will remain faithful to them. A further group of laws draws attention to the necessity of compensation for those who have been physically injured (21:18–27). In particular, it is noted that any slave who suffers serious injury at the hand of his or her master is to be released immediately (21:26–27). In the light of Israel's harsh treatment in Egypt (cf. Exod 2:11; 5:14–16) these laws justify indirectly the LORD's action in freeing the Israelites. Another set of laws focuses on the concept of restitution (22:1–15). Here also it is possible to see a connection with earlier comments about how the Israelites demanded articles of silver and gold and clothing from the Egyptians (3:21–22; 11:2; 12:35–36). These items compensated the Israelites for the way in which they had been exploited in Egypt.

Apart from their relevance in justifying prior events in the book of Exodus, the laws in this section are also significant because of the ideals and values which permeate them. The following are the most noteworthy.

MORAL SYMMETRY

The biblical laws are based on the principle that the punishment should match the crime. This is stated most clearly in the well-known, but generally misunderstood, 'law of talion': 'life for life, eye for eye, tooth for tooth, hand for hand, foot for foot, burn for burn, wound for wound, bruise for bruise' (21:23–25; cf. Lev 24:17–21; Deut 19:21). At first sight, the law of talion appears to be a rather barbaric way of ensuring justice. Yet, within the development of law in the ancient Near East it represented an important advance. In the earliest known collections of laws monetary fines were imposed in cases of assault and bodily injury. The weakness of such fines was that they failed to take into account an individual's ability to pay. (For an unemployed labourer a fine of a thousand pounds imposes great hardship; to a millionaire it is a mere trifle.) The law of talion removes all such discrepancies by ensuring that the punishment should be no less, or no more, than the crime demands.

The law of talion, however, was not necessarily applied literally. In the Book of the Covenant it is preceded by a case of wounding, the punishment for which is the cost of medical expenses and compensation for lost wages (21:18–19). Similarly, it is followed immediately by a law in which a servant is granted release as compensation for the loss of an eye or a tooth (21:26–27). Clearly, there was no literal application of the law of talion in these instances.

THE SANCTITY OF LIFE

Many modern readers of the biblical laws are likely to be disturbed by the use of capital punishment for a variety of crimes, including murder, kidnapping, physical or verbal assaults against parents, sorcery, bestiality and idolatry (21:12–17; 22:18–20).[2] Against modern standards of justice this punishment appears extremely harsh. Nevertheless, it reflects the value which the Israelites placed upon individual human life, the hierarchical structure within the family, and the purity of worship. In the case of murder the death penalty is invoked, not out of indifference for human life, but rather because each human life is of tremendous value (cf. Gen 9:6). A life for a life does not express vengefulness, but rather the idea that the only payment which can be made for the taking of a human life is a human life itself. This even applies to animals responsible for human deaths (21:28).[3]

The distinctiveness of the biblical laws is apparent when one compares the other ancient Near Eastern laws. In the earlier Laws of Hammurabi (*c*. 1750 BC), a murderer is required only to make financial compensation to the victim's family. This contrasts sharply with the biblical insistence of a life for a life. On the other hand, the non-biblical laws apply the death penalty to breaking and entering, looting at a fire, and theft. These examples reveal that in other cultures financial loss was sometimes treated more seriously than loss of life. The biblical laws consistently emphasise that human life is of greater value that material possessions.

MORAL RULES (EXOD 22:21–23:9)

The material in this passage is generally taken to be detailed statutes. However, a number of factors suggest that it should be distinguished from the laws found in 21:1–22:20. (a) The section is marked off from the surrounding material by the frame formed by 22:21 and 23:9. Both verses not only prohibit the mistreatment of aliens, but they also underline this by reminding the Israelites that they were once aliens in Egypt. (b) The way in which the material is presented does not conform to the two distinctive forms used in 21:1–22:20; rather it is reminiscent of the form adopted in the Decalogue. (c) Apart from the general comment in 22:24, 'I will kill you with the sword', no penalties enforceable by a human court are stipulated for breaking the rules outlined here. (d) The subject matter of this section is distinctive. It encourages both a caring attitude towards the weak and vulnerable members of society (i.e., aliens, widows, orphans, the needy, the poor) and a concern that the legal system be totally impartial. Those involved in disputes are to favour neither the rich, by accepting a bribe (23:8), nor the poor (23:3). Everyone, irrespective of their class, is to be treated equally (23:6,9). A witness must not be swayed by social pressure (23:2), and should ensure that his or her testimony is truthful (23:1,7).

The commands found here seek to inculcate a standard of behaviour which goes beyond the letter of the law. A human court is unlikely to prosecute someone for failing to return his enemy's straying animal; nevertheless God demands that his people should overcome evil with good (23:4–5; cf. Matt 5:43–48; Rom 12:19–21). In the light of the special relationship being established between God and the people it is surely significant that at the middle of this section is the command, 'you are to be my holy people' (22:31). We see here how God's holy people should live.

INSTRUCTIONS CONCERNING THE SABBATH AND RELIGIOUS FESTIVALS

In the third section of the Book of the Covenant the Israelites are reminded of their obligation to worship the LORD alone: 'Do not invoke the names of other gods; do not let them be heard on your lips' (23:13).[4] Such worship lies at the heart of the three annual festivals, which celebrate the LORD's benevolence towards Israel, and the Sabbath. The observance of the Sabbath is exceptionally important because it is the sign of the covenant being established between God and Israel (31:12–17). Anyone desecrating the Sabbath is guilty of renouncing this special relationship with God; the consequence is death (31:14–15).

THE RECIPROCAL NATURE OF THE COVENANT

The final part of the Book of the Covenant (23:20–33) highlights the reciprocal nature of the covenant being established between God and Israel. If the Israelites obeyed the LORD their God, then they would take possession of the land of Canaan (23:22–23). Furthermore, God's blessing would ensure their future comfort (23:25–26) and security (23:27–28). As a consequence of their relationship with the LORD, the Israelites had to distance themselves from the worship of other gods by destroying all pagan images and places of worship (23:24). For similar reasons, they were not to enter into any treaty with the inhabitants of Canaan lest this caused them to compromise their exclusive allegiance to the LORD (23:32–33). Such a warning was necessary because although God promised to remove from the land the nations already living there, they would be expelled only gradually in order to avoid the land becoming desolate (23:29–30).

THE RATIFICATION OF THE COVENANT

After descending from the mountain, Moses relayed to the people God's words. Once more they expressed their willingness to do all that God commanded (24:3; cf. 19:8). There follows a brief account of the ceremony by which the covenant between the LORD and Israel was ratified (24:4–11). Interestingly, the activities outlined here reflect the three main sections of the LORD's speech to Moses (20:24–24:2). The building of an altar and the offering of sacrifices parallel the instructions given in 20:24–26. Moses then reads to the people 'the Book of the

Covenant' (24:7), the middle section of the divine speech (21:1–23:33). After the Israelites again acknowledge their willingness to obey God (24:7), the covenant is sealed through the sprinkling of blood on the people (24:8). Finally, God's invitation to Moses and the elders to come up the mountain (24:9–11) corresponds to the third section of the divine speech (24:1–2).

REBELLION IN THE CAMP

Having successfully ratified the covenant, Moses ascended Mount Sinai in order to receive instructions for the building of the tabernacle (25:1–31:18). However, his long absence of 'forty days and forty nights' (24:18) created an atmosphere of uncertainty in the Israelite camp. Perhaps fearful of what God may have done to Moses (cf. 20:19), the Israelites sought reassurance through the construction of a image which would represent the LORD's presence in their midst. Turning to Aaron, the people asked him to make 'gods', or better 'a god' (so NIV mg.), who would go before them (32:1).[5] Although the Israelites did not consciously reject the LORD as their God, their attempt to portray him as a golden calf was a major breach of the covenant stipulations which they had earlier accepted (cf. 20:4–6; 20:23).[6] Such an obvious violation of the LORD's instructions invited fierce condemnation (cf. 32:7–10).

Abhorred by what took place, the LORD ordered Moses to return to the camp (32:7). God's anger was roused by the fact that the Israelites had so quickly turned away from his commands, and this in spite of repeated affirmations that they would do everything that the LORD had said (19:8; 24:3,7). Such disrespect for God merited the harshest of punishments, death. In contrast to the people, Moses was assured that he would become 'a great nation', echoing God's earlier promise to Abraham (Gen 12:3). Surprisingly, perhaps, Moses intervened and pleaded on behalf of the people for mercy, recalling God's marvellous deliverance of them from Egypt and his much earlier covenant with Abraham, Isaac and Jacob (32:11–13). His petition was based throughout on the character and honour of God. Moreover, he made no attempt to excuse the people's sinful behaviour. So compelling was his intercession that God relented from the immediate destruction of the people (32:14). Nevertheless, as the narrative subsequently reveals, the people did not go unpunished (32:28,35).

When Moses eventually saw what had been happening in the camp, he too became enraged. By deliberately breaking the divinely inscribed stone tablets, containing the terms of agreement, Moses indicated that the covenant relationship between God and the Israelites was now ended.

Whereas the account in chapter 32 is dominated by the rebellion of the Israelites and God's punishment of the people, attention switches in chapter 33 to Moses, the faithful servant, and his remarkable friendship with the LORD. Moses's unique relationship with God provided the opportunity for him to intercede on behalf of the people; as a result the covenant was renewed. This is attributed, not to some dramatic change of heart on the part of the people, but to the LORD's compassion and mercy. Consequently, Moses was instructed to bring up the mountain two stone tablets to replace those previously broken (34:1). Once more Moses wrote down the detailed covenant obligations (34:27; cf. 24:4),[7] and God inscribed on the new stone tablets the 'ten words' or Decalogue (34:28; cf. 20:3–17).[8]

CONCLUSION

The covenant at Sinai marked an important stage in God's relationship with the Israelites. At the centre of God's plans for his people was the hope that they should reflect his holy nature by being perfect in all they do, say and think. Unfortunately, the people soon displayed, through building the golden calf, their inability to keep the obligations set before them. As a result, the covenant relationship with God, which promised to be a source of great blessing, became for them, due to their disobedience, a source of divine cursing.

NEW TESTAMENT CONNECTIONS

For religious Jews of the New Testament period it was exceptionally important to keep the Mosaic law; it was considered the essence of God's requirements for holy living. Not surprisingly, much discussion and debate took place to determine the precise requirements of the law, and different schools of thought adopted differing views on how the Mosaic law should be interpreted and related to contemporary situations. Against this background it is no surprise that the law figured prominently both in the teaching of Jesus and in various issues addressed by the early church.

JESUS AND THE LAW

The four Gospels all indicate that Jesus frequently came into conflict with the religious leaders of his day concerning his attitude to the law. This is most apparent regarding the keeping of the Sabbath; the Gospels convey the impression that the Pharisees and teachers of the law regularly condemned Jesus' actions on the Sabbath, especially his willingness to heal (Matt 12:9–14; Mark 3:1–6; Luke 6:6–11; 13:10–17; 14:1–6; John 5:1–15; 7:21–24). Tension also existed regarding Jesus' attitude towards the laws on ritual cleanliness (Matt 15:10–20; Mark 7:1–8) and the Pharisees were quick to condemn Jesus' willingness to eat with 'sinners' (Matt 9:10–11; 11:19; Mark 2:15–16; Luke 5:29–30; 7:34; 15:2). How then did Jesus view the Old Testament law?

Two observations may be made. First, Jesus held the law in high regard. Although he did not conform to all the ways in which his contemporaries kept the Mosaic law, he constantly affirmed the importance of the law.

> I tell you the truth, until heaven and earth disappear, not the smallest letter, not the least stroke of a pen, will by any means disappear from the Law until everything is accomplished. Anyone who breaks one of the least of these commandments and teaches others to do the same will be called least in the kingdom of heaven, but whoever practises and teaches these commands will be called great in the kingdom of heaven. For I tell you that unless your righteousness surpasses that of the Pharisees and the teachers of the law, you will certainly not enter the kingdom of heaven (Matt 5:18–20).

Moreover, when asked, 'Which is the greatest commandment in the Law?' Jesus answered by stressing the need to love God and love one's neighbour (Matt 22:37–39; Mark 12:29–31). His answer summarises the two-fold division found in the Ten Commandments. Love for God must come first, but it can never to be divorced from love for one's neighbour; the former leads automatically to the latter.

Secondly, Jesus emphasised the true intention of the law. Jesus parted company from the other religious leaders of his day on the fundamental issue of the law's nature and function. His contemporaries viewed it as a line separating right and wrong behaviour. In the light of this, they sought to determine which actions were within the law and which were outside the law; that is, an individual was righteous as long as he or she did not go beyond the boundary established by the law. This approach, however, encouraged individuals to focus on the minimum requirements of the law and fostered a very legalistic attitude towards human behaviour. Furthermore, as Jesus pointed out, it created all kinds of anomalies and resulted in the law being used for unrighteous ends.[9] In marked contrast, Jesus viewed the law as a sign pointing to the type of behaviour which God desired. Jesus maintained that to keep the law fully one had to be perfect as God is perfect (cf. Matt 5:48). Hence he called on his disciples to display a righteousness which surpassed that of the Pharisees and the teachers of the law (cf. Matt 5:20). He reminded his followers that to interpret the commandments as requiring only outward obedience was to misunderstand their purpose (Matt 5:17–48). His approach is clearly seen in his understanding of the commandments, 'Do not murder' and 'Do not commit adultery'. These he interpreted respectively to mean 'Do not do, say or think anything which might lead to murder or adultery'. Furthermore, he indicated that the OT law occasionally permitted certain actions (e.g., divorce) not because it reflected God's perfect will but because God sought to accommodate the hardness of human hearts (Matt 19:3–9). While the Pharisees and the teachers of the law exploited such divine accommodations, Jesus emphasised that each individual should seek to fulfil in his or her life God's original design for human existence.

PAUL AND THE LAW

Much has been written about Paul's view of the OT law. It is possible here only to make a few brief observations. Like Jesus he condemned a legalistic understanding of the law which undermined its true purpose. In Gal 3:15–25 he argues that the divine covenant made with Abraham takes precedence over the law given several centuries later at Mount Sinai. Whereas his opponents were advocating that believers must keep the law in order to be righteous, Paul responded by noting that the law, given later to fulfil a temporary role until Christ came, could never make anyone righteous; it merely indicated the righteousness required by God, not the means of achieving such righteousness. As such it underlined the necessity of becoming righteous through faith.

THE NEW COVENANT

An important conviction among the early Christians was the belief that God had established through Jesus Christ a new covenant which superseded the covenant inaugurated centuries earlier at Sinai. Naturally such a view provoked considerable hostility from Jews whose religious outlook was centred on the Sinai covenant. This new covenant was introduced by Jesus at the last supper (Matt 26:28; Mark 14:24; Luke 22:20; 1 Cor 11:25) and sealed by his sacrificial death (Heb 9:11–28). As regards its superiority over the older Sinai covenant, the author of Hebrews, quoting Jeremiah 31:31–34, makes a number of important points. First, the new covenant is unlike the one made at Sinai (Heb 8:9). Although the Sinai covenant was intended to secure a lasting relationship between God and the Israelites, it did not succeed due to fact that the people failed to keep the divine obligations that were placed upon them; their faithlessness caused God to turn away from them (Heb 8:9). Significantly, the success of the new covenant is guaranteed by God's ability to do for the people what they themselves could not achieve. Whereas the laws of the old covenant were inscribed on stone tablets, under the new covenant God puts his laws in the hearts and minds of believers (cf. 2 Cor 3:6). Through an inner transformation, accomplished by the indwelling of the Holy Spirit, God enables his people to live as he had originally intended. A further consequence of the new covenant is a better knowledge of God: 'No longer will a man teach his neighbour, or a man his brother, saying, "Know the Lord", because they will all know me, from the least of them to the greatest' (Heb 8:11). Finally, the new covenant brings divine forgiveness for human sin and wickedness (Heb 8:12). Under the old covenant God's forgiveness was linked to the atoning duties carried out by the high priest on the Day of Atonement. Because this was repeated annually it guaranteed only limited forgiveness for the people. Since Christ's media-torial role as a high priest far exceeds that of the Aaronic high priest, the new covenant provides a greater assurance of forgiveness.[10] Those who are justified by faith in Christ are divinely pardoned for all their sins, past, present and future.

The inauguration of a new covenant by Christ influenced the early church in another way. Those bound by the old covenant were expected to demonstrate their allegiance by keeping holy the seventh day of the week; the Sabbath was the sign of the Sinai covenant (Exod 31:13–17). With the arrival of a new covenant, the strict observance of the Sabbath, like circum-cision, was no longer binding upon Christians. Rather, to commemorate Christ's resurrection the early church met for worship on the first day of the week (cf. Acts 20:7; 1 Cor 16:2). Thus, the Sabbath was replaced by the Lord's Day.

At the heart of the Sinai covenant was God's desire that Israel should be 'a kingdom of priests and a holy nation' (Exod 19:6). This thought is echoed in 1 Pet 2:9:

> But you are a chosen people, a royal priesthood, a holy nation, a people belonging to God, that you may declare the praises of him who called you out of darkness into his wonderful light. Once you were not a people, but now you are the people of God; once you had not received mercy, but now you have received mercy (cf. Rev 1:6; 5:10; 20:6).

That which the Sinai covenant failed to achieve, as a result of human disobedience, is now fulfilled through the new covenant inaugurated by Jesus Christ's death, resurrection and ascension.

NOTES

1. For a fuller treatment of the concept of holiness, see chapter 10.

2. Stoning was used as a common means of execution because it underlined that the whole community, without exception, was responsible for the judicial death of the criminal. Because of the serious consequences of their testimony in capital cases, the prosecution witnesses had to throw the first stones (Deut 17:7).

3. In the light of these observations, it might appear that Christians ought to support the death penalty for crimes like murder. However, other factors must be considered. Firstly, the ancient Israelites did not have the option of sentencing a murderer to life imprisonment; there were no facilities to imprison someone for a long period of time. Remarkably, imprisonment was never used as a means of punishment for any crime. Obviously this restricted greatly their choice of punishment. Secondly, it is likely that the death penalty was rarely utilised. This probably ensured that its use did not have the effect of devaluing human life. To make frequent recourse to capital punishment might suggest that human life is of little esteem, thus negating the very reason for adopting it. Whatever form of punishment we endorse, as Christians we must always ensure that it does not undermine the sanctity of human life.

4. The material in 23:10–19 is carefully structured, falling into two halves, centered around verse 13, with each half subdivided into two parts. The first half deals with the seventh year (23:10–11) and the seventh day (23:12). Verses 14–19 are concerned with the three main festivals which the Israelites celebrated annually: Unleavened Bread; Harvest; Ingathering. The instructions in 23:17–19 correspond with the three feasts outlined in verses 14–16; note in particular how verse 17 parallels verse 14.

5. Several factors indicate that the image of the golden calf was meant to represent the LORD. Firstly, according to the latter part of verse 4, the calf represented the god who delivered the people from Egypt; it was no new deity. Secondly, the festival, enthusiastically celebrated by the people (32:6), was described by Aaron as 'to the LORD' (32:5). Moreover, the festal activities resemble those recorded in chapter 24 regarding the ratification of the covenant between the LORD and the Israelites.

6. The narrator hints at this indirectly through his use of the Hebrew term *'ĕlohîm* 'god/gods' in verses 1, 4 and 8; when used with plural verbs *'ĕlohîm* normally refers to pagan gods; when used with singular verbs it normally refers to the LORD.

7. The terms of the covenant, outlined in 34:11–26, parallel closely those found in the last two sections of the 'Book of the Covenant' (23:14–33), except that their order is here reversed.

8. Although the subject of the verb is not clearly stated, it may be deduced from 34:1 that the tablets were inscribed by the LORD (cf. 32:16). It is not unusual in Hebrew narrative for the subject of the verb to change without this being clearly indicated.

9. We see this in his comments about making oaths (Matt 5:33–37) and the law of corban (Matt 17:3–9; Mark 7:9–13).

10. This is discussed more fully in chapter 11.

[9]

The Tabernacle

SUMMARY

The final third of the Book of Exodus focuses almost exclusively on the construction and erection of the tabernacle. The extent of the material highlights the importance of the tabernacle as God's dwelling place. Although it takes the form of a rectangular tent, the extensive use of gold and blue fabrics indicates that the tabernacle was a royal residence. Its portable nature ensured that the divine king would be with his people wherever they went. A further aspect which plays an important part in the design of the tabernacle and its furnishings is the holy nature of God's being. The outer curtain fence separates sinful people from a holy God, and the bronze altar stands as a vivid reminder that God may only be approached by those who have made atonement for their sin and uncleanness. Finally the tabernacle is designated 'the Tent of Meeting' indicating that it is the place where divinity and humanity commune together.

INTRODUCTION

The importance of the tabernacle is highlighted by the attention given to recording both God's description of how the tent and its furnishing should be manufactured (25:1–31:11), and the subsequent construction (35:1–40:33). Altogether, including the details relating to the consecration of the priests, approximately one-quarter of Exodus is given over to describing the making of the tabernacle. Chapters 25–31 consist of a very long divine speech outlining the preparations necessary for the construction of a special tent and the appointment of priests. Much of this material is repeated in 36:8–39:31, where we have an almost word for word record of the fulfilment of the instructions given by the LORD to Moses (see Table A). Such repetition is the author's way of underlining the importance of the tabernacle.[1]

TABLE A

Object	Instructions	Fulfilment
Tabernacle	26:1–11,14–29,31–32,36–37	36:8–38
Ark	25:10–14,17–20	37:1–9
Table	25:23–29	37:10–16
Lampstand	25:31–39	37:17–24
Incense altar	30:1–5	37:25–28
Anointing oil	30:25	37:29
Bronze altar	27:1–8	38:1–7
Bronze basin	30:18	38:8
Courtyard	27:9–19	38:9–20
Ephod	28:6–12	39:2–7
Breastpiece	28:15–28	39:8–21
Robe	28:31–34	39:22–26
Tunic, turban, sash	28:39	39:27–29
Gold plate	28:36–37	39:30–31

Whereas the initial divine instructions list the more important objects first, the account of their construction reflects the order in which the items were assembled when the tabernacle was erected (cf. 40:2–8,12–14; 40:17–33) and conforms to the pattern found in other summaries of the tabernacle equipment (cf. 31:7–9; 35:11–18; 39:33–40; see Table B). Occasionally the divine instructions, but rarely the fulfilment, contain additional material relating to the use of a particular object (e.g. 30:6–10; 30:18–21). The similarity between the instructions and their fulfilment indicates that the people obeyed the LORD 'to the letter'. Everything was made just as Moses had been instructed. Significantly, Exodus ends in dramatic fashion by describing how God's glory filled the tabernacle 'on the first day of the first month in the second year' (40:17) just in time for the people to celebrate the first anniversary of their deliverance from Egypt (Num 9:1–5).

A ROYAL TENT

An important theme in the final part of Exodus is God's intention to dwell among the people (25:8; cf. 29:45–46). Having rescued them from the control of Pharaoh the king of Egypt and established a special covenant relationship with them, the LORD desires to accompany them into the promised land. Consequently, he commands Moses to construct a portable dwelling. Like his people, the sovereign LORD will dwell in a tent. However, his dwelling differs in the nature of the materials used in its construction. From the inventory of precious metals and bluish coloured fabrics (25:3–7; cf. 35:5–

TABLE B

Order of presentation in Exodus 25–30 and 36–39

Instructions	*Fulfilment*
Ark 25:10–22	Tabernacle 36:8–38
Table 25:23–30	Ark 37:1–9
Lampstand 25:31–39	Table 37:10–16
Tabernacle 26:1–37	Lampstand 37:17–24
Bronze altar 27:1–8	Incense altar 37:25–28
Courtyard 27:9–19	Anointing oil 37:29
Ephod 28:6–14	Incense 37:29
Breastpiece 28:15–30	Bronze altar 38:1–7
Robe 28:31–35	Bronze basin 38:8
Gold plate 28:36–38	Courtyard 38:9–20
Tunic, turban, sash 28:39	Ephod 39:2–7
Incense altar 30:1–10	Breastpiece 39:8–21
Bronze basin 30:18–21	Robe 39:22–26
Anointing oil 30:23–25	Tunic, turban, sash 39:27–29
Incense 30:34–36	Gold plate 39:30–31

9,22–27) it is apparent that this is no common tent; it is for royal use. This is emphasised not only by the kinds of material used ('gold, silver, and bronze; blue, purple and scarlet yarn and fine linen') but also by their quantity. According to 38:21–31 approximately one ton of gold, four tons of silver and two-and-a-half tons of bronze were used to make the tabernacle and its furnishings.[2]

Initially Moses was instructed to make three items of furniture for inside the tent. The first of these was a rectangular wooden chest or box, covered 'with pure gold, both inside and out' (25:10–11). For ease of transportation the chest, or 'ark' as it is traditionally known, was to be constructed with gold rings and poles (25:12–15). Inside this container Moses would later place the stone tablets which were the 'Testimony', or 'terms of agreement', to the covenant between God and Israel (25:16,21; Deut 10:8 refers to the chest as the 'ark of the covenant'). The lid of the ark, made of pure gold, is designated an 'atonement cover' (25:17; cf. Heb 9:5, 'place of atonement'). Leviticus 16:1–34 (esp. vv. 11–17) describes the annual ritual which took place when the high priest sprinkled blood on the ark's lid to make atonement for 'the uncleanness and rebellion of the Israelites, whatever their sins have been' (Lev 16:16).[3] Two golden cherubim (or cherubs) were attached to the ends of the lid, facing each other with outspread wings.[4] Here, between the cherubim, God would later meet with Moses in order to communicate his instructions to the people (25:22; 30:36; cf. Lev

16:2). Thus, apart from being a container, the ark also functioned as a seat, or, more specifically, as a throne protected by guardian cherubim (cf. 1 Sam 4:4; 2 Sam 6:2; 2 Kgs 19:15; Pss 80:2; 99:1; Isa 37:16). Because of its importance as the LORD's throne, the manufacture of the ark is outlined first.

The second piece of furniture was a wooden table, overlaid with gold, and fitted with rings and poles (25:23–28). Plates, dishes and other utensils, all of gold, were to be provided, and the 'Bread of the Presence' was to be placed on the table at all times (25:29–30). The third main fixture to be constructed was a gold lampstand with seven lamps (25:31–40). The lampstand was to be made in the pattern of a growing tree, decorated with 'flowerlike cups, buds and blossoms' (25:31). Three branches extended to either side of the central stem; the tops of the stem and branches were designed to hold lamps. No explanation is given as to why the lampstand should resemble a tree. Possibly it was meant to look like the tree of life in Gen 3:22, symbolising the life-giving power of God. Significantly, the table and lampstand, together with the chest/seat, comprised the main items of furniture in an ancient home. As such they indicated that God lived within the tent. The abundant use of gold emphasised the importance of the occupant. The provision of bread (25:30) and light (27:21) were symbolic reminders that God was there at all times, both day and night.

Detailed instructions were provided next for the construction of the actual tent or tabernacle (26:1–37). Some uncertainty exists over how the various curtains and wooden frames fitted together. Since the entire structure was designed to be portable, its construction was probably similar to that used for other tents. The bluish fabrics and gold fittings were indicative of royalty. The rectangular structure was divided by a curtain into two rooms, one probably being twice the size of the other (26:31–33). In the smaller of these rooms, in the western half of the tabernacle, was to be placed the ark of the Testimony. Because the LORD was seated there, enthroned between the cherubim, this part was called the 'Most Holy Place' or Holy of Holies (26:34). The larger room, to the east, was designated the 'Holy Place'; it was to be furnished with the golden table and lampstand (26:35). The curtain separating the two rooms contained woven figures of cherubim as a reminder that the way into the immediate presence of God was barred to sinful man (cf. Gen 3:24).[5]

One further item of furniture was to be made for inside the royal tent, an incense altar (30:1–10). Made of acacia wood and plated with pure gold, it was to be placed in the Holy Place alongside the golden table and lampstand. Twice daily Aaron was to burn fragrant incense upon it (30:7–8), and once a year, probably on the Day of Atonement (cf. Lev 16:15–19), he was to make atonement on its horns (30:10).[6]

A HOLY TENT

Around the tabernacle or royal tent Moses was to construct a courtyard by erecting a curtain fence. The courtyard, a rectangular shape twice as long as it was broad, measured approximately 50 m. by 25 m. and was surrounded by a curtain about 2.5 m. high. The shorter sides were to the east and west. The only entrance was on the eastern side. On passing through this gateway a worshipper encountered first a large bronze altar before approaching the tabernacle which stood in the western part of the courtyard. The fence which surrounded the courtyard, along with the curtain which hung across the entrance, prevented those outside from looking into the courtyard. Separated from the rest of the Israelite encampment, the courtyard was set apart as a holy area; only the tabernacle, in which God dwelt, was considered to be more sacred.[7] This distinction between the holiness of the courtyard and the tabernacle is reflected in the value of the materials used in their construction. Whereas gold was regularly used within the tabernacle, the main metals utilised in the construction of the courtyard were silver and bronze. Just as Moses set a boundary around Mount Sinai to prevent the people from coming into the divine presence (19:12–13,21–24), so too the courtyard fence prevented them from approaching God inadvertently. As Exodus regularly emphasises only those who are holy can come into the divine presence; to approach God otherwise has fatal consequences. Without the courtyard functioning as a buffer-zone, it would have been impossible for the Israelites to dwell in safety close to the LORD.

Since the area within the courtyard was holy ground, the priests, Aaron and his sons, assigned to serve there also had to be holy. To indicate this, they were provided with 'sacred garments'. The materials used in their production, 'gold, and blue, purple, and scarlet yarn, and fine linen' (28:5), not only highlight the dignity and honour bestowed upon Aaron and his sons, but also clearly associated them with the tabernacle which was made of similar materials. As high priest Aaron was to wear a breastplate, an ephod, a robe, a woven tunic, a turban and a sash (28:4); his sons were to be given tunics, sashes and headbands (28:40).[8] Most attention is focused on the special items worn by the high priest, especially the 'ephod' (28:6–14) and 'breastpiece' (28:15–30).

The first item mentioned in the list of high priestly clothes is the ephod. Scholars refer to it by its Hebrew name '*epod* ('*ephod*) because the biblical text does not provide sufficient information to reconstruct it exactly.[9] Special reference is made to the two precious stones engraved with the names of the twelve tribes of Israel. Mounted 'in gold filigree settings' (28:11), they were fastened 'on the shoulder pieces of the ephod as memorial stones for the sons of Israel' (28:12). They were a reminder that Aaron served God as high priest, not for his own benefit, but on behalf of all the Israelites.

The next item, designated a 'breastpiece', appears from its description to have been a square pouch which the high priest wore over his chest. The pouch was made of similar materials to the ephod and was attached to it. On the outside of the pouch were four rows of precious stones, with three stones in each row; each stone was to be inscribed with the name of an Israelite tribe. Although Aaron came from the tribe of Levi, as high priest, wearing the names of the tribes on his chest, he served on behalf of all the people. The use of precious stones symbolised the value which God placed upon his people Israel; each tribe was represented by a different stone to show the individual differences which make up the whole nation. Finally, instructions were given that 'the Urim and the Thummim' should be placed in the pouch (28:30). The precise form of the Urim and Thummim remains uncertain. However, they were probably used as a means of determining God's judgement (cf. 22:8,9).[10]

Other items of clothing worn by the high priest are mentioned in 28:31–43. A blue robe, adorned with embroidered pomegranates and golden bells, was presumably worn under the ephod and breastpiece. The tinkling of the bells would serve to identify the one entering or leaving the tabernacle, enabling the high priest to come close to God in safety. As a further reminder of the sacred nature of priestly service, the front of Aaron's turban had a gold plate with the words, 'HOLY TO THE LORD' (28:36). Because he was set apart as holy, Aaron as high priest was able to mediate on behalf on the Israelites, ensuring that their sacrifices were acceptable to the LORD (28:38). Apart from the items already mentioned, Aaron was also to wear a tunic, turban and sash (28:39); the tunic appears to have been worn under the robe of the ephod (cf. 29:5). Because they do not relate directly to the 'dignity and honour' of the priests, the instructions concerning underwear were given separately. The priests were to wear 'linen undergarments' to prevent them from inadvertently exposing their genitalia in the Holy Place (cf. 20:26). Such nakedness was clearly inappropriate in the presence of the LORD (cf. Gen 3:7,10,21). Moreover, since only the priests could enter the tabernacle, the command that they should wear undergarments would reassure those outside that nothing unseemly occurred within the tabernacle.

To serve in God's holy presence the priests had to be holy. The instructions in 29:1–46 reflect the various stages (mentioned briefly in 28:41) necessary for their consecration: clothe, anoint, 'fill the hands',[11] consecrate. After assembling the appropriate items (29:1–3), Moses was to wash[12] and clothe Aaron and his sons in their priestly garments (29:4–9). Then he was to anoint them with oil.[13] Next he had to offer up three different sacrifices, involving a bull and two rams. The first (29:10–14), best understood as a purification offering, involved the bull, and followed closely the instructions given later in Leviticus 4:3–12 relating to the unintentional sin of an anointed priest. In this instance, however, the blood was probably placed on the horns of the large bronze altar in the courtyard and not on the gold incense altar within the tabernacle (29:12; cf. Lev 4:7). The blood purified the altar which had become defiled through contact with individuals who were considered unclean. The next sacrifice, a whole-burnt offering (29:15–18), follows exactly the instructions given later in Leviticus 1:10–13 for the offering of a ram. The whole-burnt offering atoned for the sins of Aaron and his sons. The total destruction of the animal was a vivid reminder that sinful man could not approach a holy God. The animal died as a substitute for those who were identified with it by the laying of their hands on its head. The third sacrifice (29:19–34) resembles closely a fellowship or peace offering made as an expression of thankfulness (cf. Lev 3:6–11; 7:12–15). However, the ritual described here has distinctive features, appropriate for this unique occasion. First, Aaron, his sons and their garments were to be consecrated by sacrificial blood (29:19–21); whatever the blood touched became holy.[14] Secondly, vv 22–35 focus on the remuneration which Aaron and his sons were to receive as priests. NIV wrongly refers to this as 'the ram for the ordination' (29:22; cf. 29:26,27,31,34); it is literally 'the ram of (the) filling'. This 'filling' refers to the portion which was to be given to the priests after they offered up different sacrifices (cf. Lev 6:14–18,25–29; 7:1–38). The ritual which Moses would later perform consecrated the right thigh and breast for priestly consumption. A distinction is drawn between the 'breast', which is 'waved', and the 'thigh', which is 'presented' (29:27). On this occasion the breast will be given to Moses as his reward for offering the sacrifice (29:26), and the thigh will be burnt on the altar, along with some bread (29:25). On future occasions, after the priests are consecrated, the breast of the fellowship sacrifice shall be presented to all the priests, and the thigh given to the priest who officiates (Lev 7:28–36). Apart from the breast, thigh, and various fatty portions, the rest of the ram of (the) filling was to be cooked and eaten, together with the remaining bread, at the entrance to the tabernacle. Only the priests were to eat this holy food.

The ritual outlined in vv 1–34 was essential for the consecration of the priests. Most commentators believe on the basis of v 35 that this ritual was repeated every day for seven days. Alternatively, the sacrifices outlined in vv 36–41 may have been offered during the next six days, with Aaron and his sons under strict instruction to remain within the courtyard of the tabernacle (cf. Lev 8:33–35). In either case the process of consecration or sanctification required time. The fulfilment of the instructions regarding the consecration of Aaron and his sons is recorded in Leviticus 8:1–36.[15]

Concerning the priests Moses was also told to make a bronze basin (30:17–21). This was to be placed between the tabernacle and the bronze altar so that Aaron and his sons could wash their hands and feet when serving within the tabernacle and courtyard (30:17–21). The requirement that the priests should wash symbolises their need to remain holy and pure (cf. 19:14; 29:4).

The Exodus narrative thus highlights in a special way the holy nature of the tabernacle and of those who served within it.

A TENT OF MEETING

The tabernacle was not only a royal and holy tent but also a tent of meeting. This is highlighted in God's comments in 29:43: 'There . . . I will meet with the Israelites, and the place will be consecrated by my glory' (29:43). Like the Garden of Eden, the tabernacle was the place where divinity and humanity could commune together. However, to enable sinful people to meet a holy God, it was necessary for them to be sanctified from their sin and uncleanness. To this end God instructed Moses to construct a portable bronze-plated altar, which was to be situated in the courtyard near the entrance to the tabernacle (27:1–8). From its dimensions, this altar dominated the area in front of the tabernacle; it was 2.5 m. wide (half the width of the tabernacle) and 1.5 m. high. It consisted of a square hollow framework made of acacia wood overlaid with bronze. To create a draught for the incineration of the animal sacrifices the lower part of each side was comprised of a grating of bronze network. Its position between the courtyard entrance and the tabernacle indicated that a worshipper could only approach God after offering a sacrifice to atone for sin.[16]

Following the erection of the tabernacle, a cloud covered it, and the glory of the LORD filled it (40:34). God now dwelt in the midst of the people, and the tabernacle was designated 'the Tent of Meeting' (40:35; cf. 27:21), replacing the tent used earlier by Moses (cf. 33:7–11).[17] It differed from this other tent, however, in that God dwelt within the tabernacle and Moses stayed outside (40:35), whereas with the earlier tent Moses went inside and God remained outside (33:9). God's presence was visible to everyone through the cloud and fire which settled upon the tabernacle. From there he guided them on their journeys (40:36–38). Thus Exodus concludes by noting the glorious presence of the sovereign God in the midst of his people Israel.[18]

THE PROVISION OF MATERIALS AND SKILLED CRAFTSMEN

The account of the making of the tabernacle also focuses on two practical matters regarding its construction. First, Moses was instructed to ask the people to make an offering to the LORD in order to provide the materials required for the construction of the tabernacle and related items (25:1–7). When Moses addressed the people (35:4–9) they responded generously (35:20–27). Indeed such was their generosity that later they had to be restrained from giving too much (36:3–7). Their freewill gifts reflect their deep gratitude to God for delivering them from Egypt.

Secondly, God informed Moses that he had chosen and equipped certain men with the skills necessary to produce the tabernacle and its furnishings (31:1–11). Singled out for particular mention are Bezalel and Oholiab whose special ability is attributed to the fact that they have been filled with the Spirit of God (31:3). Later when placed in charge of the work (35:30–36:2), they also displayed their aptitude to teach others (35:34). Elsewhere, attention is drawn to the women who devoted their natural abilities and skills to the LORD by spinning yarn (35:25–26).

CONCLUSION

Exodus 25–30 emphasises three aspects of the tabernacle: it was (a) a royal tent, (b) a holy tent, and (c) a 'Tent of Meeting'. The first two of these are clearly linked to God's nature; he is a sovereign and holy God. The third aspect focuses on the special relationship which God established with the people of Israel through the covenant at Sinai. The construction of the tabernacle enabled the people to commune more directly with their God and reassured them of his presence in their midst.

NEW TESTAMENT CONNECTIONS

Although the tabernacle was replaced by a temple, modelled upon it and constructed first by Solomon and later rebuilt at the end of the 6th century BC, it is discussed in a number of NT passages. In general these reflect important developments in the way the tabernacle (and its successor, the temple) was perceived.

(a) The early Christians emphasised the secondary nature of the tabernacle/temple. It was merely a 'copy and shadow of what is in heaven' (Heb 8:5; cf. 9:11,24). Consequently, the NT plays down the importance of the temple in Jerusalem, even to the extent of anticipating its destruction (Mark 13:1–2); rather it focuses attention on the heavenly tabernacle. The demise of the Jerusalem temple is clearly linked to how the early church understood the death and resurrection of Jesus Christ. First, Matt 27:51 records that when Jesus died the curtain in the temple, separating the Holy of Holies from the Holy Place, was torn from top to bottom. The tearing of this curtain revealed that, by his sacrificial death, Christ removed the barrier which existed between God and humanity (cf. Heb 9:1–8). Second, Jesus was viewed as entering the heavenly sanctuary, rather than the earthly sanctuary, to serve as a high priest: 'For Christ did not enter a man-made sanctuary that was only a copy of the true one; he entered heaven itself, now to appear for us in God's presence' (Heb 9:24; cf. 9:11–28).[19] This emphasis upon the heavenly sanctuary, rather than the earthly temple in Jerusalem, is also reflected in Jesus's comments to a Samaritan woman concerning the right place to worship God:

> Believe me, woman, a time is coming when you will worship the Father neither on this mountain nor in Jerusalem. You Samaritans worship what you do not know; we worship what we do know, for salvation is from the Jews. Yet a time is coming and has now come when the true worshippers will worship the Father in spirit and truth, for they are the kind of worshippers the Father seeks. God is spirit, and his worshippers must worship in spirit and in truth (John 4:21–24).

Here Jesus anticipates a time when worship will not be restricted to any particular earthly location.

(b) From another perspective the NT draws a close parallel between Jesus and the tabernacle/temple. In Jesus, God is viewed as inhabiting human flesh just as he previously inhabited first the tabernacle and then the temple. John alludes to this when he writes, 'The Word became flesh and made his dwelling (lit. tabernacled) among us. We have seen his glory . . .' (John 1:14). The same idea clearly underlies Jesus' own comment in John 2:19, 'Destroy this temple, and I will raise it again in three days.' John clarifies the meaning of this statement by observing, 'The temple he had spoken of was his body' (John 2:21; cf. Mark 14:58).

(c) According to Paul every believer, due to the indwelling of the Holy Spirit, is a temple (1 Cor 6:19; cf. 1 Cor 3:16–17; 2 Cor 6:16). Moreover, the Spirit's presence causes God's glory to be reflected in the lives of those who are Christ's followers: 'We, who with unveiled faces all reflect the Lord's glory, are being transformed into his likeness with ever-increasing glory, which comes from the Lord, who is the Spirit' (2 Cor 3:18).

NOTES

1. Remarkably, in spite of the space devoted to recording the making of the tabernacle, the present account does not provide all the information necessary to reconstruct fully the original tent.

2. Although the quantities involved appear large, they are by no means unusual when compared with contemporary practices in the ancient world. See K. A. Kitchen, 'The Tabernacle – A Late Bronze Age Artefact' *Eretz Israel* 24 (1993) 119–29.

3. The Day of Atonement ritual is discussed more fully in chapter 11.

4. Cherubim were the traditional guardians of holy places in the ancient Near East. Apart from the two described here, others were woven into the curtains which surround the tabernacle and which separate the Holy of Holies from the Holy Place (26:1,31).

5. For a fuller discussion of the problems involved in reconstructing the tabernacle, see 'Tabernacle', *IBD* 1506–1511.

6. The altar had four horns, one at each of its top corners.

7. The two rooms of the tabernacle also differed in their degree of holiness. The Holy of Holies which contained God's throne could only be entered by the high priest on the Day of Atonement. The Holy Place, however, was entered daily by some of the priests who ministered there. The bronze basin was used for washing feet.

8. The lack of reference to footwear may indicate that the priests served barefooted; when God appeared in the burning bush Moses was commanded to remove his sandals because the ground was holy (cf. Exod 3:5).

9. It appears to have been either a waistcoat or a waist-cloth.

10. For a brief description and picture of a modern reconstruction of the breastpiece, see 'Breastpiece of the High Priest', *IBD* 207.

11. NIV 'ordain' does not translate accurately the Hebrew original.

12. Purity and cleanliness are closely associated with being holy (cf. 19:10,14).

13. Special oil was to be manufactured for the anointing of the tabernacle, its furnishings, and the priests who served there (30:22–30). Since everything touched by this particular oil became holy, restrictions were placed upon its production and use (30:31–33). Similar instructions were given for the making and use of the incense which was to be burned within the tabernacle (30:34–38).

14. 'The priest must have consecrated ears ever to listen to God's holy voice; consecrated hands at all times to do holy deeds; and consecrated feet to walk evermore in holy ways' (A. Dillmann, *Die Bücher Exodus und Leviticus* [2nd ed.; Leipzig: Hirzel, 1880], 465).

15. For a brief discussion of the process by which the priests were consecrated, see chapter 10.

16. Instructions for the consecration of the altar are given in 29:36–37. Leviticus 1:1–7:38 details the various sacrifices which individuals were expected to offer.

17. Exodus 33:7–11 records how Moses, prior to the erection of the tabernacle, was in the custom of pitching a tent at some distance from the main encampment in order to meet with God. Given its specific function, this tent was known as the 'tent of meeting' (33:7). Here Moses enjoyed a unique and personal relationship with God: 'The LORD would speak to Moses face to face, as a man speaks with his friend' (33:11). Although they were in close proximity to one another, even Moses the faithful servant was not permitted to look directly upon God; 33:9 implies that the tent curtain shielded Moses who was within from the LORD who was without.

18. Although the Exodus narrative portrays the LORD as coming to dwell within the tabernacle, there are indications that the tabernacle was not viewed as his main residence. As Jacob Milgrom observes:

> From the fact that Moses is commanded to build the Tabernacle and its appurtenances according to the pattern that was shown to him on Mount Sinai (Exod 26:30; cf. Exod 25:9,40; 27:8; Num 8:4), it is possible that he was shown the earthly sanctuary's heavenly counterpart. (*Leviticus 1–16* [Anchor Bible 3; New York: Doubleday, 1991] 141).

In the light of this, it is interesting to note Moses' comment in Deut 26:15: 'Look down from heaven, your holy dwelling place, and bless your people Israel'

19. On Christ's role as a high priest within the heavenly tabernacle, see chapter 11.

[10]

Be Holy

SUMMARY

Leviticus is dominated by the topic of holiness. Its prominence derives from the fact that God is holy. Although Leviticus emphasises God's power to sanctify or make holy other people or objects, it also highlights the danger posed by the moral and ritual uncleanness associated with human behaviour. Holiness and uncleanness are presented as mutually exclusive. Consequently, for the Israelites to enjoy a meaningful and fruitful relationship with God, they must reflect his holiness in their daily lives. Since differing degrees of holiness and uncleanness exist, the Israelites are divinely exhorted, 'Be holy because I, the LORD your God, am holy' (19:2; cf. 11:44–45; 20:26).

INTRODUCTION

The book of Leviticus continues the story of Exodus by describing what took place in the thirteenth month after the Israelites' divine deliverance from Egypt (cf. Exod 40:17; Num 1:1). As a result, the books of Exodus and Leviticus, and, as we shall later observe, also Numbers, are closely connected. Leviticus both assumes the erection of the tabernacle which forms the climax of the book of Exodus (40:1–38), and records the consecration of Aaron and his sons as priests, fulfilling the instructions given to Moses by the LORD in Exodus 29:1–46. Leviticus must, therefore, be read in conjunction with Exodus, both books forming part of the continuous and carefully composed narrative which comprises the Pentateuch.

Although Leviticus continues the story of the Israelites' journey from Egypt to Canaan, almost 90 per cent of the book consists of divine speeches on a variety of topics. As a result, apart from numerous short introductions to these discourses (cf. 1:1; 4:1; 5:14; 6:1; 6:8; etc.), there are only two sections in which the narrator describes events rather than reports God's

110

words. The first of these focuses on the consecration of the priests and the subsequent sin of Nadab and Abihu (8:1–10:20). The second passage is much briefer and deals with a man who blasphemes by cursing God (24:10–23). Even in this short episode more than half of the verses record what the LORD said to Moses (24:13–22). Leviticus is thus composed almost entirely of divine speeches. In this regard it resembles closely Exodus 20:22–24:2 and 25:1–31:17.

In Leviticus Moses continues his role of mediator between God and the Israelites. While the LORD nearly always speaks directly to Moses alone — on a few occasions Aaron is also included (11:1; 13:1; 14:33; 15:1) — his words are usually intended for either the Israelites (e.g. 1:2; 4:2; 7:23,29; 11:2) or the priests (6:9,20,25; 21:2; 22:2). This distinction between the majority of Israelites and the selected few who were divinely appointed as priests is a significant feature in Leviticus. Not only is it reflected in many of the divine speeches, but more importantly it lies at the very heart of the account of the consecration of Aaron and his sons as priests in chs. 8–9. Here the narrative highlights the three stages by which Aaron and his sons were set apart from the rest of the Israelites. First, they were brought out from the midst of the community (8:6) to be consecrated as priests. The special ritual, involving washing, clothing and anointing, endowed them with a degree of holiness which surpassed that of other Israelites (8:6–30).[1] Moreover, because Aaron was treated differently from his sons, he was recognised as being even holier. Secondly, the priests were to stay at the entrance to the tabernacle for seven days (8:31–36). Not only did this further emphasise their separation from the people, but it also confirmed their holy status; unlike the rest of the population they remained in close proximity to God. Thirdly, on the eighth day there was a rite of incorporation by which the priests were once again brought into contact with the rest of the community (9:1–24). Although Moses provided instructions, the newly appointed priests offered up the sacrifices on behalf of the community, with Aaron, as high priest, performing the main tasks. By recording that 'fire came out from the presence of the LORD and consumed the burnt offering and the fat portions on the altar' (9:24), the account of the consecration of the priests concludes by highlighting God's acceptance of Aaron and his sons as the community's cultic representatives.[2] Leviticus thus emphasises the important distinction which God instituted between the priests and all other Israelites.

As well as stressing the differing degrees of holiness which existed between the priests and other Israelites, the book of

Leviticus, especially in chs. 11–15, also draws attention to the fact that ordinary Israelites belonged to one of two categories: clean or unclean. Various factors, including eating particular foods, suffering from certain types of skin disease[3] or experiencing particular bodily discharges, caused an individual, and sometimes even those who came into contact with him or her, to become unclean. Significantly, anyone designated as unclean had to undergo a process of purification before they could participate fully in the religious life of the community.

HOLY, CLEAN AND UNCLEAN

The features noted briefly in the preceding paragraphs draw attention to three related categories which permeate almost all of the material in Leviticus; these are holy, clean/pure, and unclean/impure. The importance of these three categories is underlined by the very frequent occurrence of these and associated words throughout Leviticus. Terms based on the Hebrew root *qādaš* (*qādash*) (e.g. 'holy', 'holiness', 'sanctify') come 152 times in Leviticus, representing about one-fifth of all occurrences in the OT. *Ṭāhôr* (*ṭakhôr*) 'clean' and associated words occur 74 times, representing more than one-third of all OT occurrences. *Ṭāmēʾ* 'unclean' and cognate terms come 132 times, representing more than half of the total occurrences in the OT. These statistics highlight the significance of the categories holy, clean/pure and unclean/impure in Leviticus.

The existence of these three categories is reflected in the layout of the Israelite camp. At the heart of the camp stood the tabernacle courtyard, a holy area, the rest of the camp had the status of a clean area, and everywhere outside the camp was unclean.[4] This same three-fold division was also found among the people; the priests were considered to be holy, the Israelites clean, and non-Israelites unclean. Moreover, the places and people corresponded directly: the priests were associated with the tabernacle, the Israelites with the camp, and the non-Israelites with those outside the camp (see Diagram D).

Within these main categories, sub-divisions also existed. As regards holiness, this is evident in a number of different spheres. First, differing degrees of holiness existed within the priesthood and laity. The high priest was distinguished from the other priests in a variety of ways. Not only was the ritual for his consecration distinctive, as were his clothes, but he alone enjoyed the title of 'high' priest. At any time there could

DIAGRAM D

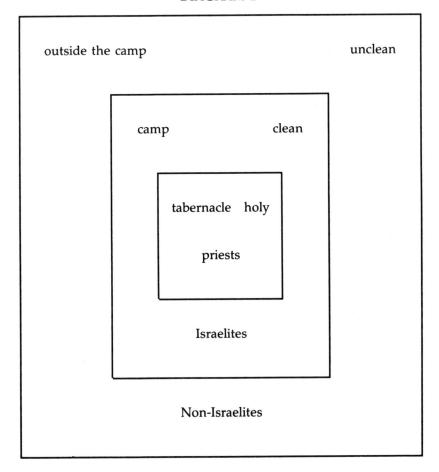

only be one high priest, and each new appointee had to undergo a special consecration ritual. Of all the priests he alone was permitted to enter the Holy of Holies. The high priest was also required to adhere to much stricter rules regarding marriage, purity and mourning. A lesser category of priests consisted of those who suffered from some form of physical defect. Although they were prohibited from offering sacrifices, they were allowed to eat from the portions of sacrifices allocated to the priests. Next to the priests in holiness were the Levites. While they were not permitted to offer sacrifices, they assisted the priests with other duties concerning the tabernacle, especially its transportation and erection (Num 4:1–49).[5] Whereas the priests and Levites enjoyed a special status of holiness arising from their ancestry and divine appointment, other Israelites were given the opportunity to have a higher degree of holiness by becoming Nazirites. To attain this holier status an individual took 'a vow of separation to the LORD' which entailed (a) abstaining from the produce of the vine and (b) not cutting one's hair (Num 6:1–21). These sub-divisions of people surface in different contexts within Leviticus. For example, whereas ordinary Israelites might touch any corpse, regular priests were only permitted to touch the corpse of a close relative (21:1–4), and the high priest was prohibited from contact with any corpse (10:1–7).

Second, the tabernacle was divided into at least three distinct areas, each with differing degrees of holiness. The tent itself consisted of two rooms, the Holy of Holies and the Holy Place. The former of these, containing the ark of the covenant, was considered to be much holier than the adjacent room, the Holy Place, which contained the lampstand, the table for the 'Bread of the Presence' and the incense altar.[6] The tabernacle courtyard was less holy than the tent itself, although holier than the camp from which it was separated by a curtain fence. These different degrees of holiness within the tabernacle are also reflected in the access which people had. Only the most holy of the priests, the high priest, could enter the Holy of Holies, and even he was limited to one day in the year, the Day of Atonement. Although any priest could enter the Holy Place, ordinary Israelites were barred; they had access only to the courtyard.

Third, the tabernacle furnishings also reflect the three-fold pattern of holiness found within the different areas of the tabernacle. They do so in a number of ways depending upon (a) their location, (b) the materials used in their manufacture, (c) their accessibility to human beings, and (d) their use in religious rituals. Whereas the holiest furniture, made of pure gold, was placed within the tent, the altar and laver, made of bronze, were located in the courtyard. Although ordinary Israelites were permitted to view the bronze altar and laver, only priests could look upon the gold furnishings in the Holy Place with immunity (Num 4:18–20). Within the tent, the ark of the covenant was set apart from the other items of furniture by being placed in the Holy of Holies. It was so holy that only the high priest could approach it, and even then he possibly used smoke from incense to conceal the top of the ark from view (16:12–13).[7]

Fourth, particular days of the week and year exhibited differing degrees of holiness. The weekly Sabbath and the annual Day of Atonement were marked as especially holy by the prohibition of all work (23:3,28). The pilgrimage festivals of Unleavened Bread, Weeks and Tabernacles and certain other days were considered less holy and therefore required only abstinence from regular work (23:7,21,25,35). Finally, while the Israelites were expected to make special offerings on the first day of each month, they were permitted to work on these days, indicating that they were the least holy of all special days.

In the light of these four factors it is apparent that the book of Leviticus envisages a world in which people, places, objects and even periods of time have differing degrees of holiness.

Just as there were varying degrees of holiness, so too with uncleanness. First, the strength or weakness of an impurity was judged by its ability to communicate impurity to other objects or persons. Only more serious forms of impurity could pollute other people or objects. For example, if a man lay with a woman during her monthly period, she caused him to become unclean for seven days, and, in turn, any bed upon which he lay also became unclean (15:24). Furthermore, anyone who touched this bed became unclean; however, this latter uncleanness lasted only for one day and could not be transferred to other people or objects.

Second, differing degrees of impurity were reflected by the way in which they polluted the sanctuary. The location of the pollution is indicated by where the blood of the purification offering was placed. Deliberate or intentional sins polluted the ark of the covenant in the Holy of Holies (cf. 16:16); unintentional or inadvertent sins by the high priest or the community polluted the incense altar in the Holy Place (4:2–21); lesser sins or impurities polluted the bronze altar in the courtyard (4:22–35).

Third, Leviticus distinguishes between those impurities which could be rectified and those which could not. Regarding the former, considerable attention is given in chs. 12–15 to the rectification of uncleanness arising from skin diseases and various bodily discharges. In marked contrast, among those impurities which could not be rectified were sexual sins (18:20,23–25,27–30), idolatry (20:2–5), murder (Num 35:16–21,31) and profaning the sacred (e.g. 7:19–21; 22:3,9). In these cases only the death of the guilty party could remove the pollution caused by his or her sin.

When rectification was possible, the process by which any uncleanness was purified varied depending upon its seriousness. Normally, a person or object was purified by (a) the passage of time, and (b) washing and/or laundering; those objects which could not be washed were disposed of by burial, burning or some other method. For minor impurities the length of time required for purification was one day (e.g. for touching the carcass of an animal, 11:39). More serious impurities required the passing of seven days (e.g. touching a human corpse, Num 19:11). Longer periods of forty and eighty days respectively were necessary for a woman who gave birth to a son or daughter (12:2–5). As regards the washing of the body and the laundering of clothes, requirements again differed depending upon the degree of impurity. For example, whoever *touched* an animal carcass was unclean for a day; whoever *carried* an animal carcass sustained greater impurity and was required to wash his or her clothes (11:24–25,27–28).[8]

From these observations concerning holiness and uncleanness/impurity, it is apparent that they formed a spectrum of closely associated categories. On the one side there was holiness, in the middle cleanness, and on the other side uncleanness/impurity (see Diagram E). The further one moved

DIAGRAM E

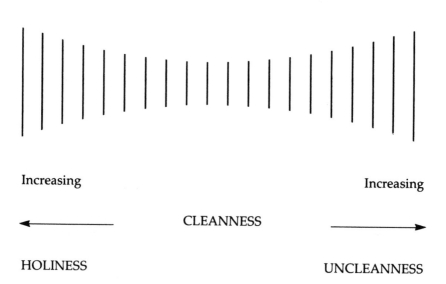

Increasing   Increasing

←——————   CLEANNESS   ——————→

HOLINESS   UNCLEANNESS

from the middle of this spectrum the greater the intensity of either holiness or uncleanness. For the ancient Israelites every person, object, place and period of time could be located somewhere on this spectrum.

So far we have discussed the concepts of holiness and uncleanness without attempting to define them. It is necessary, therefore, to clarify what was meant by these terms within the context of Leviticus. What was holiness? What was uncleanness?

HOLINESS

In Leviticus, holiness is always associated with God. Four aspects of this are very significant. (a) God is innately holy; he is the supreme manifestation of holiness. To be holy is to be god-like. (b) Holiness emanates from God; he is the sole source of holiness. He alone endows other objects, places or people with holiness. Everything that is given to God or belongs to him is holy. Since God radiates holiness to all that is close to him, the ark of the covenant, which functioned as his earthly throne, was the most holy item of furniture in the tabernacle. For the same reason the Holy of Holies was the holiest part of the tabernacle; indeed God's presence made it the holiest location upon the entire earth. (c) Holiness describes the moral perfection and purity of God's nature. For this reason God's command to the Israelites, 'Be holy because I, the LORD your God, am holy' (19:2), comes in the context of imperatives governing the people's behaviour. Their actions and attitudes were to reflect God's perfect nature. (d) Sanctification, the process by which someone or something becomes holy, is the result of divine activity. It is God who sanctifies. This is reflected in the refrain 'I am the LORD, who makes you holy (who sanctifies you; NIV margin)' (20:8; 21:8,15,23; 22:9,16,32). Yet, while Leviticus notes the divine side of sanctification, it also emphasises the human side. Those made holy by God were expected to remain holy by doing nothing which would compromise their special status (cf. 11:44). The Israelites were also to keep holy anything sanctified by God. This applied, for example, to the Sabbath day. Because God had sanctified it, the Israelites were commanded to maintain its sanctity by refraining from all work (Exod 20:8–11).

A natural extension of the belief that God is holy is the idea that holiness means wholeness or perfection. To be holy is to be unblemished or unmarred. It is to experience life in all its fullness as God had originally intended it to be. On one level this is reflected in the divine requirements regarding both priests and sacrifices. Priests with physical defects are not permitted to offer sacrifices (21:17–23). Similarly, it is regularly stated that the sacrificial offerings had to be without defect (1:3, 10; 3:1, 6; 4:3, 23, 28, 32; 5:15, 18; 6:6; 9:2–3; 14:10; 22:19–25; 23:12, 18; cf. Exod 12:5); only in the case of a free-will offering was an exception made (22:23).[9] On another level, holiness is associated with perfect moral behaviour (cf. 20:7; 22:32–33). This is revealed especially in ch. 19 (but compare also chs. 18 and 20) which contains a long list of commands governing personal behaviour. Interestingly, the material in this chapter echoes closely the Decalogue or Ten Commandments (Exod 20:2–17) and the collection of moral instructions found within the Book of the Covenant (Exod 22:21–23:9). To be holy is to live in a way that reflects the moral perfection of God; it is to live a life marked by love, purity and righteousness, these being the three most important hallmarks of perfect behaviour.

UNCLEANNESS

In simple terms, uncleanness is the opposite of holiness. It represents all that is less than God-like. Although Leviticus never identifies the original source of uncleanness, we may surmise that it was believed to emanate from that which opposed God. Interestingly, uncleanness is associated with human beings in two ways. First, certain forms of uncleanness or impurity arise as a natural consequence of being human. These included suffering from specific skin diseases and experiencing bodily discharges. Significantly, these and related forms of uncleanness all appear to be linked in one way or another to death. By associating some bodily diseases and conditions with death, the regulations of Leviticus indicate that death dominates human existence. Only by becoming holy can a human being escape the domain of death and experience the life-giving power of God.

Secondly, there are other forms of uncleanness which human beings have the power to control. These occur when individuals by their actions transgress any boundary established by God. People who wilfully ignore God's commands, decrees, or laws are a source of uncleanness and defile all that they touch. Their actions both distance them from God and bring them further under the domain of death.

THE RELATIONSHIP BETWEEN HOLINESS AND UNCLEANNESS

Leviticus highlights two important factors regarding the relationship between holiness and uncleanness. First, holiness and uncleanness are totally incompatible. Not only was it impossible for anyone or anything to be holy and unclean at the same time, but, more importantly, no holy object or person was normally permitted to come into contact with anything unclean.[10] This incompatibility between holiness and uncleanness accounts for the existence of many of the regulations found in Leviticus. For example, it explains the necessity of the complex sacrificial system, outlined in chs. 1–7, which enabled those who were by nature unclean to become pure and holy.

Without the offering of sacrifices, it would have been impossible for the Israelites to live in close contact with the LORD their
God.[11]

Second, both holiness and uncleanness were perceived by
the ancient Israelites as being dynamic in nature; that is, they
had the ability to transmit their nature to other people or
objects. In this regard they differ significantly from the state of
cleanness/purity; it was merely neutral, and was unable to
make anything else clean or pure. Consequently, any clean
person or thing was constantly in the middle of a struggle
between the powers of holiness and uncleanness.[12] Since the
status of an individual could change, Leviticus consistently
underlines the danger posed by uncleanness to those who are
holy or pure. This danger was greatest for the priests who
worked within the tabernacle, a holy area, and handled the
tabernacle furniture, holy objects. For a priest to serve in the
tabernacle, it was essential that he remained holy. If he became
unclean, he could no longer carry out his duties; to do so would
have meant death.[13]

The dynamic nature of holiness and uncleanness also
explains the antagonism which we find in Leviticus towards
the inhabitants of Egypt and Canaan (cf. 19:1–37). Due to their
uncleanness they were viewed as a major threat to the well-
being of the Israelites. Because their uncleanness was dynamic
and opposed to the holiness of the LORD, it had the potential to
make the Israelites unclean and, therefore, threaten their
special relationship with the LORD. For this reason the inhabitants of Canaan had to be removed from the land. Any form of
compromise would inevitably pollute the Israelites and subsequently God's sanctuary. To be a holy nation, Israel had to set
itself apart from all that was unclean.

NEW TESTAMENT CONNECTIONS

The concepts of holiness and uncleanness are frequently
mentioned in the NT and reflect closely what we observe in
Leviticus. As regards uncleanness Jesus focused attention on
those actions or attitudes which make a person unclean:

> What comes out of a man is what makes him 'unclean'. For from
> within, out of men's hearts, come evil thoughts, sexual immorality,
> theft, murder, adultery, greed, malice, deceit, lewdness, envy,
> slander, arrogance and folly. All these evils come from inside and
> make a man 'unclean' (Mark 7:20–23; cf. Matt 15:17–20).

In doing so he was highly critical of the Pharisees and teachers
of the law who neglected these causes of uncleanness while

concentrating on relatively minor aspects of ritual purity (cf. Matt 23:23–28; Luke 11:37–41). Paul, likewise, associated impurity with wickedness and immorality (e.g. Rom 1:24; 6:19; 2 Cor 12:21; Eph 4:19; 5:3,5). According to Paul, such sinful behaviour was to be shunned by believers 'for God did not call us to be impure, but to live a holy life' (1 Thess 4:7; cf. 1 Cor 1:2; 2 Tim 2:8).

The NT references to purification highlight two complementary aspects. On the one hand, they underline that it is God who purifies those who are unclean (cf. Acts 15:9). More specifically, it is emphasised that purification is achieved through the sacrificial death of Jesus Christ: 'But if we walk in the light, as he is in the light, we have fellowship with one another, and the blood of Jesus, his Son, purifies us from all sin' (1 John 1:7; cf. John 15:3; Titus 2:14; Heb 1:3; 1 John 1:9). On the other hand, believers are exhorted to purify themselves: 'Since we have these promises, dear friends, let us purify ourselves from everything that contaminates body and spirit, perfecting holiness out of reverence for God' (2 Cor 7:1; cf. Jas 4:8).

The concept of holiness figures prominently in all of the NT Epistles. Holiness of life is to be the ambition of every believer. Peter expresses this most clearly, quoting in the process Leviticus: 'But just as he who called you is holy, so be holy in all you do; for it is written: "Be holy, because I am holy" ' (1 Pet 1:15–16; cf. Rom 6:19,22; 2 Cor 1:12; Eph 4:24; Col 3:12; 1 Thess 2:10; 3:13; 1 Tim 2:15; Titus 1:8; Heb 12:14; 2 Pet 3:11). The importance of holiness is underlined by the author of Hebrews: 'Make every effort to live in peace with all men and to be holy; without holiness no-one will see the Lord' (Heb 12:14). Such holiness is clearly linked to behaviour that is morally exemplary. Jesus instructed his followers: 'For I tell you that unless your righteousness surpasses that of the Pharisees and the teachers of the law, you will certainly not enter the kingdom of heaven . . . Be perfect, therefore, as your heavenly Father is perfect' (Matt 5:20,48). Significantly, there are thirty-three occasions in the NT (excluding Revelation) when believers are designated as 'saints' or 'holy ones' (e.g. Acts 9:13,32; 26:10; Rom 1:7; 8:27; 15:25,26,31; 16:2,15).

Although believers are constantly exhorted to be holy, God's role in the process of sanctification is also recognised (1 Thess 5:23). In Hebrews he is pictured as a father disciplining his children in order to produce holiness of character: 'But God disciplines us for our good, that we may share in his holiness' (Heb 12:10). Most attention, however, tends to be focused on the role played by Jesus Christ and the Holy Spirit. On three occasions both are mentioned together in connection with the sanctification of believers (1 Cor 6:11; Heb 10:29; 1 Pet 1:2). 2 Thessalonians 2:13 refers specifically to 'the sanctifying work of the Spirit' (cf. Rom 15:16). This is obviously linked to the belief that the Holy Spirit dwells within believers: 'Do you not know that your body is a temple of the Holy Spirit, who is in you, whom you have received from God' (1 Cor 6:19)? As God's presence made the tabernacle holy, so too the presence of the Holy Spirit sanctifies believers. Elsewhere, the sanctifying work of Jesus Christ is highlighted; he is 'the one who makes men holy' (Heb 2:11; cf. Acts 26:18; 1 Cor 1:2). Significantly, this is linked to Christ's death: 'we have been made holy through the sacrifice of the body of Jesus Christ once for all' (Heb 10:10; cf. Col 1:22; Heb 10:14; 13:12).

A number of incidents recorded in the Gospels focus on the relationship between the holy and the unclean. When Jesus touched those who were unclean with skin diseases, he displayed his power both to heal and to purify (Matt 8:1–4; Mark 1:40–44; Luke 5:12–14). The same was true when Jesus was touched by the woman suffering from bleeding for twelve years (Matt 9:20–22; Mark 5:24–34; Luke 8:42–48). Similarly, when Jesus restored the dead to life, he revealed his power over death, a primary source of uncleanness (Matt 18:23–25; Mark 5:35–43; Luke 7:11–17; 8:49–56). Jesus' holy nature was also recognised by his disciples (John 6:69; cf. Acts 3:14; 4:27,30; Heb 7:26) and by the unclean spirits or demons who refer to him as 'the Holy One of God' (Mark 1:24; Luke 4:34).

NOTES

1. For a fuller discussion of the different elements which comprised the ritual for the consecration of the priests, see chapter 9.

2. The appearance of the glory of the LORD to all the people in 9:23 parallels what occurred immediately after the erection of the tabernacle (Exod 40:34–35). On both occasions God expressed his approval and acceptance of what had just taken place by displaying his presence to the people.

3. Although these skin diseases have in the past been understood to be a form of leprosy, it is most unlikely that this was the case.

4. Although the entire area outside the camp was considered unclean, selected places were set apart as clean for the disposal of the ashes from the altar in the tabernacle courtyard (4:12,21; 6:11; cf. the burning of the bull of the purification offering [Lev 16:27]).

5. While the Levites and the priests were all descended from Levi, the third oldest son of Jacob, only Aaron and his sons were designated priests. See chapter 13 for a fuller discussion of the relationship between the priests and Levites.

6. For a detailed discussion of the layout of the tabernacle, see chapter 10.

7. These distinctions between the items of furniture are also reflected in the instruction given in Num 4:5–33 regarding the activities of the Kohathites, Gershonites and Merarites in helping the priests transport the tabernacle.

8. According to J. Milgrom, *Cult and Conscience: The ASHAM and the Priestly Doctrine of Repentance* (Leiden: Brill, 1976) 108–121, when an individual expressed remorse regarding a deliberate sin this had the effect of lessening the resulting pollution and thereby reduced the amount of rectification required.

9. Interestingly, the defects which disqualified both priests and sacrificial animals correspond very closely (21:18–20 and 22:22–24).

10. When such contact occurred it either had a purifying or defiling effect, depending upon the specific circumstances.

11. For a fuller treatment of sacrifice, see chapter 11.

12. Elsewhere in the OT this conflict is presented in terms of Yahweh's conflict with death.

13. The danger posed by the holy furnishing of the tabernacle to an unclean person is also reflected in the regulations concerning an individual who unintentionally killed another person. They are instructed to cling to the horns of the altar. Only one who was morally clean might expect to touch the altar with immunity.

[11]

The Sacrificial System

SUMMARY

When Moses and the Israelites completed the building of the tabernacle it became possible for God to dwell in their midst. However, to enable the people to live in close proximity to the Holy One of Israel, God instituted through Moses a sacrificial system by which the people could atone for their sins. At the heart of this system lay a number of different sacrifices which complemented each other by addressing differing facets of human wrongdoing. This is most apparent with the purification offering which cleansed the tabernacle of pollution caused by sin. Of all the sacrifices offered throughout the year those presented on the Day of Atonement were the most important. Annually the high priest entered the Holy of Holies to atone for the sin of the whole nation and to purify the most sacred part of the tabernacle. Without this and other rituals it would have been impossible for the people to live in harmony with the LORD their God.

INTRODUCTION

The first seven chapters of Leviticus consist of regulations governing the offering of sacrifices. These come between the account of the erection of the tabernacle in Exod 40 and the consecration of the priests in Lev 8–9. Since the instructions for the erection of the tabernacle and the consecration of the priests were given together in Exod 25:1–31:17, we might have expected the description of their fulfilment to be placed side by side. They are separated, however, by the sacrifice regulations. Nevertheless, the present location of the sacrifice instructions is very apt. First, their location at the very beginning of Leviticus emphasises their importance; they are central to Israel's relationship with God. Second, overseeing the offering of

123

sacrifices was the foremost duty of the priests. It is, therefore, quite appropriate that these instruction should be placed immediately prior to the account of the consecration of the priests in chs. 8–9.

Several features of the material in chapters 1–7 are noteworthy. First, the information provided about the sacrifices is in the form of instructions or regulations. These fall into two sections. Whereas the instructions in 1:2–6:7 and 7:22–34 are addressed to the Israelite laity, those in 6:8–7:21 are for the priests. Two sets of instructions are provided because the ordinary Israelites and the priests performed different functions when it came to offering sacrifices.

Second, the instructions given cover five different types of sacrifices. In the New International Version of the Bible these sacrifices are termed burnt offering, grain offering, fellowship offering, sin offering and guilt offering. Some scholars, however, prefer the designations peace, purification and reparation for the fellowship, sin and guilt offerings respectively. As we shall see below, these alternative titles reflect more accurately the distinctive functions of these offerings. The differences between the various types of sacrifices will be discussed later.

Third, the order in which these sacrifices are presented differs in the two sections. This is due to the location of the peace (fellowship) offering (see Table C). Whereas it comes in

TABLE C

Regulations for laity	Regulations for priests
Burnt offering 1:2–17	Burnt offering 6:8–13
Cereal offering 2:1–16	Cereal offering 6:14–23
Peace offering 3:1–17	Purification offering 6:24–30
Purification offering 4:1–5:13	Reparation offering 7:1–10
Reparation offering 5:14–6:7	Peace offering 7:11–21

the middle of the list of regulations addressed to the laity, it comes at the end of the rules for the priests. In the first list the peace offering is grouped with the burnt and grain because all three are 'food offerings' which produce 'a soothing aroma for the LORD'. The purification and reparation offerings are discussed separately due to their distinctive functions. In the second section the order is determined by the holiness of the meat associated with each sacrifice. The peace offering was placed last in the list because ordinary Israelites could eat this meat. In both sections the burnt offering comes first because it was viewed as the most important of all the sacrifices.

Fourth, for both sections the order of the sacrifices does not reflect the sequence in which they were normally offered. Although the burnt offering, as the most important sacrifice, is mentioned first, it was often only presented after a purification offering had been made. This is evident in the case of the sacrifices offered by a Nazirite at the end of his or her period of separation. Although the burnt offering is mentioned first in Num 6:14–15, in practice it was presented after a purification offering (Num 6:16–17). A similar situation can be observed regarding the purification ritual for someone suffering from a skin disease. The purification offering is made first (Lev 14:19–20), although in the list of offerings it comes after the burnt offering (14:10; the ewe lamb for the purification offering is mentioned after the male lamb for the burnt offering).[1] Interestingly, the presentation of a purification offering prior to other sacrifices appears to have been a common pattern in the sacrificial rituals of other ancient Near Eastern societies.

THE GENERAL PATTERN FOR ANIMAL SACRIFICES

Of the five main types of sacrifices listed in the early chapters of Leviticus all but one involve the offering up of an animal. Although there are important differences in detail regarding the procedure for these animal sacrifices, which will be considered below, a common pattern was adopted for each offering. This falls into two parts: the first involves the actions of the Israelite worshipper; the second concerns the duties of the priest. An individual wishing to make a sacrifice brought an animal to the tabernacle courtyard (1:3; 4:4,14). There the worshipper laid a hand on the animal's head (e.g. 1:4; 3:2,8,13), before slaughtering it (e.g. 1:5,11; 3:2,8,13). The blood from the animal was collected by the priest and usually sprinkled against the sides of the bronze altar (1:5,11,15; 3:2,8,13); in the case of the purification offering some of the blood was put to special use (4:7–8,16–18,25,30,34). Next the whole animal, or selected parts, was placed on the altar to be consumed by fire (e.g. 1:6–9,12–13,16–17; 3:3–5,9–11,14–16; 4:8–10,19–20,26,31,35). Finally, any meat that was not burnt up upon the altar was usually consumed by the priests or Israelites (e.g. 6:26–29; 7:6; 7:15–21).

Two aspects of this pattern require further consideration. (a) The laying of a hand upon the animal's head has been understood in a variety of ways. It probably indicated at the very least ownership of the animal. By leaning on the animal the worshipper signalled that this was his or her sacrifice to God. An extension of this idea is that of association. The worshipper associated himself or herself with what happened to the animal. Since the death of the animal was meant to atone for the sin of the worshipper, by touching the animal the worshipper acknowledged that in reality he or she should be put to death. This understanding may even have extended to the belief that the animal was a substitute for the worshipper.[2] Some scholars have argued that the laying of a hand on the animal symbolised the transference of sin from the worshipper to the animal. However, a clear distinction needs to be drawn between the act of placing *one* hand on the animal's head and placing *two* hands. With two hands it is undoubtedly a case of transference. This is clearly illustrated in the ritual of the scapegoat which was sent off into the wilderness on the Day of Atonement (16:20–22). The high priest was instructed 'to lay both hands on the head of the live goat and confess over it all the wickedness and rebellion of the Israelites' (16:21). The text then specifically states, 'The goat will carry on itself all their sins to a solitary place' (16:22). In the case of a single hand being laid on the head of an animal no passage states clearly that the transference of sin took place.

(b) For all the animal sacrifices special instructions are given regarding the use or disposal of the animal's blood. As we shall see in more detail below, with the purification offering the sacrificial blood was used to cleanse sacred objects within the sanctuary which were defiled or polluted due to human sin or impurity. With the other types of sacrifices the blood was collected and sprinkled against the sides of the bronze altar (1:5,11,15; 3:2,8,13; 7:2). These ritual actions reflect the importance with which the ancient Israelites viewed blood; it symbolised life. For this reason sacrificial blood was a powerful antidote to the deathly consequences of sin and impurity.[3]

THE FIVE TYPES OF SACRIFICES

The early chapters of Leviticus provide instructions for five main types of sacrifices. Although they share common features, each type has its own distinctive elements. Naturally, the existence of five different types of sacrifices suggests that each type had its own function. For the purification and reparation offerings it is possible to be reasonably certain about their differing purposes. As regards the other sacrifices we can only make tentative suggestions.

(a) THE BURNT OFFERING (LEV 1:2–17; 6:8–13)

The burnt offering was easily distinguished from all the other sacrifices by the fact that the entire animal was burnt upon the altar. For all other sacrifices only selected portions of the offering were placed upon the altar, with the remainder of the offering being eaten by the priests and/or other worshippers.[4] Of the different sacrifices the burnt offering was viewed as the most important. It comes first in both sets of instructions and the worshipper is clearly expected to present his or her best animal; this is implied by the brief comment that the offering was to be 'a male without defect' (1:3,10). Although the burnt offering was intended to be a costly offering to make, allowance was made for those who were poor and were able only to bring 'a dove or a young pigeon' (1:14).

Few details are given regarding the specific function of the burnt offering. The repetition of the phrase 'an aroma pleasing to the LORD' (1:9,13,17) suggests that it was intended to gain divine favour (cf. Gen 8:20–21). This understanding of the sacrifice is probably to be linked to the comment in 1:4, 'it will be accepted on his behalf to make atonement for him'. The concept of atonement in the OT has two distinctive meanings: it can mean either 'to cleanse' or 'to pay a ransom'. In the case of the burnt offering the latter of these meanings seems the more likely. Within the judicial systems of ancient Israel and her neighbours it was sometimes possible for a guilty party to substitute in place of the death penalty a ransom (cf. Exod 21:30). Thus, the animal offered as a burnt offering was presented as an alternative to the death penalty imposed by God for human sin. By paying this 'ransom' the worshipper appeased God's righteous anger against his or her own sin and uncleanness. God's justice demanded the death of an animal as a substitute for the judicial death of the worshipper. Given that burnt offerings were used to restore broken relationships between God and human beings, it is hardly surprising that such offerings figure prominently in the ratification of divine/human covenants (e.g. Gen 8:20–9:17; 22:1–19; Exod 24:3–11).

(b) THE CEREAL OFFERING (LEV 2:1–16; 6:14–23)

The cereal offering is unique in that of the five main types of sacrifices it was the only one not involving animals. It consisted of an offering made of fine flour, which could be presented either cooked (2:4–7) or uncooked (2:1–2). After the worshipper presented the offering, part of it was burnt upon the bronze altar, the rest being allocated to the priests who were dependent upon it for their daily food.

Like the burnt offering, the cereal offering was clearly intended to evoke a pleasing response from God (cf. 2:2,9). However, whereas the whole of the burnt offering was consumed by fire, only a portion of the cereal offering was burnt on the altar. Most of it was handed over as a gift to the priests in recognition of their unique service for the people (cf. 8:22–31). Interestingly, the Hebrew term for a 'cereal offering' (*minḥâ*) (*minkhâ*) is translated in other contexts as 'gift' or 'tribute'. Sometimes it has the idea of a gift intended to ingratiate the giver to someone else (e.g. Gen 32:13–21; 2 Kgs 8:7–8). Elsewhere it can refer to the money given by a lesser king to a greater in order to guarantee a peaceful relationship (e.g. Judg 3:15–18; 1 Kgs 4:21; 10:23–25; 2 Kgs 17:3–4). This suggests that the cereal offering was possibly viewed as a gift or tribute paid to God in recognition of his divine sovereignty. In this case the priests received it as God's representatives.

(c) THE PEACE OFFERING (LEV 3:1–17; 7:11–21)

The peace offering is distinguished from the other offerings by the fact that most of the meat from the sacrificial animal was retained by the worshipper for a festive meal. Certain portions, however, were set apart for God and the priests: the fat associated with the kidneys and liver was burnt on the altar to produce 'an aroma pleasing to the LORD' (3:5,16); the right thigh was given to the officiating priest, and the breast shared among the other priests (7:28–34). Whereas the burnt offering required that the larger sacrificial animals be male, for the peace offering females could also be offered. Since a meal was an important aspect of the sacrifice, doves and pigeons were excluded as suitable offerings. Under the general heading of peace offerings further divisions existed. According to Leviticus 7 the peace offering could be an expression of thankfulness (vv. 12–15), the result of a vow or a freewill offering (vv. 16–21). For the first of these the meat of the animals had to be consumed on the day it was offered. In the second and third cases the meat could also be eaten on the second day, but if any remained until the third day it had to be burnt up.

Due to the festive nature of the peace offering it is sometimes referred to as the fellowship offering (cf. NIV). The Hebrew name for the sacrifice *šĕlāmîm* (*shĕlāmîm*) has traditionally been linked to the concept of peace (cf. Hebrew *šālôm* [*shalom*]). Since 'peace' in Hebrew thought implied well-being in general it is likely that an important element of the peace offering was the acknowledgement of God as the source of true peace.

(d) THE PURIFICATION OFFERING (LEV 4:1–5:13; 6:24–30)

The distinctive nature of the purification offering is highlighted by the special use made of the animal's blood to cleanse sacred items within the tabernacle. Although Leviticus 4 focuses on different types of purification offering, attention is drawn on each occasion to how the priest placed or sprinkled the sacrificial blood on particular items within the tabernacle. The examples in ch. 4 are given in descending order, with the most serious offences being listed first. If the anointed priest or whole community of Israel sinned, the blood was placed on the horns of the golden incense altar which stood within the Holy Place (4:7,18). If the sin was committed by a leader, the blood was put on the horns of the bronze altar which was located in the tabernacle courtyard (4:30,34).

Traditionally the purification offering has been known as the 'sin offering'. This is due to the fact that the Hebrew word used to designate the sacrifice ḥaṭṭā't (khaṭṭā't) frequently means 'sin'. However, the title 'purification offering' is preferable because it indicates more precisely the purpose or function of the sacrifice. As we have already noted in chapter 10, sin and uncleanness had the power to defile or pollute sacred objects. The more serious the sin, the greater the pollution. Consequently, if the anointed or high priest,[5] who was expected to be especially holy and blameless, sinned unintentionally this polluted the golden incense altar in the Holy Place. In contrast a tribal leader's sin defiled the bronze altar. Significantly, for the purification offerings outlined in Lev 4:1–5:13, the blood was placed on the sacred furnishings and not on the people responsible for the sin, indicating that it was the pollution caused by the sinner which was being cleansed rather than the actual sinner. On other occasions, however, the blood was applied to people in order to cleanse and sanctify them (e.g. making of the covenant at Sinai; the consecration of the priests).

(e) THE REPARATION OFFERING (LEV 5:14–6:7; 7:1–10)

Few details are given concerning the ritual of the reparation offering. Most attention is focused on the circumstances requiring such a sacrifice. Regarding the sacrifice itself, special emphasis is placed upon the bringing of a 'ram from the flock, one without defect and of the proper value in silver, according to the sanctuary shekel' (5:15 cf. 5:18; 6:6). The animal was slaughtered, its blood sprinkled against the altar, and the fatty portions associated with the kidneys and liver were burnt upon the altar (7:2–5). The rest of the animal was given to the priests who alone were permitted to eat the meat (7:6).

Some English translations refer to this sacrifice as the 'guilt offering'. The Hebrew name 'āšām ('āshām) can mean 'guilt'.

However, it can also mean 'reparation' or 'compensation'. This latter understanding seems to be more appropriate as regards the function of this sacrifice. The emphasis placed upon the value of the ram and the references to adding 'a fifth of the value' in order to make restitution suggest that the sacrifice was intended to compensate God for wrongs committed against him (cf. 5:16; 6:5). In this regard the reparation sacrifice resembles in part the practice of redemption outlined in Leviticus 27.

From the preceding survey of the five main types of sacrifices mentioned in Lev 1–7, it is clear that each sacrifice had a distinctive function. These functions reflect the different ways in which the divine/human relationship is affected by human sin and uncleanness. Together these different sacrifices sought to restore human beings to a harmonious relationship with God.

THE DAY OF ATONEMENT (LEV 16:1–34)

The ritual associated with the Day of Atonement was also important for maintaining a harmonious relationship between God and the people of Israel. This ritual falls into three main parts: (a) the purification of the sanctuary, (b) the sending away of the scapegoat, and (c) the presentation of two burnt offerings. The first part parallels closely the ritual noted above for the offering of a purification offering. The second part is unique to the Day of Atonement. The final part is mentioned only briefly, fuller details being unnecessary in the light of those already given in 1:2–17 and 6:8–13. An important aspect of the ritual on the Day of Atonement was that it centred on the high priest, named here as Aaron. He alone bore responsibility for what took place and the onus was on him to ensure that atonement was achieved for all the people.

(a) THE PURIFICATION OF THE SANCTUARY

Annually on the Day of Atonement the high priest, wearing his special clothing (16:4), passed through the curtain which separated the Holy of Holies from the Holy Place. Inside the Holy of Holies he sprinkled blood on and before the cover of the ark of the covenant, cleansing it and the Holy of Holies from pollution caused by sin. This process was repeated twice. On the first occasion a bull was sacrificed as a purification offering; its blood atoned for the sins of the high priest and his family. Afterwards one of two male goats was sacrificed and its blood brought into the Holy of Holies by the high priest to atone for the sins of the whole community of Israel (16:15–16). The high priest entered the Holy of Holies a second time and placed some of the goat's blood on the cover of the ark of the covenant before sprinkling more blood seven times before the ark of the covenant. He then performed a similar ritual in the Holy Place before the golden altar of incense.[6] The high priest next put some of the blood from the bull and the goat on the horns of the bronze altar in the courtyard (16:18). Finally, he sprinkled more of this blood seven times on the altar to cleanse it (16:19). Later, the remains of the bull and the goat were taken outside the camp and burned (16:27). The man designated to perform this task had to wash himself before returning to the camp (16:28).

(b) THE SCAPEGOAT

At a preliminary stage in the Day of Atonement ritual two goats were brought before the high priest. Lots were cast to determine which of the two would be sacrificed as a purification offering. After the high priest had purified the tabernacle with the blood of the first goat, he took the second goat and, placing both hands upon it, confessed over it 'all the wickedness and rebellion of the Israelites — all their sins' (16:21). This goat was then led to an uninhabited place in the desert and released. Finally, the man responsible for taking the goat into the wilderness washed himself before coming back into the camp (16:26).

(c) THE BURNT OFFERINGS

Apart from the animals listed as purification offerings, it is mentioned that two rams were sacrificed as burnt offerings. The first was provided by the high priest (16:3); the second by the Israelites (16:5). Following the purification of the sanctuary and the sending away of the scapegoat, the high priest took off his special garments and washed himself. He then offered up both rams in order to atone for himself and the people (16:23–24).

The Day of Atonement was probably the most important occasion in the cultic calendar of ancient Israel, designed to atone for those sins which were not covered by sacrifices offered throughout the rest of the year. The seriousness of the pollution caused by these sins is indicated by the fact that the high priest had to cleanse with the blood of the purification offering the most sacred part of the tabernacle, the Holy of Holies. The expulsion of the scapegoat which removed the people's sin from the camp was a visible sign of the special cleansing achieved on this important occasion.

NEW TESTAMENT CONNECTIONS

The concepts associated with the OT sacrificial rituals influenced strongly the way in which NT writers viewed the death of Jesus Christ. In particular, they believed that through the offering of a unique sacrifice by a unique high priest it was possible for the divine/human relationship to be restored to complete harmony. While this was central to the faith of the early Christians, we should not overlook the brief observation by the author of Hebrews that it was never God's desire that sacrifices should be offered. Their existence was due to the failure of human beings to keep God's commands (Heb 10:5–9).

JESUS CHRIST AS A SACRIFICE

The New Testament writers frequently understand the death of Jesus Christ in sacrificial terms. This is highlighted, for example, by the description of Jesus as 'the Lamb of God, who takes away the sin of the world' (John 1:29; cf. 1 Pet 1:19) and various references to the 'blood' of Jesus Christ (e.g. Acts 20:28; Rom 5:9; Eph 2:13; Col 1:20; 1 Pet 1:2; Rev 7:14; 12:11). Similarly, Paul refers to the death of Jesus as a 'sacrifice of atonement' (Rom 3:25), and it is recorded in Heb 9:26 that Christ 'appeared once for all at the end of the ages to do away with sin by the sacrifice of himself.'

For the author of Hebrews Christ's death was the ultimate sacrifice, of which the Old Testament sacrifices were merely an illustration (Heb 9:9–10; 10:1). The inadequacy of the Old Testament sacrifices is highlighted by the fact that they had to be repeated; they could never make perfect for all time those who offered them (Heb 10:1). Christ, however, constituted the perfect offering. Consequently, his sacrificial death was all-sufficient, and further animal sacrifices became unnecessary. For this reason the early Church believed that Christ's death superseded the temple sacrifices in Jerusalem. Nevertheless, the Old Testament regulations about sacrifices had continuing significance because they shed light on the nature of the atonement achieved through Christ's death.

Special attention is drawn to the cleansing associated with Christ's sacrificial blood. Whereas the blood of animals was able to cleanse objects and people who outwardly were ceremonially unclean, the blood of Christ is viewed as superior in that it can cleanse or purify inner, human consciences (Heb

9:14; cf. Titus 2:14). Since the forgiveness of sins comes through the shedding of blood (Heb 9:22; cf. Matt 26:28; Eph 1:7), those cleansed by the blood of Christ need no longer feel guilty (Heb 10:2; cf. 1 John 1:7).

A further link with the Old Testament sacrifices may be observed in the celebration of the Lord's Supper or Eucharist. Paul alludes to this in 1 Corinthians 10:14–22 when he emphasises how believers, by eating bread and wine which represent respectively the body and blood of Jesus Christ, participate in his sacrificial death (cf. John 6:53–56). As a result of Christ's atoning death individuals are made holy and perfect (cf. Heb 10:10,14; cf. 10:1; 13:12).

JESUS CHRIST AS HIGH PRIEST

Closely associated with the description of Christ's death in sacrificial terms is his portrayal as a high priest. To this end the author of Hebrews argues that although Jesus did not belong to the family of Aaron, he was divinely appointed to be a high priest in the 'order of Melchizedek' (5:10; 7:11–22).[7] Furthermore, he differs from all previous high priests by the fact that he alone is 'holy, blameless, pure, set apart from sinners, exalted above the heavens' (7:26). Also, whereas the Aaronic priests served in the earthly tabernacle, 'a copy and shadow of what is in heaven' (8:5; cf. 9:24), Christ serves in the heavenly tabernacle (8:1–5). While the Aaronic high priest of necessity had to purify the earthly tabernacle each year on the Day of Atonement, Christ, by the offering of himself, purified the heavenly temple once and for all (Heb 9:23; 13:11–12). Moreover, because his priestly mediation was completely acceptable to God, having entered the heavenly temple, there was no need for him to leave. Consequently, he is able continually to represent others before God (Heb 9:25), and, because God accepts Christ's high priestly mediation, believers may have confidence that they also are accepted by God.[8]

By emphasising that Jesus Christ, as God's unique son, provided the sacrifice necessary to atone completely for human sin, the New Testament highlights two important aspects of God's character: his justice and his love. Motivated by love, God provides the sacrifice necessary to meet the demands of his own justice. It is God, in the person of his own son, who pays the price of forgiveness for human sin.

NOTES

1. In this case a reparation offering (14:12–18) preceded both the purification offering and burnt offering.

2. Against the idea of substitution, however, is the fact that the meat of some sacrifices was consumed by the priests or even by the worshipper.

3. The special importance of blood is also highlighted in the food regulations; see chapter 12.

4. For this reason the burnt offering is sometimes described as the whole burnt offering or holocaust.

5. The title 'anointed priest' is used only in Lev 4:3,5,16 and 6:22. Although all priests were anointed, most commentators accept that this designation must be a reference to the high priest who was viewed as having received a special anointing (cf. Num 35:25).

6. This is implied in 16:16–17.

7. By associating Jesus with Melchizedek the author of Hebrews presents Jesus as both a priest and a king. A further dimension to this may be noted. In Genesis 1–3 Adam is presented as a priest-king. Not surprisingly, therefore, Jesus was viewed as the Second Adam (Rom 5:12–21; cf. Luke 3:38 and 4:3).

8. Another OT idea which may be linked to the death of Jesus Christ as a high priest is the belief that a high priest's death purged pollution.

[12]

The Clean and the Unclean Foods

SUMMARY

The food regulations contained in the book of Leviticus highlight two important theological principles. The distinction between clean and unclean foods emphasises the divine calling of Israel to be a holy nation, different from the other nations of the earth; the clean and unclean animals symbolise Israelites and non-Israelites respectively. The law prohibiting the eating of blood derives from the idea that all life, both human and animal, is sacred. Although God sanctions the eating of meat, due respect must be shown for the life of any animal slaughtered for food; blood, as the symbol of life, must not be eaten.

INTRODUCTION

As we have already noted, most of Leviticus consists of divine speeches mediated through Moses to the Israelites. Although these speeches cover various topics, a major unifying theme is God's concern that the people should be a holy nation. To this end Leviticus contains regulations governing the offering of sacrifices (chs. 1–7) and the procedures for being purified from various forms of uncleanness (chs. 12–15). Significantly, this latter block of material is preceded immediately by rules concerning those animals which the Israelites may and may not eat (11:1–47). These regulations divide all living creatures on the basis of specific criteria into two groups: clean and unclean. Only those animals which belong to the former category may be eaten by the Israelites. These regulations are repeated later in Deut 14:3–20.

At first sight it is difficult to see any connection between these food regulations and the divine desire that Israel should be a holy nation. In what way did the eating of particular animals fulfil Israel's calling to be a holy people?

THE FOOD REGULATIONS SUMMARISED

The regulations defining clean and unclean animals are divided into three sections which correspond with the three main regions of habitation: land (11:1–8), sea (11:9–12) and air (11:13–23). All animals were categorised as clean or unclean on the basis of a single principle governing each location:

(a) Only cloven-hoofed, cud-chewing land animals were clean; all other mammals were unclean.

(b) Only fish with fins and scales were clean; all other sea creatures were unclean.

(c) Birds of prey and flying insects that walked, rather than hopped, were unclean; all other birds and insects were clean.

While the general principles are clearly stated in Leviticus 11 for land animals, fish and flying insects, in the case of birds it has to be deduced from the different types listed. However, even when the principle is given, further details are usually added to clarify particular cases. For example, regarding land animals special attention is given to the camel, the coney, the rabbit and the pig; they are all declared unclean even though they meet one of the two criteria for clean animals given in the general principle.[1]

THE FUNCTION OF THE FOOD REGULATIONS

Various explanations have been offered to account for the dietary rules in Leviticus 11 and Deuteronomy 14. Some commentators have suggested that the classification of the animals into two types symbolised people and their behaviour. An animal which chewed its cud resembled a human being who meditated on the divine law. The sheep was designated clean because the ancient Israelites viewed God as their heavenly shepherd. The pig was unclean because of its dirty habits which were reminiscent of a sinner's behaviour. Although the arbitrary nature of such explanations has led contemporary scholars to reject them, the basic idea that the two type of animals are symbolic of people is probably correct.

Other writers have proposed that these ancient food regulations anticipate the findings of modern science regarding hygiene. Whereas the clean animals were safe for human consumption, the unclean animals were not. Several factors argue against this proposal. (a) While pork is often cited as an example of an unclean meat that is dangerous to human health, this is only true when the meat is not properly cooked. Thoroughly cooked, pork is as safe to consume as any of the meats which are classified as clean. Similarly, camel meat poses little danger to health; indeed it is viewed by Arabs as a delicacy. (b) If a danger to health was the reason behind the food regulations, it is strange that this motive is never mentioned in the Bible. Might we not have expected that the Israelites would have been warned of this danger in order to encourage them not to eat the unclean meats? In the light of these factors, the explanation of hygiene is unconvincing.[2]

Some commentators suggest that the Israelites were instructed to avoid the unclean animals because of their close association with non-Israelite religions. For example, archaeological evidence suggests that the pig was eaten in Canaanite rituals. Yet, while some unclean animals were clearly used in the cultic activities of ancient Israel's neighbours, it is not possible to demonstrate this for all the animals designated unclean. Furthermore, if this was the rationale behind the classification of the animals, it is surprising that the bull, which was prominent in both Egyptian and Canaanite religious rituals, was not included among the unclean animals. While the rationale of religious associations might account for certain cases, it fails to explain all of the distinctions made between clean and unclean animals.

The most satisfactory explanation of the food regulations rests on the observation that for the Israelites the animal world was structured in the same way as the human world. The clean and unclean animals parallel clean and unclean people (i.e. Israelites and non-Israelites). Within the category of clean animals two further classes may be observed, sacrificial and non-sacrificial; these correspond with the human classes of priestly and non-priestly.[3] By restricting their diet to clean animals the Israelites were reminded of their obligation to be a clean people, distinct from others.[4] Consequently, each meal at which meat was served had religious implications for the Israelites; it spoke of their divine calling to be a holy nation. This link between the food regulations and Israel's divine election is clearly reflected in 20:24-26:

> I am the LORD your God, who has set you apart from the nations. You must therefore make a distinction between clean and unclean animals and between clean and unclean birds. Do not defile yourselves by any animal or bird or anything that moves along the ground — those which I have set apart as unclean for you. You are to be holy to me because I, the LORD am holy, and I have set you apart from the nations to be my own.

Moreover, the food regulations made it difficult for an Israelite to participate in meals provided by non-Israelites. Thus, they not only symbolised that Israel was to be a clean nation in contrast to other nations, but they also had the practical effect of limiting contact with other people which might compromise Israel's special status.

THE RATIONALE BEHIND THE CLEAN/UNCLEAN CLASSIFICATION

While the distinction between clean and unclean peoples accounts for the purpose of the food regulations, it is still necessary to explain why some animals were considered clean and others unclean. Why, for example, was a sheep categorised as clean, but a pig unclean? Was this classification merely arbitrary, or were there particular reasons for designating some animals clean and others unclean? Although most scholars accept that some rationale must have governed the categorisation of the animals as clean and unclean, no explanation commands unanimous support. One factor, however, deserves special consideration.

A common factor among many of the unclean animals is that they depend upon the death of other creatures in order to survive.[5] A survey of those animals which are declared unclean reveals that most of them eat meat. All of the birds listed as unclean in verses 13–19 are birds of prey; their diet consists of the meat of other animals. The same is true regarding the land animals; those designated unclean have paws (e.g. cats and dogs) and such animals are carnivorous. In marked contrast cloven-hoofed animals do not eat meat. This distinction between carnivores and non-carnivores (or ruminants) is emphasised by the inclusion of the criterion of chewing the cud. The idea that animals associated with death should be viewed as unclean is in keeping with what we have observed in chapter 12; in Leviticus death and uncleanness are generally linked, being the opposites of life and holiness. By eating clean animals the Israelites distanced themselves from death which was perceived as the source of uncleanness.

THE BLOOD PROHIBITION

Before concluding our discussion of the food regulations in Leviticus 11, it is important to say something about the prohibition against eating blood which is highlighted in 17:1–16 (cf. 3:17; 7:26–27; Deut 12:16,23–25). So serious was this prohibition that God commanded anyone who ate blood to 'be cut off' (17:14).

To understand the reason for this, it is necessary to refer back to the book of Genesis. Although God had initially created human beings to be vegetarian (Gen 1:29), one result of Adam and Eve's rebellion in the Garden of Eden was that humanity thereafter desired to eat meat. As a result, human beings killed animals for food, apparently adding to the general violence of humankind which ultimately caused God to send the flood (6:11–13). After the flood God made a concession to Noah and his descendants regarding the eating of meat. They were permitted to do so, on the condition that they 'must not eat meat that has its lifeblood still in it' (Gen 9:4). Although God allowed the taking of an animal's life, the prohibition against eating blood drew attention to the importance which he placed upon all life. Thus, the Israelites' attitude to the killing of animals, even for food, was to differ from that of their neighbours. They were to behave in a way that reflected their belief that God was the source of all life. Since God was the giver and sustainer of life, he alone had the right to sanction the taking of a life.[6]

In passing it should be observed that animal meat did not form part of the regular diet of the Israelites, especially during the wilderness wanderings. The absence of such meat was a recurring reason for complaints against God. When meat was eaten it appears to have been within the context of religious celebrations.

CONCLUSION

From the preceding discussion it is clear that the food regulations contained in Leviticus reflect important theological ideas. On the one hand, the distinction between clean and unclean animals emphasises the special calling of Israel to be a holy nation. On the other hand, the prohibition against eating blood underlines the value which God places upon all life, animal as well as human. Thus, in a remarkable way religious truths were reflected in the daily routine associated with eating.

NEW TESTAMENT CONNECTIONS

The concept of clean and unclean foods appears in a number of NT passages. In the Gospels, the parallel passages in Matt 15:1–20 and Mark 7:1–23 focus on Jesus' attitude towards eating something which is unclean. In these passages it is not specifically stated that the meat was unclean; rather the issue centres on the fact that the disciples 'were eating food with hands that were "unclean", that is, unwashed' (Mark 7:2). In response Jesus commented to the people:

Nothing outside a man can make him 'unclean' by going into him. Rather, it is what comes out of a man that makes him 'unclean' (Mark 7:15; cf. Matt 15:11).

Later, Jesus explained the saying to his disciples:

Don't you see that nothing that enters a man from the outside can make him 'unclean'? For it doesn't go into his heart but into his stomach, and then out of his body . . .What comes out of a man is what makes him 'unclean'. For from within, out of men's hearts, come evil thoughts, sexual immorality, theft, murder, adultery, greed, malice, deceit, lewdness, envy, slander, arrogance, and folly. All these evils come from inside and make a man 'unclean' (Mark 7:19–23; cf. Matt 15:17–20).

Significantly Mark adds the brief observation: 'In saying this, Jesus declared all foods "clean" ' (7:19).

The topic of clean and unclean foods also arises in the account of Peter's visit to Cornelius, a God-fearing Gentile (Acts 10:1–11:18). This is an important incident within the book of Acts because it marks the first occasion on which the gospel was proclaimed to Gentiles. Prior to being asked to visit Cornelius, Peter was commanded by God in a vision to kill and eat animals which were unclean. Although Peter objected strongly, God warned him not to 'call anything impure that God has made clean' (Acts 10:15). Later, when he visited Cornelius he commented on the significance of the vision:

You are well aware that it is against our law for a Jew to associate with a Gentile or visit him. But God has shown me that I should not call any man impure or unclean (Acts 10:28).

Whereas God had previously introduced the concept of clean and unclean foods in order to separate the Israelites from other nations, the distinction between clean and unclean foods was abandoned in the NT period in order to show that God no longer distinguished between 'clean' Jews and 'unclean' Gentiles. With the death, resurrection and ascension of Jesus Christ, the Gentiles were now recipients of God's grace and mercy. In the light of this, it was only natural that the divinely instituted regulations concerning clean and unclean foods should be abandoned; they no longer served any meaningful purpose. So significant was Peter's vision in shaping the outlook of the early church that it is recorded twice in Acts (10:9–16; 11:5–10). Later, at the Council of Jerusalem, Peter defended his action in taking the gospel to the Gentiles by commenting that God no longer made a distinction between Jews and Gentiles (Acts 15:7–9).

Although the early church abandoned the distinction between clean and unclean foods on theological grounds, it is interesting to observe that they still insisted that Gentiles should adhere to the principle of not eating blood. This is seen in the conclusion reached by the Council of Jerusalem which was called to clarify the position of Gentiles regarding circumcision and the law of Moses. James summarised the council's findings by noting that Gentile believers should be instructed 'to abstain from food polluted by idols, from sexual immorality, from the meat of strangled animals and from blood' (Acts 15:20; cf. 15:29). Whereas the OT regulations concerning clean/unclean foods were no longer relevant under the new covenant established by Jesus Christ, the theological basis for the OT prohibition against the eating of blood remained unchanged as a result of the new covenant. Thus, there was good reason for insisting that both Jewish and Gentile believers should adhere to it.

Remarkably, although the early church insisted on maintaining the OT regulation concerning the eating of the blood of animals, several NT passages contain startling statements about eating the blood of Christ. The most striking of these is John 6:53–56:

> Jesus said to them, 'I tell you the truth, unless you can eat the flesh of the Son of Man and drink his blood, you have no life in you. Whoever eats my flesh and drinks my blood has eternal life, and I will raise him up at the last day. For my flesh is real food and my blood is real drink. Whoever eats my flesh and drinks my blood remains in me, and I in him.'

These comments, which highlight a special relationship between Jesus and those who eat his flesh and drink his blood, are clearly related to the celebration of the Lord's Supper or Eucharist. In commemorating the new covenant believers are to eat bread and wine, representing the body and blood of Jesus Christ (Matt 26:27–28; Mark 14:23–24). By doing so, they acknowledge their association with Jesus and participate in the benefits derived from his death (1 Cor 10:16–21; 11:23–26). Thus, at the very heart of the meal instituted by Jesus Christ is communion with God.

NOTES

1. There are three basic ideas which underlie current Jewish dietary laws: (a) it is forbidden to consume blood (Deut 12:23); (b) meat and dairy produce must not be eaten together (Exod 23:19); (c) certain types of animals, birds and fish are classified as unclean and should not be consumed (Lev 11:1–47; Deut 14:3–21). Food which meets these requirements is described in Hebrew as *kāšēr* (*kāshēr*; cf. Kosher) 'ritually fit', 'wholesome'.

2. From a Christian perspective, a further reason can be added. How could Jesus Christ have abolished rules which were supposed to protect the health of those who abided by them?

3. We have already noted the importance of the three categories of holy, clean, and unclean, in chapter 10. It is, therefore, not surprising that they should reappear in the context of the food regulations. Regarding the correspondence between priests and sacrificial animals, it is interesting to observe how chs. 21 and 22 parallel each other; ch. 21 deals with blemished priests and ch. 22 with blemished sacrificial animals.

4. Interestingly the dietary rules are placed immediately after material dealing with the separation of the priests from the rest of the Israelites. As the priests were set apart as holy from the rest of the Israelites, so too was Israel set apart as holy from the rest of the nations.

5. As if to highlight this association with death, much of chapter 11 focuses on the uncleanness which occurs through touching or carrying the carcasses of unclean animals (cf. vv. 24–38). Even the carcasses of clean animals — those which die by some means other than ritual slaughtering — communicate uncleanness to human beings (vv. 39–40).

6. On the significance of blood within the sacrificial system, see chapter 11.

[13]

Towards the Promised Land

SUMMARY

Although the Israelites' encounter with the LORD at Sinai lies at the heart of the Pentateuch, Sinai is not their final destination. Consequently, the initial chapters of Numbers focus on the preparations carried out by the people prior to leaving Sinai for the land of Canaan. Significantly, these preparations show that the Israelites will be required to defeat militarily the nations which already occupy the land. The middle chapters of Numbers reveal, however, as we shall examine in more detail in the next chapter, that the people's trust in God wavered in the face of opposition and as a result they failed to take possession of what God had promised them. Of all those who left Egypt as adults, only Joshua and Caleb would enter the promised land. Nevertheless, in spite of this initial failure, the final chapters of Numbers reveal that the promise of land was renewed with the next generation of adults. God's promise to Abraham would not be thwarted by human disobedience.

INTRODUCTION

Whereas the book of Leviticus is dominated by divine speeches outlining regulations and laws for the people of Israel, with few descriptions of events, the reverse occurs in Numbers. Most of the book records events which took place in the forty-year period beginning shortly after the making of the covenant at Sinai and ending with the Israelites camped on the plains of Moab ready to enter the land of Canaan. Interspersed among these narrative passages are a number of sections which record further regulations and laws (e.g. chs. 5–6; 15; 18–19; 28–30).

Although the book of Numbers spans a forty-year period, the coverage is uneven: chapters 1–10 record events which fall within a two month period; chapters 11–24 focus on selected

143

experiences scattered throughout the next forty years; chapters 25–36 concentrate on developments which take place in the fortieth year. Whereas the opening and closing chapters are generally favourable in their portrayal of the Israelites, the middle section consists of a series of incidents which highlights the failure of the people to trust and obey the LORD. These observations suggest that the book falls into three major parts and this is further supported by several other features. (1) The first and third sections begin with censuses of all those men who were twenty years old or more (1:1–54; 26:1–65). Significantly, the account of the second census specifically mentions that of all those included in the first census only Caleb and Joshua remained alive (26:64–65). This second census marks a new stage in the narrative and highlights an important difference between the second and third sections of the book: whereas chapters 11–25 record various events which describe the death of large numbers of Israelites, chapters 26–36 mention no deaths; even during a battle with the Midianites no Israelite soldier was killed (31:49). (2) All of the material in chs. 27–36 relates directly in one way or another to the occupation of the land of Canaan. This is highlighted by the fact that the final section of Numbers is framed by two episodes which focus on problems concerning the inheritance of land by the daughters of Zelophehad (27:1–11; 36:1–13).

In this chapter we shall concentrate on the first and last sections of Numbers. The middle section of the book will be considered in the next chapter.

PREPARATIONS FOR THE JOURNEY

The events recorded in the initial chapters of Numbers all took place close to Mount Sinai. Although the material in these chapters appears somewhat diverse a common theme ties much of it together: chapters 1–10 describe how the Israelites prepared to leave Sinai to occupy the land of Canaan.[1] The following features of these preparations are noteworthy.

First, the Israelites were to prepare for war against the inhabitants of Canaan. This is highlighted in the very first chapter of the book which records a census of the people that took place 'on the first day of the second month of the second year after the Israelites came out of Egypt' (1:1). The census was intended to number 'all the men of Israel twenty years old or more who are able to serve in the army' (1:3; cf. 1:45). This emphasises an idea, alluded to elsewhere (cf. Exod 13:18), that the Israelites were expected to fight for the land which God had promised them. The Levites, however, were excluded from this census due to their special association with the tabernacle. Because of their responsibility for its care and transportation, they were not to be involved directly in any killing which might occur during the taking of the land.[2]

Second, linked to the preparations for conflict was the requirement that those living in the camp should be pure. Anything which might defile the camp was a potential danger to the success of the Israelites' occupation of the land of Canaan. Thus, anyone, whether male or female, who was unclean, as a result of a skin disease, a bodily discharge or contact with the dead, was to be sent outside the camp (5:1–4). For the same reason instructions regarding restitution for wrongs (5:5–10) and suspected adultery (5:11–31) are included here. Nothing was to be allowed to defile the camp.[3]

Third, instructions are given regarding the layout of the camp (2:1–34). While these specify the location of the tribes around the tabernacle or Tent of Meeting in terms of north, south, east and west,[4] they also indicate the order in which the tribes were to set out when they journeyed from one location to another (cf. 2:9,16,24,31). The travel aspect of these arrangements is especially emphasised in the comments regarding the tabernacle and the tribe of Levi (2:17).

Fourth, apart from specifying the arrangement of the tribes when they journeyed, various other practical details are mentioned. In outlining the duties of the Levitical clans, special attention is drawn to the transportation of the tabernacle and its furnishings (4:5,10,12,15,19,24,25,27,31,32). The account of the census of all the Levites ends by noting that 'At the LORD's command through Moses, each was assigned his work and told what to carry' (4:49). Subsequently, it is noted that the tribal leaders presented to the LORD 'six covered carts and twelve oxen' (7:3) which were handed over by Moses to the Levites in order to assist them with the transportation of some of the tabernacle furnishings. However, the holiest items of the tabernacle were to be carried on human shoulders rather than transported by animals (7:9). It is also noted that the LORD commanded Moses to make two silver trumpets which were to be used, among other things, 'for calling the community together and for having the camps set out' (10:2; cf. 10:5–6).

Fifth, the concept of travel is prominent in remarks about the cloud which covered the tabernacle in 9:15–23. This passage explains, even before the Israelites leave Sinai, how God will lead them during the journey from Sinai to Canaan. Attention is repeatedly drawn to the way in which the movement of the cloud determined whether the Israelite camp moved or remained where it was.

THE ROLE OF THE LEVITES

Apart from highlighting the preparations necessary for the Israelites' journey to Canaan, the early chapters of Numbers also give prominence to the setting apart of the Levites. This is evident in a number of ways. At the outset the tribe of Levi is excluded from the census, the reason being that they were appointed to be in charge of the tabernacle and its furnishings (1:47–53; cf. 2:33). Moses is subsequently instructed by God to present the Levites to Aaron the high priest as special assistants (3:6–9). There follows immediately a lengthy passage which associates the setting apart of the Levites with the sparing of the Israelite firstborn in Egypt (3:11–51; cf. Exod 13:1–16). This passage also notes how God assigned different responsibilities regarding the tabernacle and its furnishings to the main Levite clans. More detailed instructions, which relate primarily to the transportation of the tabernacle by the three main branches of the Levites, are given to Moses in 4:1–49. Later, the LORD instructs Moses regarding the process by which the Levites were to be set apart (8:5–19). These instructions underline that the Levites were to purify themselves in order to 'do the work at the Tent of Meeting on behalf of the Israelites and to make atonement for them so that no plague will strike the Israelites when they go near the sanctuary' (8:19).[5] The actual setting apart of the Levites is recorded briefly in 8:20–22. This is followed by further instructions regarding the age of Levitical service at the tabernacle (8:23–26). It should also be noted that the Levites were given gifts of oxen and carts which were presented by the other tribes for the service of the tabernacle (7:2–9). Thus, in a variety of ways the opening chapters of Numbers highlight the special role of the Levites.

The setting apart of the Levites resembles in some respects the appointment of Aaron and his sons as priests (cf. Exod 29:1–46; Lev 8:1–36). However, it is clear that the Levites were not granted the same holy status as the priests. Although, like the priests, they served within the tabernacle, they were not permitted to touch directly the holiest of the tabernacle furnishings or to perform the duties assigned to the priests regarding the offering of sacrifices.

This distinction between the priests and the Levites is significant. Prior to the book of Numbers there are few references to the Levites. Their loyalty to God is noted in Exod 32:26–28 and, apart from a brief mention in Exod 38:21, there is only one other minor reference to them (Lev 25:32–33). In the light of this the detailed attention given to them in the early chapters of Numbers is striking. Their prominence at this stage is probably tied to later developments within the book. As we shall observe in more detail in the next chapter, the account of the rebellion of Korah in 16:1–50 centres on the relationship between the priests and the Levites. As a leading Levite, Korah is found guilty and punished for trying to usurp the position of the divinely appointed priests.

Closely associated with the appointment of the Levites are the instructions in 6:1–21 for the setting apart of ordinary Israelites as Nazirites. The inclusion of this material in the early chapters of Numbers reveals that the taking of a special holy status was freely available to all Israelites. Although non-Levites were restricted from serving in the tabernacle, they were not excluded from adopting a special degree of holiness.

FURTHER PREPARATIONS TO ENTER THE LAND OF CANAAN

The final part of the book of Numbers (26:1–36:13), like the first, begins with a census of 'all those twenty years old or more who are able to serve in the army of Israel' (26:2; cf. 1:3). The significance of this second census lies in the fact that of all those included in the previous census, forty years earlier, only Caleb and Joshua remained alive (26:64–65; cf. 32:11–12). This fact is clearly linked to the earlier account of the rebellion of the Israelite spies following their reconnaissance of the land (13:1–14:45) and the LORD's prediction that 'not one of you will enter the land I swore with uplifted hand to make your home, except Caleb son of Jephunneh and Joshua son of Nun' (14:30). Even Moses, as recorded later in Deuteronomy 34:1–8, died outside the promised land due to his failure to honour God in the sight of the Israelites at the waters of Meribah (Num 20:9–12; cf. 27:13–14).

Whereas chs. 11–25 catalogue a series of events that result in the death of the entire adult generation which was delivered from Egypt, chs. 26–36 record no comparable events; no deaths are mentioned in the final section of the book. Even when the narrative recounts a major battle against the Midianites (31:1–24), it is specifically noted that not one soldier failed to return alive from the conflict (31:49). This contrast between the second and third sections of the book is particularly striking and highlights the fact that the death of the exodus generation was due to their failure to trust God. As we shall observe in the next chapter, the middle section of Numbers highlights various occasions on which large numbers of Israelites perished as a result of disobeying God.

All of the material coming after the census in ch. 26 focuses in one way or another on the future occupation of the land of Canaan. With the death of all those who failed to enter the promised land on the first occasion, the narrative now focuses on the preparations for the second generation to possess Canaan. These preparations are framed by two accounts which involve the daughters of Zelophehad (27:1–11; 36:1–12). Significantly, both episodes address the topic of land inheritance. In the first instance Zelophehad's daughters are guaranteed that they shall have 'property as an inheritance among their father's relatives' (27:7). On the second occasion they are required to marry within their own tribe in order that their inheritance should not pass to another tribe. In both episodes questions concerning inheritance are resolved before the Israelites enter the promised land.

Of the other episodes in the final section of Numbers, the land of Canaan figures prominently in chs. 32 and 34–35. The first of these chapters focuses on the request of the tribes of Reuben and Gad to settle on the east side of the Jordan in the 'lands of Jazer and Gilead' (32:1). Their wish is only granted when it is made clear that they are prepared to assist the other tribes in obtaining their inheritance on the west side of the Jordan. Moses is deeply concerned that the desire of the tribes of Reuben and Gad to stay on the east side of the Jordan does not arise from wrong motives; they are not to follow the rebellious example of their fathers who refused to enter the promised land. Towards its conclusion chapter 32 also notes that 'the descendants of Makir son of Manasseh went to Gilead, captured it and drove out the Amorites who were there' (32:39). As a result half of the tribe of Manasseh was permitted to settle on the eastern side of the Jordan.

Chapter 34 falls into two parts, each focusing on the land of Canaan. The first half delineates the boundaries of the land to be possessed by the Israelites. The rest of the chapter lists the names of the leaders appointed from each tribe to assist Eleazar the priest and Joshua in assigning the land between the nine and a half tribes (34:17). Because of their separation from the other tribes to serve in the tabernacle, the Levites are not allocated a specific region of the land of Canaan. Rather they are given forty-eight towns, each with some pasture-land surrounding it, distributed throughout the twelve tribal regions. Significantly, six of these towns are designated 'cities of refuge, to which a person who has killed someone may flee' (35:6). Further details are added to explain how these cities should function as places of refuge for those who unintentionally kill another person (35:9–28). Interestingly, the chapter concludes by highlighting yet again the theme of land: the Israelites must not defile the land because the LORD will be dwelling in their midst (35:34).

CONCLUSION

The opening and final sections of the book of Numbers are clearly linked to the overall development of the narrative plot in the Pentateuch. Whereas chapters 1–10 describe the final preparations of the people before they leave Sinai to enter the promised land, chapters 25–36 anticipate the next major development in the narrative, the possession of the land. However, as we shall observe in detail in the next chapter, chapters 11–24 record a series of events which result in the death of the generation which left Egypt to go to the promised land. It is an entirely new generation of adults that prepares to occupy the land of Canaan.

NEW TESTAMENT CONNECTIONS

Most of the main links with the New Testament will be considered at the end of the next chapter when we consider the central section of Numbers. As regards the theme of land, we have already discussed the relevant NT material in chapter 3.

NOTES

1. It should be noted in passing that the material in chs. 1–10 is not in strict chronological order.

2. A further reference to battle comes in 10:9 concerning the sounding of silver trumpets by the priests.

3. Uncleanness also figures in ch. 9 regarding the celebration of the Passover in the second month. For a fuller discussion of the topic of cleanness/uncleanness, see chapter 10.

4. The east side of the tabernacle was viewed as the most important due to the fact that the entrance to the Tent of Meeting was located there.

5. In the light of this the rebellious actions of Korah, a Levite, take on added significance.

[14]

Murmurings

SUMMARY

Whereas the opening and concluding chapters of Numbers describe the preparations which the Israelites made before entering the promised land, the middle chapters provide a contrasting picture. Here various incidents portray the true nature of the exodus generation of adult Israelites. In spite of all that they had witnessed in Egypt and at Sinai, they display a remarkable lack of faith in the LORD's ability (a) to provide for their daily needs and (b) to ensure their safety in the land of Canaan. Their complaints against the LORD form a recurring pattern in these chapters. Furthermore, there are frequent challenges to the hierarchical structures which God has introduced for the well-being of all the people. As a consequence of their rebellious actions the entire adult generation, with the exception of Caleb and Joshua, is consigned to remain in the wilderness for forty years until they all die.

INTRODUCTION

After highlighting certain preparations for the next stage of the journey from Egypt to Canaan, the early chapters of Numbers reach a climax in 10:11 with the departure of the Israelites from Sinai. The narrative now focuses on their future progress. At the outset a very positive picture is presented with the tribes setting out just as the LORD had commanded them (10:11–28). To underline this the narrator includes material which displays Moses' optimism as regards the future. When his brother-in-law Hobab talks of returning to his own land and people, Moses responds by commenting: 'If you come with us, we will share with you whatever good things the LORD gives us' (10:32). A similar confidence underlies Moses' words each time the ark sets out and comes to rest. 'Rise up, O LORD! May your enemies be scattered; may your foes flee before you' (10:35). 'Return, O

LORD, to the countless thousands of Israel' (10:36). In these ways the second half of chapter 10 conveys a sense of confidence that the LORD will successfully bring the Israelites into the promised land of Canaan.

Against this brief optimistic introduction the events of chapters 11–25 contrast markedly. God's anger turns against the Israelites, eventually resulting in the death of the entire generation of those adults who left Egypt. As we shall explore in more detail below, a number of themes are prominent. We frequently encounter the people complaining about the conditions under which they must now live during their journey to the promised land. Significantly, these complaints reflect a deep-seated failure to trust the LORD. A second related theme is that of rebellion against those exercising authority. Associated with both of these are two other motifs: the divine punishment of those at fault, and the role of Moses and the Aaronic priests as mediators on behalf of the people. It should also be noted that various episodes in Numbers parallel closely Exodus 15:22–17:17 where the theme of 'testing' is prominent.

MURMURINGS AGAINST THE LORD

As soon as the journey from Sinai to Canaan begins we encounter the first of a number of incidents in which the Israelites express their dissatisfaction with the LORD (11:1–3). While this brief account does not specify the reason for the people's unrest, it sets the tone for much that follows in chapters 11–25. Various elements in this episode will reappear later. (a) God's anger is roused against the people because of their complaints (11:1; cf. 11:10,33; 12:9; 21:5). (b) As a result they are divinely punished (11:1; cf. 11:33; 12:10; 21:6). (c) Moses prays to the LORD on behalf of the people (11:2; cf. 12:13; 14:13–19; 21:7). (d) The punishment is limited (11:2; cf. 12:13; 21:8–9). (e) A particular name, reflecting some aspect of what occurs, is given to the location of the event. On this occasion the place is called Taberah, which means 'burning', on account of the punishment by fire which comes upon the people (11:3; cf. 11:34; 20:13).

The incident at Taberah is immediately followed by another which is recorded in much more detail (11:4–34). As is often the case, the reason for the people's dissatisfaction with God is linked to their craving for food. In spite of the fact that the LORD has provided them with manna the Israelites yearn to return to Egypt. The narrative conveys well this sense of longing: 'If only we had meat to eat! We remember the fish we ate in Egypt at no cost — also the cucumbers, melons, leeks, onions and garlic'

(11:4–5). Their complaint is full of irony. They forget, on the one hand, the terrible conditions under which they had laboured as slaves in Egypt, and, on the other hand, the fact that they are journeying towards a land 'flowing with milk and honey'. The former reflects their lack of gratitude for all that God has done for them in the past, and the latter displays their lack of faith regarding all that God will do for them in the future. Not surprisingly, their complaint is interpreted by the LORD as a personal rejection of him (11:20). Although the LORD provides quails in abundance, he sends at the same time a severe plague, killing some of the people. Thereafter the place is called Kibroth Hattaavah (Graves of Craving; 11:34).[1]

The next occasion on which the people murmur against the LORD occurs following the return of the twelve spies from the land of Canaan. Sent to discover the nature of the promised land, the spies report back that the land 'does flow with milk and honey' (13:27). As evidence of this they display before the people a single cluster of grapes which two men are required to carry. However, they also describe the inhabitants of the land as powerful, living in large, fortified cities (13:28). While Caleb, and later Joshua, speaks up in favour of entering the land (13:30; cf. 14:6–9), the rest of the spies discourage the people from doing so. As a result the Israelites grumble against Moses and Aaron, indicating their desire to return to Egypt (14:1–4). The implications of this are outlined by Joshua and Caleb: not only will the people miss out on the opportunity to possess a land which is 'exceedingly good', but they are also rebelling against the LORD (14:7–9). This is confirmed by the LORD's comments to Moses: 'How long will these people treat me with contempt? How long will they refuse to believe in me, in spite of all the miraculous signs I have performed among them' (14:11)? In the light of this the LORD states that he will destroy the Israelites with a plague and create a new nation through Moses. Moses, however, argues against the destruction of the people on the grounds that it will cause other nations to doubt the LORD's ability to bring his own people into the promised land.[2] While the LORD relents from wiping out the entire nation, he makes it abundantly clear that not one of the adults who witnessed his glory and miraculous power, both in Egypt and in the desert, will enter the promised land; the only exceptions will be Joshua and Caleb. Consequently, on account of the unfaithfulness of their parents, the children are subjected to forty years in the desert — one year for each of the forty days which the spies spent in the land.

As regards the story of the spies two further points are noteworthy. First, the spies who speak out against entering the land are punished immediately; a plague strikes them dead (14:36–38). Second, the people belatedly attempt to enter the land of Canaan. This, however, is viewed as a further act of disobedience, the LORD having just stated that they shall remain in the desert forty years. Consequently, they are defeated by the Amalekites and Canaanites (14:39–45).

A further report of the people grumbling against Moses and Aaron comes in ch. 16, following the divine execution of Korah and his followers.[3] This time criticism is levelled at Moses and Aaron because they have 'killed the LORD's people' (16:41). The making of such a comment is a further indication of the distorted outlook of the people. Even in the dramatic and terrible death of Korah and his followers they fail to recognise the hand of God. Once more the LORD threatens to kill the whole assembly. Before Aaron, at Moses' command, can atone for them, 14,700 are struck dead by a plague.

Another incident involving grumbling is recorded in 20:1–13. This time it is a lack of water which prompts the people's complaint. Apart from wishing to return to Egypt, the Israelites state that it would have been better for them, like their brothers, to have been struck dead by God (20:3). Once again the narrative highlights the rebellious nature of their comments (cf. 20:10). On this occasion, however, it is the actions of Moses and Aaron which come in for severest criticism by the LORD. By striking the rock twice and saying, 'Must we bring you water out of this rock?' Moses and Aaron dishonour God (20:10). As a result, the LORD announces that they shall not enter the promised land (20:12).[4]

Numbers records one further occasion when the people speak against God and Moses: 'Why have you brought us up out of Egypt to die in the desert! There is no bread! There is no water! And we detest this miserable food' (21:5)! Yet again their criticisms focus on food and water. When the LORD sends venomous snakes to attack the people, they soon acknowledge their sin and seek help from Moses. Significantly, this is the first occasion when the people themselves acknowledge their sin. As a result, the LORD commands Moses to place a bronze snake on the top of a pole. Remarkably, when those bitten by the venomous snakes look to this bronze snake they do not die.

All of the episodes considered so far are linked by the common motif of the people's lack of trust in the LORD. Interestingly, their complaints about food and water echo earlier incidents in Exod 15:22–17:12. In the light of this it is no surprise that Num 14:22 picks up the idea that through their disobedience the Israelites tested God. Although the concept of testing is only mentioned once in Numbers, it is clear from the material in Exodus that, whereas God intended the desert experience to test the faith and obedience of the Israelites (cf. Exod 15:25–26; 16:4; cf. 19:20), it was they who tested God (Exod 17:2,7; Num 14:22). Furthermore, Exodus 15:26 emphasises that if the people obey him, God will not bring upon them any of the diseases which came upon the Egyptians. In the light of this it is interesting to observe the frequent references to plagues in Numbers 11–25.[5] Ironically by longing to be back in Egypt, the Israelites bring upon themselves the same suffering that earlier afflicted the Egyptians.

CHALLENGES AGAINST THOSE IN AUTHORITY

Interspersed between the episodes about the murmurings of the Israelites are others which focus on various challenges to those appointed by God to positions of authority. Remarkably, the first such challenge comes from the least likely source. Miriam and Aaron, Moses' own sister and brother, contest the uniqueness of his claim to speak on the LORD's behalf (12:1–2). No doubt their challenge was prompted by the authority which they already had, Aaron as the high priest and Mirian as a prophetess (Exod 15:20). The LORD, however, soon responds and confirms Moses's special status: whereas the LORD speaks to prophets in visions and dreams, he speaks to Moses 'face to face, clearly and not in riddles' (12:8). Consequently, the LORD's anger burns against Aaron and Miriam with the result that Miriam is afflicted with a skin disease. Although her punishment is reduced due to the intercession of Moses, she is still required to remain outside the Israelite camp for seven days (12:15).

The sinful nature of the challenge by Miriam and Aaron is highlighted by the comment, 'Moses was a very humble man, more humble than anyone else on the face of the earth' (12:3). This clearly indicates that Moses himself did not emphasise unduly his own importance. In the light of Moses' attitude towards his own position the challenge of Miriam and Aaron is all the more serious. Furthermore, because Moses did not relish the idea of having absolute authority over the nation, he involved seventy of the elders in the task of leading the people (11:24–30).

The next challenge to authority comes in chapter 16 and centres on an attempt by Korah and certain Reubenites — Dathan and Abiram — to usurp the special position of Moses and Aaron. Once again the challenge comes from those who already enjoy a special standing within the nation; Korah as a Levite has been previously set apart to assist in the work of the tabernacle; his supporters are described as 'well-known community leaders who had been appointed members of the council' (16:2). Their challenge is against the hierarchical structure introduced by God whereby Aaron and his sons, as priests, had a holier status than that of the Levites and other Israelites (cf. 8:5–26). In the light of the early chapters of Numbers there can be little doubt that Korah's actions run counter to God's instructions for the people.[6] Furthermore, Korah's sin is all the greater because he himself enjoyed a more privileged status than that of the majority of Israelites. While he should have been grateful for the opportunity to serve in the tabernacle, he uses this as a springboard to aspire to priestly status (see the comments of Moses in 16:8–11). As the basis for his challenge to Moses and Aaron, Korah claims that 'the whole community is holy, every one of them, and the LORD is with them' (16:3). Implicit in this is the idea that there is no reason for Moses and Aaron to restrict others from approaching the LORD.[7] The attitude of Dathan and Abiram to Moses is highlighted in 16:12–14. As far as they are concerned, Egypt, not Canaan, is the 'land flowing with milk and honey' (16:13). Not only has Moses led them away from all that is best materially, but he has failed to provide them with anything better; his motive throughout has been to lord it over the people and kill them in the desert. The response of God to both these challenges is dramatic. The families of Korah, Dathan and Abiram are swallowed up into the earth (16:31–34), and a further group of 250 supporters are consumed by fire (16:35). In passing it should also be noted that once again Moses is portrayed as interceding on behalf of the whole community (16:20–22).

In the light of Korah's challenge to the authority of Aaron, chapters 17–19 take on a special significance. In the first of these Moses demonstrates the unique standing of the tribe of Levi by having twelve staffs, one for each ancestral tribe, placed in the Tent of Meeting.[8] When these are removed on the next day the staff of Aaron has 'budded, blossomed and produced almonds' (17:8), indicating the unique, and life giving, status of the tribe of Aaron. Moses then commands that the staff be kept as a sign to 'the rebellious' that they should not 'grumble' against the LORD (17:10). To emphasise further the uniqueness of Aaron's position as high priest chapter 18 records divine instructions regarding the relationship between the priests and Levites. Here it is noted that the Levites are a 'gift' to Aaron 'to do the work of the Tent of Meeting' (18:6). Furthermore, the 'service of the priesthood' is also a divine gift (18:7). Since the priest and the Levites are divinely appointed to fulfil specific roles, it is wrong for others to usurp their positions. Chapter 19 also alludes back to the rebellion of Korah by focusing on the ritual involving the water of cleansing. First, it highlights the special mediatorial role of the divinely appointed priests. Secondly, it emphasises that anyone who sins becomes unclean and of necessity must undergo a process of purification. Korah's claim in 16:3 that the whole community is holy was clearly presumptuous.

Alongside these challenges to those in authority, we might also include the reaction of Moses and Aaron to the people's demand for water in 20:2–13. In their impatience with the people they claim responsibility for the miraculous appearance of the water, thus failing to acknowledge the LORD as the one who provided it from the rock.

RELIGIOUS APOSTASY

The long line of episodes in which the exodus generation of Israelites exhibit their lack of trust in the LORD comes to a conclusion in ch. 25. On this occasion they are guilty of both religious apostasy, worshipping the Baal of Peor, and sexual immorality, having relationships with Moabite women. Once more the LORD's anger burns against the people with the result that 24,000 of them are killed by a plague. Three factors stand out in the story as significant. (a) After the LORD's condemnation of their activity, the Israelites display a spirit of repentance, 'weeping at the entrance to the Tent of Meeting' (25:6). (b) Phinehas, the grandson of Aaron, is commended for his willingness to kill a fellow Israelite who blatantly ignores the LORD's condemnation of idolatrous and immoral behaviour. The execution of the guilty party is presented as an act of atonement, with the result that the plague against the Israelites stops. Afterwards Phinehas is rewarded through being divinely granted 'a covenant of a lasting priesthood, because he was zealous for the honour of his God and made atonement for the Israelites' (25:13). (c) As confirmed by the census of ch. 26 (cf. 26:63–65), this incident marks the death of the last of the Israelite who left Egypt as adults. The forty-year period in the desert is almost complete.

DESTINATION — THE PROMISED LAND

In spite of the people's rebellion and the death of the entire exodus generation of adult Israelites, the central chapters of Numbers contain clear indications that the occupation of the land of Canaan is still a priority in God's dealings with the Israelites. This is reflected in the following ways. First, instructions given by the LORD in ch. 15 begin with the words, 'After you enter the land I am giving you as a home . . .' (15:2). This introduction is significant in that it follows immediately the account of the people's failure to enter the land of Canaan. Furthermore, the instructions in ch. 15 presuppose a situation in which the people are able to grow crops of grain and grapes. Secondly, ch. 21 records the defeats of the Canaanite king of Arad (21:1–3), Sihon king of the Amorites (21:21–31) and Og king of Bashan (21:33–35). These victories contrast with the defeat recorded earlier in 14:44–45[9] and the backing away from battle with the Edomites in 20:14–21, and indicate a first step towards the possession of the promised land (cf. 31:1–24). Thirdly, the lengthy account of the activities of Balaam son of Beor in chs. 22–24 reveals God's desire to bless rather than curse Israel. Although Balaam is hired by Balak king of Moab to curse the Israelites, he blesses them on four separate occasions (23:7–10; 23:18–24; 24:3–9; 24:15–19; cf. 22:12). Significantly, in doing so he echoes briefly the promises made earlier to the patriarchs in Genesis: 'Who can count the dust of Jacob' (23:10; cf. Gen 13:16; 15:5); 'The LORD their God is with them' (23:21; cf. Gen 17:8); 'May those who bless you be blessed and those who curse you be cursed' (24:9; cf. 23:8,20; Gen 12:3); 'A star will come out of Jacob; a sceptre will rise out of Israel' (24:17; cf. Gen 17:6,16; 49:10).[10] In the light of these factors it is apparent that, in spite of the death of the exodus generation, God still intends to bring his people into the promised land. This is further emphasised by the fact that almost all of the material in chs. 26–36, as noted in the previous chapter, anticipates in various ways the possession of the land.

CONCLUSION

The central chapters of Numbers provide a very negative portrait of the Israelites. This is highlighted in a number of ways. In spite of their remarkable deliverance from slavery in Egypt, they are unwilling to enter the promised land. Contemptuous of all that God has already done for them, they constantly complain and desire to return to Egypt. Furthermore, they challenge those whom God has placed in authority over them, and fail to see in the divine punishment of others, God's power at work, believing that those struck dead are the LORD's people. Finally, they commit idolatry, the ultimate rejection of and rebellion against the LORD. In the light of all these shortcomings it is hardly surprising that the entire adult generation of those who came out of Egypt die in the desert, outside the promised land.

Whereas the exodus generation of Israelites shows no sign of learning from its experience in the desert, their children, while initially revealing similar characteristics of unbelief and rebellion, demonstrate a greater capacity to trust the LORD. They, at least, willingly acknowledge their own sin (21:7; 25:6). For this reason, the book of Numbers portrays them as making progress towards inheriting the land promised to the patriarchs.

NEW TESTAMENT CONNECTIONS

The account of the Israelites' time in the wilderness is picked up in a number of ways in the NT. One of the most striking uses comes in the account of the temptation of Jesus (Matt 4:1–11; Luke 4:1–13). Indeed, it is impossible to understand fully the gospel temptation story without appreciating how Jesus is contrasted with the Israelites who came out of Egypt. Whereas the ancient Israelites were tested in the wilderness and failed, Jesus, as the new Israel, succeeds. This theme is reflected in all three temptations. In the first, Jesus, hungry after having fasted for forty days, is asked to turn stones into bread. Had he, however, like the ancient Israelites, given priority to his own physical appetite, he would have implied dissatisfaction with God's provision for him. The second temptation, following Matthew's order, focuses on God's ability to save. Here Jesus is challenged to follow the example of the earlier Israelites and test, rather than trust, God's might to protect him. The third temptation focuses on God's capacity to give to Jesus those kingdoms which are under the control of another. Whereas the Israelites had doubted God's strength to give them the land of Canaan, Jesus expresses complete confidence in God. Thus, in various ways Jesus' faith in God contrasts sharply with that of the Israelites who came out of Egypt.

Several passages in John's Gospel refer directly to the OT account of the Israelites' sojourn in the wilderness. In his conversation with Nicodemus Jesus mentions briefly the incident of the bronze snake in Num 21:4–9:

> Just as Moses lifted up the snake in the desert, so the Son of Man must be lifted up, that everyone who believes in him may have eternal life (John 3:14–15).

Here Jesus draws an important parallel between himself and the bronze snake. While the ancient Israelites received life by trusting in the bronze snake, those who trust in Jesus will receive eternal life.

Later in John's Gospel, in a discussion which takes place shortly after the feeding of the five thousand, Jesus compares himself to the manna provided in the wilderness (John 6:25–59). Like the manna, he has been sent from heaven to give life to those who feed upon him (6:33,35–40,50–51,54–58). However, the life which Jesus offers, in contrast to that given by the manna, is eternal (6:47–51,58). Significantly, John observes that many of the Jews responded to Jesus' words by grumbling (6:41,43). Like their unbelieving ancestors, they failed to appreciate what had happened in their midst. For them the miraculous feeding of the five thousand, which should have been a sign of Jesus' divine origin, conveyed nothing of significance.

The experience of the Israelites in the wilderness is also used by Paul to warn the Corinthian Christians against pursuing various unrighteous practices. He writes:

> Now these things occurred as examples to keep us from setting our hearts on evil things as they did. Do not be idolaters, as some of them were; as it is written: 'The people sat down to eat and drink and got up to indulge in pagan revelry.' We should not commit sexual immorality, as some of them did — and in one day twenty-three thousand of them died. We should not test the Lord, as some of them did — and were killed by snakes. And do not grumble, as some of them did — and were killed by the destroying angel (1 Cor 10:6–10).

Because Paul views the wilderness experience as a time of testing, he concludes by exhorting his readers to resist temptation:

> No temptation has seized you except what is common to man. And God is faithful; he will not let you be tempted beyond what you can bear. But when you are tempted, he will also provide a way out so that you can stand up under it (1 Cor 10:13).

Here Paul shares an understanding of the Numbers material similar to that found in the gospel account of Jesus' temptation.

Before leaving Paul's comments in 1 Corinthians 10, one other issue deserves mention. This concerns his comment that the ancient Israelites 'drank from the spiritual rock that accompanied them, and that rock was Christ' (1 Cor 10:4). At first sight it seems remarkable that Paul should associate Jesus with an inanimate object. Two observations, however, are important. First, Paul seeks in 1 Corinthians 10 to draw a parallel between the wilderness experience of the Israelites and that of the Corinthian believers. He argues that because the ancient Israelites perished on account of eating food associated with idols, the Corinthian believers should not indulge in such activities. As part of this argument Paul compares the food and drink which the ancient Israelites received from God (1 Cor 10:3–4) with the food and drink which the Corinthians eat at the Lord's Supper (1 Cor 10:16–17). To strengthen the parallels between the two situations Paul associates the food and drink of the wilderness with Christ; the source of the drink is a 'spiritual rock' and that rock is Christ. Second, in the OT God is sometimes entitled a Rock. In this regard the Song of Moses in Deuteronomy 32 is significant, given that it is presented as having been composed at the end of the Israelites' period in the wilderness. On five separate occasions God is designated 'the Rock' (Deut 32:4,15,18,30,31; cf. 32:37), making this one of the main divine titles in the entire song. Undoubtedly, Paul's reference to Christ is influenced by the designation of God as a Rock. Paul does not think of Christ as a physical rock; rather he is a 'spiritual rock'. By presenting Christ as the source of the drink which the ancient Israelites received, Paul, first, affirms Christ's divine status and oneness with the God of Israel, and, secondly, reinforces the parallel which he wishes to demonstrate between the situation of the Corinthians and the ancient Israelites.

The author of Hebrews also highlights the failure of the wilderness generation and uses this as a warning to his readers (Heb 3:7–19). Quoting Ps 95:7–11, which is one of a number of psalms to recount the Israelites' experience in the wilderness, he observes that they did not enter the promised land 'because of their unbelief' (Heb 3:19).

NOTES

1. The dissatisfaction of the people at Kibroth Hattaavah provides the setting for and also frames the account of God appointing seventy of Israel's elders to assist Moses in the task of leading the people.

2. One sees here various echoes of the golden calf incident at Sinai when God made a similar suggestion to make a new nation (Exod 32:9–10). On this latter occasion Moses intercedes for the people by quoting the LORD's earlier comment about being 'slow to anger, abounding in love and forgiving sin and rebellion' (14:18). Interestingly, this statement was first made in the context of the people's rebellion at Sinai (Exod 34:6–7).

3. See below, pp. 154–155.

4. Although the narrative does not make it explicitly clear, it seems likely that this episode occurs in the fortieth year (compare 20:1 with 33:36–38). If so, this incident reveals that the next generation of adult Israelites is in danger of copying the rebellious behaviour of their parents.

5. Note how the different terms used for the plagues in Egypt are also used in Numbers.

6. On the role of the Levites, see chapter 13.

7. In believing that all of the Israelites are holy and can draw near to the LORD, Korah failed to appreciate one of the distinctive roles given to the Levites; they were to act as a barrier between the LORD and the other tribes (1:53; cf. 8:19).

8. The Hebrew word for 'staff' can also mean 'branch' or 'tribe'.

9. Note the mention of Hormah in 14:45 and 21:3.

10. Although the Balaam story shows signs of being a once independent unit, it picks up a number of important themes found in Genesis. As it stands it has been carefully integrated into the Pentateuch as a whole.

[15]

Love and Loyalty

SUMMARY

The book of Deuteronomy brings the Pentateuch to a significant climax. As the Israelites stand on the verge of entering the
promised land, Moses outlines God's agenda for the future.
This centres on the special covenant relationship which exists
between the LORD and Israel. At the heart of this covenant is a
commitment by both parties to love the other wholeheartedly
and faithfully. For the Israelites this commitment will require
them to be completely obedient to all of the obligations placed
upon them by God. Obedience will ensure blessing in terms of
material prosperity and national security; disobedience will
have the opposite consequence, resulting in the expulsion of
the Israelites from the promised land. As Moses invites the
people to renew their covenant relationship with the LORD, he
sets before them an important choice, a choice between 'life
and death, blessings and curses' (30:19).

INTRODUCTION

The setting of the events described in Deuteronomy is
introduced in the opening verses of the book. It is the end of
the fortieth year since the Israelites left Egypt and the people
are camped to the east of the river Jordan. At last they are on
the brink of entering the land which God had promised to their
ancestors, Abraham, Isaac and Jacob. Following the death of
the first generation of adults who came out of Egypt, the next
generation of Israelites is at a decisive point in its relationship
with God. Will they like their parents fall at the hurdle before
them, or will they through faith in the LORD cross the Jordan
and possess the promised land?

Given the importance of the setting it is hardly surprising
that the people are addressed at length by Moses. Having led

162

their parents out of Egypt he reminds a new generation of adult Israelites of all that has happened in the preceding years and challenges them to affirm their personal commitment to the special covenant relationship with the LORD initiated at Mount Sinai. At the heart of Deuteronomy is the future of the relationship between Israel and her God.

Only in Deuteronomy does Moses address the people at length using his own words. Elsewhere he usually repeats what the LORD has told him. Here he speaks on his own behalf, persuading the Israelites to follow the LORD. As a result Deuteronomy often reads like a sermon with frequent exhortations and much repetition. This gives the book a character not found elsewhere in the Pentateuch.

Moses' speeches take on added significance in that they were given shortly before his death, which is recounted in the final verses of the book (34:1–12). They are the final words of an elder statesman to his people, a father to his children, encouraging them to proceed in the right direction for the future.

Apart from brief comments by the book's narrator, the bulk of Deuteronomy consists of the words of Moses. Two main speeches dominate the book, the first coming in 1:6–4:40 and the second in 5:1–26:19. The former speech begins with a survey of Israel's relationship with the LORD since leaving Mount Sinai forty years earlier and concludes with exhortations to obey the LORD in the future. This provides a suitable introduction for the second speech which begins in 5:1 and continues unbroken until 26:19, constituting approximately two-thirds of the entire book of Deuteronomy. The narrator's introduction to this second speech (4:44–49) indicates that it forms the law (Hebrew, *tôrâ*) which 'Moses set before the Israelites' (4:44). This understanding of the speech is confirmed by later comments which refer (a) to 'all the words of this law (*tôrâ*)' being inscribed on stones coated with plaster (27:2–8) and (b) to Moses 'writing in a book the words of this law (*tôrâ*) from beginning to end' (31:24). This 'Book of the Law (*tôrâ*)' was subsequently to be placed beside the ark of the covenant of the LORD (31:26). Instructions are also given by Moses to the priests and elders that they are to read this law (*tôrâ*) to the people every seventh year (31:9–13). We shall say more on the 'Book of the Law' below.

The concluding chapters of Deuteronomy consist mainly of a number of shorter addresses, not all by Moses, introduced by brief narrative comments. The first of these speeches is comprised of instructions for the inscribing of the Book of the Law (*tôrâ*) on plaster-coated stones once the people have crossed the Jordan and entered the land of Canaan (27:1–8). The next speech, which also looks to the future occupation of the land, begins with instructions to the tribes of Israel for the pronouncement of blessings from Mount Gerizim and curses from Mount Ebal (27:11–13; cf. 11:26–32), followed by the recital of a list of curses by the Levites (27:14–26). To these instructions Moses adds a further exhortation encouraging the people to obey the LORD (28:1–68). Interestingly, Moses' exhortation mirrors the previous instructions by highlighting the blessings which will flow from obedience (28:2–14) and the curses which will come as a result of disobedience (28:15–68). While it might have been anticipated that equal weight would be given to both blessings and curses, this is not the case; in both parts of Moses' speech, greater prominence is given to the curses (27:15–26; 28:15–68). Following the blessings and curses, Moses once more exhorts the people to keep the terms of the covenant by highlighting that the choice before them is one of life or death (29:2–30:20). Next there is a brief passage which focuses on Joshua's appointment as Moses' successor (31:1–8). After this Moses commands the priests and elders regarding the reading of the law (*tôrâ*) every seven years (31:9–13). Significantly, the LORD then predicts that after entering the promised land Israel will soon forsake him and break the covenant (31:16–18). Consequently, Moses is instructed to teach them a song 'so that it may be a witness' for the LORD against them (31:19–22). Before reciting this song to the people (31:30–32:43), Moses tells the Levites to place the Book of the Law (*tôrâ*) beside the ark of the covenant so that it also may witness to the waywardness of the people (31:24–29). The remaining sections of Deuteronomy focus on the death of Moses. The LORD instructs Moses to go up Mount Nebo in order that he may see the promised land before dying (32:48–52). Before doing so Moses pronounces a series of blessing upon the Israelites (33:1–29). Finally, Moses' death is recorded, ending with a brief statement concerning his greatness as a prophet (34:1–12).

DEUTERONOMY AND ANCIENT NEAR EASTERN TREATIES

As we have already noted Deuteronomy is concerned with the renewing of the special covenant relationship between the LORD and the Israelites. Since the mid-1950s biblical scholars have discussed in some detail the similarities which exist between the covenant in Deuteronomy and other ancient documents, in particular political treaties and law-codes. While some scholars have argued that the book of Deuteronomy as a whole conforms to the pattern of certain second millennium BC treaties, others have challenged this by observing that either the parallels are not particularly close or those parallels which do exist may be accounted for on the basis of mid first-millennium BC treaties. Without wishing to enter into this debate in detail some further comments are necessary.

The closest parallels to the covenant found in the book of Deuteronomy appear to come in ancient treaties made between kings of powerful nations and the rulers of weaker, vassal states. These treaties have a formal structure which may be outlined as follows:

1. a preamble: this introduces the treaty and those participating in it;
2. a historical prologue: this describes prior relationships between the parties;
3. stipulations: these set out the obligations placed upon the weaker party to the covenant. They fall into two parts: (a) general, and (b) detailed;
4. document clause;
5. witnesses: this section lists the gods who witness the making of the treaty;
6. curses and blessings: these list the consequences of either keeping or breaking the covenant stipulations.

According to some scholars this very treaty form is reflected in the text of Deuteronomy as it stands. Consequently, attempts are made to assign the material in Deuteronomy between the various elements of the treaty form. This can result in a proposal such as follows:

1. preamble:	1:1–5
2. historical prologue:	1:6–3:29
3a. general stipulations:	4:1–40; 5:1–11:32
3b. detailed stipulations:	12:1–26:19
4. document clause:	27:1–26
5. witnesses:	not applicable due to the monotheistic outlook of Deuteronomy
6. curses and blessings:	28:1–68

Other scholars, however, adopt a more cautious approach, suggesting that it is mistaken to find the treaty form replicated in the book of Deuteronomy as it stands. While the essential elements of the treaty form are reflected in the present narrative form of the text, the book itself is not an actual treaty document. There is much to commend this view, especially since Deuteronomy in its entirety does not claim to be a self-contained covenant document. At the very most only 5:1–

26:19, including possibly 28:1–68, is presented as an independent document within the present text.[1]

Although formal correspondence between the whole of Deuteronomy and ancient near-eastern vassal treaties is lacking, the process by which the covenant was ratified between the Israelites and the LORD does bear a striking resemblance to that found in vassal treaties. In each we have the formalising of a special relationship between two parties, one strong and one weak, with the listing of extensive obligations and the pronouncement of blessings and curses. While scholars will undoubtedly continue to debate the precise nature of this correspondence, there can be little doubt that an awareness of it enables us to appreciate better the main characteristics of the covenant in Deuteronomy.

LOVE THE LORD

Although the book of Deuteronomy focuses on a formal renewal of the relationship between the LORD and the Israelites, considerable attention is given to the fact that the formal act of renewal by itself does not constitute the relationship. Rather the relationship between the LORD and his people is to be based on the twin pillars of love and loyalty. To appreciate this better it may be helpful to consider a modern, and biblical, analogy. The relationship between God and Israel can in part be compared to that between husband and wife. In many societies the relationship between husband and wife is formally instituted by the taking of marriage vows. While the wedding ceremony formalises the relationship of husband and wife, it cannot of itself sustain the relationship. For the marriage relationship to exist and develop in a meaningful way, it is essential that there be mutual love and loyalty. If love and/or loyalty disappear from the relationship between a husband and wife, the fact that they have been formally united will mean little. Indeed, both partners may seek to have this formal bond removed by instituting another formal procedure, divorce. The making of the treaty between God and Israel resembles a marriage ceremony. While both parties promise allegiance to each other, the strength of the relationship between them depends not on the covenant ceremony itself but on the love and loyalty which each has for the other. For this reason, Moses emphasises that the Israelites are to love the LORD with their whole being. He expresses it thus: 'Love the LORD your God with all your heart and with all your soul and with all your strength' (6:5; cf. 11:13;

13:3; 30:6). Without such love the covenant relationship will be meaningless.

Moses' frequent exhortations to love the LORD suggest that this was likely to prove difficult for the Israelites. Significantly, their ability to love stands in marked contrast to that of the LORD. Nowhere is there any suggestion that his love might cease towards Israel. On the contrary, Moses highlights God's lasting faithfulness towards his people. From the outset he was the one who initiated the relationship. Motivated by love he chose Israel and delivered her from slavery in Egypt (4:37; 7:8; cf. 10:15). For the same reason, he did not allow Balaam to curse his chosen people (23:5). Elsewhere Moses expresses confidence regarding God's love for the future; his love will continue for a thousand generations (5:10; 7:9)

Although Moses is absolutely certain that the LORD loves Israel and that he will be completely faithful to her, this is no open-ended guarantee of divine blessing and favour. On the contrary, the covenant relationship involves a commitment from each Israelite to love the LORD. Should they fail to love the LORD, the consequences are clearly set out; they will experience God's disfavour in the form of various curses which are listed at length in 27:15–26 and 28:15–68.

In the light of this, love in Deuteronomy is never presented as something emotional; it is not just a matter of feelings. On the contrary loving God had very practical implications for the people. They must fulfil the obligations placed upon them by the covenant. Thus Moses repeatedly draws attention to the link between loving the LORD and keeping 'his requirements, his decrees, his laws and his commands always' (11:1; cf. 5:10; 7:9; 10:12; 11:13,22; 19:9; 30:16). True love will demonstrate itself in perfect obedience. On the other hand, disobedience indicates a failure to love God (cf. 13:3).

Given this link between love and obedience — if you love me, you will obey me — it is no surprise that the central core of Deuteronomy consists of a long list of obligations which the Israelites were expected to keep. These obligations constitute the Book of the Law (*tôrâ*), a designation used in 28:61, 29:21 and 31:26. Although the Hebrew word *tôrâ* has traditionally been translated as 'law', this is partially misleading. While it includes laws which might be enforced by a legal court, it also embraces commands or stipulations which by their nature are not 'laws'; for example, it would be wrong to categorise the divine commands in 6:6–9 — to teach *tôrâ* to one's children — as 'law'. For this reason some scholars prefer to translate *tôrâ* 'instruction'. While this avoids the legal connotations of the term 'law', it fails to convey adequately the judicial aspect of *tôrâ*. As 17:8–13 reveals, *tôrâ* includes legal decisions taught by Levitical priests. Since it is difficult to find in English a single word which reflects accurately the full meaning of the term *tôrâ*, it is perhaps best to retain the Hebrew term and understand it in terms of all the material found in 5:1–26:19.

The importance of *tôrâ* is underlined throughout Deuteronomy. Reference is made to it at the very beginning of the book in the brief comment, 'East of the Jordan in the territory of Moab, Moses began to expound this law (*tôrâ*)' (1:5). According to the narrator's remark in 4:44, the Book of the Law (*tôrâ*) begins in 5:1. Later Moses instructs the people to have the Book of the Law (*tôrâ*) inscribed on plaster-coated stones on Mount Ebal (27:1–8), with a further copy being placed beside the ark of the covenant (31:24–26). Elsewhere, attention is drawn to the importance of the Book of the Law (*tôrâ*) in that future kings are to make a copy of it for their own use and are expected to read it all the days of their lives (17:18–20). It is also mentioned in the last of the curses recited by the Levites: 'Cursed is the man who does not uphold the words of this law (*tôrâ*) by carrying them out' (27:26).

Since Israel's obedience to the '*tôrâ*' demonstrates her love for the LORD, Moses underlines the importance of being familiar with all that it demands. Consequently, he instructs the Israelites not only to meditate on all that he commands them, but also to teach it to their children:[2]

> These commandments that I give you today are to be upon your hearts. Impress them on your children. Talk about them when you sit at home and when you walk along the road, when you lie down and when you get up. Tie them as symbols on your hands and bind them on your foreheads. Write them on the door-frames of your houses and on your gates (6:6–9; cf. 4:4; 11:18–21; 31:9–13).

For Moses the stipulations of the covenant were to be a vital part of everyday life for all God's people, both young and old. Familiarity with them was essential for the maintenance of a harmonious relationship with the LORD; to ignore them would bring disaster.

Conscious of the Israelites' strong tendency towards disobedience (see next chapter), Moses incorporates within his exhortations various comments to encourage obedience. These motivation statements are found throughout Deuteronomy. Interestingly, apart from the longer section of curses in ch. 28, Moses generally motivates the people by highlighting the positive aspects of obedience. Only rarely does he mention the consequences of disobedience (e.g. 8:19–20). The most common motive is the promise of divine blessing, mentioned on a number of occasions within the Book of the Law. When, for example, in 15:7–10 Moses encourages the Israelites to be generous towards the poor, he adds the comment: 'then because of this the LORD your God will bless you in all your work and in everything you put your hand to' (15:10). Similar remarks are found in 7:12–15; 14:29; 15:4,18; 23:10. The promise of blessing, however, is developed most fully in ch. 28 where Moses lists not only the blessing which will flow from obedience (28:3–14), but also the curses which will result from disobedience (28:16–68). Here Moses spells out in detail the practical consequences of experiencing divine blessing or cursing. Since a detailed examination of this chapter lies beyond the scope of this work, some general observations must suffice. First, there is an emphasis upon fruitfulness and prosperity. Blessed by God, the people will increase numerically, as will their livestock. Moreover, the land will produce abundant harvests enabling the people to prosper richly, so much so that other nations will come to borrow from them. Under God's curse, however, the reverse will occur. Diseases will strike down the people, as well as their animals and crops.[3] Such will be the decline in their fortunes that the Israelites will be forced to borrow from the aliens living in their midst. Second, under God's blessing the Israelites will enjoy as a nation security from their enemies who will be easily defeated. Implicit in this promise, and in the references to the fruitfulness of the land, is the assurance that the Israelites will occupy the promised land. This picture of national security is reversed, however, should the people come under God's curse. Not only will they be defeated by their enemies, but significantly, they will be led out of the promised land into captivity elsewhere.[4] Interestingly, these two aspects of blessing and cursing — prosperity and security — occur frequently in the briefer motivation statements made by Moses. References to life and prosperity come in the following passages: 4:1,40; 5:29,33; 6:2–3,18,24; 7:13–15; 8:1; 11:9,14–15; 12:25,28; 16:20; 29:9; 30:16,20; 32:47. The land is mentioned in 4:1,40; 5:33; 6:3,18; 7:13; 8:1,6–9; 11:8–9,14–15,23; 16:20; 17:20; 23:20; 30:16,20; 32:47.[5] Stated briefly Moses constantly reminds the Israelites that obedience brings life, disobedience brings death. Significantly, this choice between life and death, prosperity or destruction, comes at the climax of Moses' final speech to the Israelites:

> See, I set before you today life and prosperity, death and destruction. For I command you today to love the LORD your God, to walk in his ways, and to keep his commands, decrees and laws; then you will live and increase, and the LORD your God will bless you in the land you are entering to possess. But if your heart turns away and you are not obedient, and if you are drawn

away to bow down to other gods and worship them, I declare to you this day that you will certainly be destroyed. You will not live long in the land you are crossing the Jordan to enter and possess (30:15–18).[6]

BE LOYAL TO THE LORD

While Moses stresses the importance of love for a secure relationship between the Israelites and God, he also emphasises equally the necessity of loyalty. The Israelites must be faithful in loving only the LORD. In religious terms this means that they are not to practise idolatry; they must worship the LORD alone. Significantly, this aspect of the covenant relationship heads the list of obligations found in the Decalogue: 'You shall have no other gods before (besides) me' (5:7; cf. Exod 20:3).

A number of important ideas are associated with idolatry in the book of Deuteronomy. While most of these are found in the Exodus account of the Sinai covenant, they are developed in greater detail at this stage. First, Moses commands the people not 'to follow other gods' (6:14; 8:19; 11:28; 28:14; cf. 13:2). They are to neither 'serve' or 'worship'[7] these gods (7:4,16; 8:19; 11:16; 17:3; 28:14,36,64; 29:18; 30:17; cf. 13:2,6,13; 29:26), nor 'bow down' to them (8:19; 11:16; 17:3; 30:17; cf. 5:19; 29:26). Underlying this terminology is the idea that the relationship between the worshipper and deity resembles that between slave and master. Since for the Israelites true worship involved total obedience to all that the LORD demanded, it was not possible for them to give allegiance to any other deity. Ironically, by being restricted to worship only the LORD, the Israelites were freed from the difficulty of trying to meet the sometimes conflicting demands of different deities. Not only were the Israelites prohibited from worshipping other gods, but they were also prohibited from worshipping anything that God had made, in particular the sun, moon or stars (4:19; 17:3)

Second, Moses highlights the danger posed by the religious beliefs of the nations living in the land of Canaan; the Israelites will be enticed to worship their gods. In an attempt to prevent this occurring, they are commanded not to copy their religious practices (16:21–22; 18:14); such practices are described as 'detestable' to the LORD (12:31; 13:14; 17:4; 18:9,12; 20:18).[8] The Israelites are also to destroy everything associated with the worship of other gods in the land of Canaan: 'Break down their altars, smash their sacred stones, cut down their Asherah poles and burn their idols in the fire' (7:5; cf. 7:25; 12:2–3). Most significantly, because they will encourage the Israelites to worship their gods, the nations of Canaan are to be destroyed completely (7:16; 20:17–18).

Third, picking up another of the obligations found in the Decalogue (5:8–10; cf. Exod 20:4–6), Moses warns the people against making idols (4:15–31). Since the LORD did not reveal his form at Sinai, the Israelites must not try to depict him using human or animal forms (4:15–18). Elsewhere in Deuteronomy it is made very clear that all idols are 'detestable' to the LORD (7:25–26; 23:16; 27:15; 29:17; 32:16; cf. 32:21).

Fourth, those who engage in idolatrous activities are guilty of 'doing evil in the eyes of the LORD' (4:25; 9:18; 17:2; 31:29; cf. 13:5,11; 17:5,7). One consequence of this is that they provoke him to anger (4:25; 6:15; 7:4; 11:7; 29:24–29; cf. 9:7–8,18–20; 13:5,11; 17:5,7). Consequently, those guilty of idolatry should be put to death (6:15; 7:4; 13:15; cf. 9:8,14,19–20,25–26). Furthermore, the regulations within the Book of the Law (*tôrâ*) make it very clear that anyone who entices others to worship foreign gods must be put to death. The Israelites were to execute those who, possibly claiming to be prophets either of the LORD or some other deity, enticed others to worship gods they had not previously known (13:1–5; cf. 18:20). This rule applies even to the closest of relatives or friends (13:6–11). Moreover, entire Israelite communities were to be wiped out should they commit idolatry (13:12–16).[9] Ultimately, should the nation as a whole be guilty of idolatry, the punishment would be destruction and exile (4:26–28; 29:24–28). Ironically, as part of this punishment the people 'will worship man-made gods of wood and stone, which cannot see or hear or eat or smell' (4:28; 28:36,64).

In the light of these regulations against idolatry it is clear that the Israelites were expected to remain completely loyal to the LORD their God.

CONCLUSION

In the book of Deuteronomy the story of the LORD's relationship with Israel reaches an important landmark. As they stand poised to take possession of the land of Canaan, Moses sets before a new generation of adult Israelites the obligations which they must fulfil in order to enjoy God's blessing there. At the heart of these obligations is the requirement to love the LORD wholeheartedly. Significantly, Israel's future in the promised land is tied directly to their willingness and ability to fulfil their covenantal duties. While Deuteronomy holds out the prospect of divine blessing in the promised land, as we shall examine in more detail in the next chapter, it also envisages a future in which Israel, through failure to fulfil the covenant obligations, will come under God's curse.

NEW TESTAMENT CONNECTIONS

The book of Deuteronomy is one of the most frequently quoted books in the New Testament.[10] Since, of all the OT books it sets out most fully the essential requirements for a harmonious relationship with God, this is hardly surprising. It is often quoted as stating what the OT law requires (e.g. Matt 5:31,38; 15:4; 18:16; 19:18–19; Mark 7:10; 10:19; Luke 18:20; 1 Cor 5:13; 9:9; 2 Cor 13:1; Eph 6:2–3; 1 Tim 5:18).

Deuteronomy's influence pervades the teaching of Jesus. When asked by 'an expert in the law', 'Which is the greatest commandment?' (Matt 22:36), Jesus responds by quoting first Deuteronomy 6:5: 'Love the Lord your God with all your heart and with all your soul and with all your mind.'[11] Elsewhere his commitment to the agenda set by Deuteronomy is clearly seen in the parallel accounts of his temptation (Matt 4:1–11; Luke 4:1–13). On each occasion that he is tested by the devil Jesus replies by quoting from Deuteronomy.[12] Significantly, in doing so he highlights one of the principle tenets of the book: 'Worship the LORD your God, and serve him only' (Deut 6:13, quoted in Matt 4:10 and Luke 4:8).

Even when the text of Deuteronomy is not quoted directly, its influence is still apparent. We see this in Jesus' insistence that his followers must be single-minded in their commitment to God:

> No-one can serve two masters. Either he will hate the one and love the other, or he will be devoted to the one and despise the other. You cannot serve both God and Money (Matt 6:24).

Later, this principle is highlighted in the story of the rich young man (Matt 19:16–30; Luke 18:18–30). By insisting that he give his wealth to the poor, Jesus reveals that the man has divided allegiances. The idea of wholehearted commitment to God also appears in the parables of Jesus, especially those which involve a master/servant relationship (Matt 18:23–35; 24:45–51; 25:14–30; Luke 12:42–48; 19:12–27); these parables commonly emphasise the importance of loyalty and faithfulness.

Another aspect of Deuteronomy which is developed briefly in the NT is that of cursing. Paul picks this up in his letter to the Galatians where he notes that 'All who rely on observing the law are under a curse for it is written: "Cursed is everyone who does not continue to do everything written in the Book of the Law" ' (Gal 3:10, quoting Deut 27:26). Since, according to Paul, no-one can keep the law fully, all are cursed. However, this for Paul is not the end of the matter. He then confidently affirms that Christ has 'redeemed us from the curse of the law by becoming a curse for us, for it is written: "Cursed is everyone who is hung on a tree" ' (Gal 3:13, quoting Deut 21:23).

NOTES

1. Two references suggest that chapter 28 and perhaps other material should be included in the Book of the Law (see 28:58,61)

2. It should be noted that the noun *tôrâ* is closely related to the Hebrew verb 'to teach' (cf. 17:11). *Tôrâ* is that which is taught (by God).

3. The description of what will happen to the Israelites echoes the punishments which fell upon the Egyptians at the time of the exodus.

4. We shall have more to say on this in the next chapter. Interestingly, the promise of blessing was both national and personal. This is reflected in comments concerning the future king who is promised a long reign for obeying the law (17:18–20).

5. Deut 8:7–9 provides a very vivid picture of the 'good land':

> For the LORD your God is bringing you into a good land — a land with streams and pools of water, with springs flowing in the valleys and hills; a land with wheat and barley, vines and fig-trees, pomegranates, olive oil and honey; a land where bread will not be scarce and you will lack nothing; a land where the rocks are iron and you can dig copper out of the hills.

6. There are close links between Deuteronomy and Genesis as regards the concept of blessing and cursing.

7. The same Hebrew verb may be translated by the English words 'serve' or 'worship'.

8. It is interesting to note that in 25:16 dishonesty is included among the various things which are described in Deuteronomy as 'detestable' to the LORD.

9. It is important to note that as regards idolatry the Israelites are treated in the same way as the nations already living in the land of Canaan. The same punishment applied to them.

10. It is quoted some 83 times. The only other OT books to be referred to as often in the NT are Genesis, Psalms and Isaiah. Two factors, however, should be borne in mind in considering the number of times Deuteronomy is quoted in the NT. First, many of the quotations come in parallel accounts recorded in the Synoptic Gospels. Secondly, on a few occasions part of the Decalogue is quoted; in such instances it is possible to see the source of the quotations as either Exodus ch. 20 or Deut ch. 5 (e.g. Rom 7:7; 13:9; Jas 2:11).

11. Parallel accounts come in Mark 12:28–34 and Luke 10:25–28. To emphasize an important consequence of loving God, Jesus also quotes Lev 19:18: 'Love your neighbour as yourself.'

12. He quotes Deut 8:3; 6:16 and 6:13.

[16]

Why Israel?

SUMMARY

By establishing a special covenant relationship with the Israelites, the LORD set them apart from all other nations as his people. Significantly, God's choice of Israel is not linked to any special quality which they possess; it is not due to their righteousness or size. When the LORD promised them the land of Canaan, this was because the nations living there had forfeited, by their wickedness, their right to the land. Yet, whereas the Israelites were commanded to destroy completely the nations living in Canaan, it was God's intention that they should be a light to other nations, reflecting the righteousness which he expected of all people. Although the Israelites stood to benefit greatly from the privilege of being God's holy nation, their calling also carried with it important responsibilities. Failure to fulfil these would bring upon them God's disfavour.

INTRODUCTION

The book of Deuteronomy, as we have already noted in the previous chapter, revolves around the covenant which is renewed between the LORD and Israel. As a consequence of this Israel enjoyed a relationship with the LORD which differed markedly from that experienced by other nations. Various passages within Deuteronomy focus on the nature and purpose of this special relationship and indirectly a number of important theological issues are addressed. Why did the LORD choose Israel and deliver her from Egypt? Did the LORD display favouritism in wiping out the nations of Canaan in order to give their land to the Israelites? Did Israel, as a result of her special relationship with God, have an unfair advantage over all the other nations of the earth? The answers to these questions permeate the book of Deuteronomy.

174

✓ THE ELECTION OF ISRAEL

Throughout Deuteronomy it is made clear that Israel as a nation had a unique relationship with the LORD. Moses summarised this as follows:

> For you are a people holy to the LORD your God. The LORD your God has chosen you out of all the peoples on the face of the earth to be his people, his treasured possession (7:6; cf. 14:2).[1]

Here we encounter several distinctive ideas which occur elsewhere in Deuteronomy and which point to God setting Israel apart as his own special nation. First, on a number of occasions it is stated that God chose Israel 'out of all the nations on the earth' (14:2; cf. 4:37; 7:6–7; 10:15). Significantly, the emphasis rests on the fact that it was the LORD who chose Israel, not Israel who chose the LORD. Second, the Israelites were to be *his* people (4:20; 7:6; 26:18; 27:9; 28:9–10; 29:13; cf. 9:26,29; 21:8; 26:15). Israel alone was the LORD's people; no other nation could claim this. The uniqueness of this relationship is underlined by the comment that Israel was God's 'treasured possession' (7:6; 14:2; 26:18). The Hebrew term *sĕgullâ* 'treasured possession' is used elsewhere in the OT to describe the jewels and value objects in a king's treasury (1 Chr 29:3; Eccl 2:8); Israel was precious to the LORD. Elsewhere the closeness of this bond is presented in terms of a parent/child relationship (32:18–20). Third, the distinctive relationship between Israel and the LORD is reflected in the designation 'holy nation' (7:6; 14:2,21; 26:19; 28:9). Of all the nations on earth Israel alone was under a special obligation to exhibit the holiness of God's nature.

Further evidence pointing to the LORD's choice of Israel comes in the many references to what he had already done for them in the past. Some of these focus on the special promises, chiefly concerning the possession of the land of Canaan, which God made to the patriarchs (4:31; 6:18,23; 7:8; 8:1; 9:5; 13:17; 19:8; 26:15; 31:20; 34:4). Others deal with their divine redemption from Egypt (5:6; 6:12; 7:8; 8:14; 9:26; 13:5; 15:15; 21:8; 24:18) and the defeat of their enemies (2:24–3:11). Deuteronomy frequently highlights how the LORD has acted uniquely and decisively on the people's behalf. One passage which is particularly vivid in this regard is the poetic description in 32:8–15:

> When the Most High gave the nations their inheritance, when he divided all mankind, he set up boundaries for the peoples according to the number of the sons of Israel. For the Lord's portion is his people, Jacob his allotted inheritance. In a desert land he found him, in a barren and howling waste. He shielded him and cared for him; he guarded him as the apple of his eye, like an eagle

that stirs up its nest and hovers over its young, that spreads its wings to catch them and carries them on its pinions. The LORD alone led him; no foreign god was with him. He made him ride on the heights of the land and fed him with the fruit of the fields. He nourished him with honey from the rock, and with oil from the flinty crag, with curds and milk from herd and flock and with fattened lambs and goats, with choice rams of Bashan and the finest kernels of wheat. You drank the foaming blood of the grape. Jeshurun grew fat and kicked; filled with food, he became heavy and sleek.

Deuteronomy, however, looks not only to the past to highlight Israel's relationship with the LORD, but also to the future. The concluding words of Moses' second speech emphasise in a special way one important aspect of the LORD's future for Israel:

He (the LORD) has declared that he will set you in praise, fame and honour high above all the nations he has made and that you will be a people holy to the LORD your God, as he promised (26:19).

Elsewhere the future benefits of Israel's election are highlighted indirectly through those sections of the legal material which presuppose the occupation of the land of Canaan. Although the Israelites have yet to cross the river Jordan and take possession of the promised land, many of the regulations outlined by Moses to the people anticipate their settlement in the land. Thus, to mention but some, rules are given regarding the eating of animals away from the tabernacle (12:15–25),[2] pilgrimage festivals (16:1–17), and the giving of tithes (14:22–27). All of these presuppose that the Israelites will occupy a large territory, with many of them living at a considerable distance from the tabernacle. Similarly, the giving of instructions to establish cities of refuge (19:1–9) also implies that the Israelite will be dispersed throughout the whole of Canaan.

Apart from providing evidence that Israel was set apart by God from all other nations, the book of Deuteronomy also sheds light on the reason for Israel's divine election. What caused the LORD to choose Israel rather than some other nation? Interestingly, in Deuteronomy this question is mainly answered by excluding certain possibilities. First, Israel's election is not due to her righteousness. This is clearly stated in 9:4–6:

After the LORD your God has driven them out before you, do not say to yourself, 'The LORD has brought me here to take possession of this land because of my righteousness.' No, it is on account of the wickedness of these nations that the LORD is going to drive them out before you. It is not because of your righteousness or your integrity that you are going in to take possession of their land; but on account of the wickedness of these nations, the LORD your God will drive them out before you, to accomplish what he swore to your fathers, to Abraham, Isaac and Jacob. Understand, then, that it is not because of your righteousness that the LORD your God is giving you this good land to possess, for you are a stiff-necked people.

This passage is not alone in emphasising Israel's lack of righteousness. There are frequent references to Israel's way-wardness. Moses reminds the people that when God tested their obedience through the wilderness experience (8:2–5), they rebelled and were punished (1:26–46; 9:7–24), and, but for the intercession of Moses, the LORD would have rejected them completely (9:18–20,25–29; 10:10). Not only are they occasionally described as a stiff-necked people (9:4–6; 9:13; 10:16; 31:27), but Moses comments, 'You have been rebellious against the LORD ever since I have known you' (9:24; cf. 31:27). In these and other ways Israel is consistently portrayed as failing to achieve the high standard of righteousness demanded by the LORD. Even as regards the future, Deuteronomy highlights the Israelites' inability to fulfil the obligations placed upon them (e.g. 31:16–18; 32:15–35).[3] Clearly, God's election of Israel is not determined by the fact that they were morally superior to others.

Another factor which is briefly mentioned as regards the election of Israel is that of size. According to Moses, 'The LORD did not set his affection on you and choose you because you were more numerous than other peoples, for you were the fewest of all peoples' (7:7). It was not because of Israel's superiority in numbers and strength that God chose her; on the contrary, when God initiated his dealings with Israel, he started with one individual, Abraham.

If Deuteronomy dismisses Israel's righteousness and size as reasons for her divine election, is any other explanation provided? The only other factor mentioned is God's oath with her forefathers (7:8; 9:5; cf. 4:31; 6:18,23; 8:1; 13:17; 19:8; 26:15; 31:20; 34:4). Yet, even here the emphasis rests on God's love and faithfulness to the oath which he swore (7:8–9). The part played by the patriarchs in the process of election is secondary to that of the LORD. Deuteronomy is consistent in emphasising that the LORD's election of Israel was not due to some inherent quality found in the people; rather it resulted from his unmerited love for them.

Having observed how Deuteronomy emphasises the divine election of Israel, what does it say about the purpose underlying this? What did the LORD hope to achieve through choosing the Israelites to be his own people? The clearest answer to this question comes in 4:6–8:

> Observe them (God's decrees and laws) carefully, for this will show your wisdom and understanding to the nations, who will hear about all these decrees and say, 'Surely this great nation is a wise and understanding people.' What other nation is so great as to have their gods near them the way the LORD our God is near us whenever we pray to him? And what other nation is so great as to have such righteous decrees and laws as this body of laws I am setting before you today?

Underlying this passage is the idea that Israel is divinely chosen to be an example for others to emulate. Two aspects of this are highlighted here. First, the nearness of the LORD's presence is emphasised. Israel will enjoy an intimate relationship with God which will be seen in the LORD's willingness to hear the people's prayers. Second, the *tôrâ* ('body of laws' NIV) by which the nation shall regulate its affairs will be praised by others because of the inherent righteousness of its decrees and laws. Naturally, this required that the Israelites should be consistent in keeping all the demands of the *tôrâ*. Israel's election is linked to her obligation to be a holy nation (cf. 7:7–11). Because the LORD has chosen Israel and promised to bless her abundantly, she has the responsibility of living up to her divine calling. Moses expresses this link between election, obedience to the LORD, and other nations, as follows:

> The LORD will establish you as his holy people, as he promised you on oath, if you keep the commands of the LORD your God and walk in his ways. Then all the peoples on earth will see that you are called by the name of the LORD, and they will fear you (28:9–10).

Given the importance that is placed upon Israel being a light to the nations, it is not surprising that much of Deuteronomy is devoted to outlining the regulations and laws which are intended to make Israel more righteous that other nations. While it is not possible to provide here a detailed survey of all the material in the Book of the Law (*tôrâ*), a number of general observations can be made. At the outset it should be noted that the regulations in Deuteronomy seek to promote a sense of brotherhood. An example of this comes in the regulations concerning kingship (17:14–20). Not only is it stated that the king 'must be from among your own brothers' (17:15) but later it is added that he 'must not consider himself better than his brothers' (17:20). The Law (*tôrâ*) required that the king should not use his special status to promote his own interests above those of others. Linked to the concept of brotherhood is a concern for the weaker members of society. Throughout the Book of the Law (*tôrâ*) special mention is made of the fatherless, the widow, the slave, the poor and the alien.[4] Because of their vulnerability, they must not be mistreated or exploited; all are to be shown dignity and respect. Furthermore, the Law (*tôrâ*) is also concerned to promote a generous spirit (e.g. 10:18–19; 15:12–14). In their dealings with others, the Israelites must reflect the LORD's generosity towards them.[5]

Deuteronomy also emphasises throughout the importance of Israel being a righteous nation. We see this highlighted, for example, in the refrain which occurs often in the Book of the Law (*tôrâ*): 'You must purge the evil from among you' (13:5; 17:7; 19:19; 21:21; 22:21; 22:24; 24:7; cf. 17:12; 19:13; 21:9; 22:22). It is also reflected in the LORD's description of Israel as Jeshurun 'the upright one' (32:15; 33:5,26).[6] However, although Deuteronomy stresses the importance of Israel being righteous, it also allows for the possibility that should Israel fail in this regard, she would still be a witness to God's righteousness (cf. 29:24–28).[7]

Although Israel was the LORD's 'treasured possession', this did not give to the people a firm guarantee that they would always enjoy divine favour. As we have noted in the previous chapter, the covenant established between the LORD and Israel only guaranteed blessing when the people fulfilled the obligations placed upon them. Failure to meet these obligations would bring upon them the curses outlined at the end of the Book of the Law (*tôrâ*). While the Israelites enjoyed a unique and privileged position as regards their relationship with the LORD, they were expected to be especially righteous.

ISRAEL AND THE NATIONS

Thus far we have focused our attention on the LORD's choice of Israel to be his people out of all the nations of the earth. What, however, does the book of Deuteronomy reveal about the LORD's attitude towards other nations? In addressing this question it needs to be noted that in Deuteronomy an important distinction is drawn between the nations living in the land of Canaan and those living elsewhere. To appreciate this it may be best to consider first what Deuteronomy has to say about the nations of Canaan.

Given that the whole movement in the book of Deuteronomy is towards the Israelite occupation of the land of Canaan, it is hardly surprising that considerable attention should be devoted to the issue of what should happen to those nations already living there. Since the land was in the possession of seven nations — the Hittites, Girgashites, Amorites, Canaanites, Perizzites, Hivites and Jebusites — how would Israel come to possess it? The response of Deuteronomy is unambiguous. The Israelites were to destroy totally all those inhabiting the land of Canaan. As Moses instructs the people:

> When the LORD your God has delivered them over to you and you have defeated them, then you must destroy them totally. Make no treaty with them, and show them no mercy (7:2; cf. 20:16–17).

To justify such a policy towards these nations, Moses highlights two factors. First, the destruction of these nations is an act of divine punishment.[8] As Moses emphasises in 9:4–6 the Israelites were not being given the land as a reward for their own righteousness, 'but on account of the wickedness of these nations, the LORD your God will drive them out before you' (9:5; cf. v. 4). Although the nature of their wickedness is not explicitly mentioned, a major factor was their idolatrous worship and its associated practices.[9] Second, the complete annihilation of the nations living in the promised land is necessary in order to prevent the Israelites from worshipping their gods (20:16–18). For this reason, Moses commands the total destruction of everything associated with the worship of these gods (7:5,25–26) and forbids the people from following their religious practices (16:21–22; 18:14). Although the treatment of the nations living in Canaan appears exceptionally severe, it should be noted that their punishment was not arbitrary. As Deuteronomy makes clear, the Israelites themselves would suffer similar punishment for idolatry.

In spite of the strength of the nations already in Canaan — 'seven nations larger and stronger than you' (7:1) — the Israelites are assured that the LORD will give them the victory (7:16–24; 9:1–3; 11:22–25; 31:3–8). Although the victory will be decisive, it will also be gradual (7:22). Furthermore, their victory is linked to their obedience to God's decrees and laws (11:22–23).

While the book of Deuteronomy adopts a very negative attitude towards the inhabitants of Canaan, the same is not true of all other nations. This is reflected in a number of ways. First, Moses draws attention to the fact that during their journey to the promised land the Israelites were not permitted by the LORD to attack certain nations in order to take possession of their land (2:1–23). This was so for the Edomites, Moabites and Ammonites. Concerning each of these nations Moses observes that the LORD was responsible for giving them their land (2:5,9,19). Since the land was granted to them by the LORD, the Israelites had no right to take any part of it. Interestingly, Moses observes a number of parallels between the Edomites, Moabites and Ammonites; all were given land by the LORD,[10] and all of them overcame powerful enemies in order to take possession of the land (2:10–12,20–23). Implicit in Moses' comments is the suggestion that if the LORD has done this for these nations, then the Israelites should have confidence that he will achieve the same for them.

Second, when the Book of the Law (*tôrâ*) addresses the topic of war against other nations, a clear distinction is drawn between how the Israelites should deal with the nearby nations of Canaan and more distant peoples. While they were to spare none of the members of the nearby nations (20:16–17) — all were to be put to death, men and women, young and old — a different policy was to be adopted towards other nations. At the outset of any conflict an offer of peace was to be made (20:10). If this was accepted, then no deaths resulted. If, however, this was refused, the Israelites were to 'put to the sword all the men' but spare 'the women, the children, the livestock and everything else in the city' (20:13–14).[11]

Third, various minor remarks within Deuteronomy also suggest that the Israelites were expected to adopt a positive attitude towards the well-being of the nations outside of Canaan. Thus, they are commanded not to 'abhor an Edomite' or 'an Egyptian' (23:7). In spite of all that had happened in Egypt the Israelites were to allow 'the third generation of children' born to Egyptians to 'enter the assembly of the LORD' (23:8). A positive attitude towards foreigners is also reflected in the numerous references to aliens within the Book of the Law (*tôrâ*). As noted above, they, like widows and the fatherless, were to be cared for in a special way.

These differing approaches towards foreign nations are in keeping with what we observed earlier regarding the election of Israel. Since the nations of Canaan, through their wickedness, had forfeited their right to the land of Canaan, the land was to be given to the Israelites. It was in this territory that Israel was to establish herself as a holy nation. Furthermore, because Israel was to be a light to the nations, it was important that she reflected in her national life the lifestyle and values which were consistent with the single-minded service of the LORD. This required that the land be purged of everything that might undermine the divine purpose underlying Israel's election. Hence the Israelites were to destroy completely the nations already living in Canaan. However, as regards other nations, a different attitude was to prevail. At all times Israel was to follow a policy of non-aggression towards them. Only if they threatened the national security of Israel would they be in danger of attack.

ELECTION AND RESPONSIBILITY

Although the LORD chose the Israelites to be his people, at no stage were they forced against their will to accept him as their God. At Sinai and on the Plains of Moab they are invited to enter freely into a covenant relationship with the LORD. However, once they entered into such an agreement, they were committed by the terms of the covenant to remain loyal to the LORD. While Moses emphasises in his speeches the benefits available to the Israelites as a result of their divine election, the book of Deuteronomy also highlights the serious consequences which would result from a failure to fulfil this calling. If the Israelites were to enjoy the benefits of being the LORD's people, they had to keep the obligations placed upon them by the covenant.

Significantly, although Moses strongly exhorts the people to obey the covenant obligations, Deuteronomy as a whole conveys the idea that the Israelites will fail to keep them. While the possibility of failure is introduced as early as 4:25–31, it is in the concluding chapters that it becomes most prominent. First, the likelihood that Israel will break the covenant obligations is suggested by the space devoted to the curses in chs. 27 and 28. Whereas twelve verses are given over to outlining the blessing which will reward obedience (28:3–14), the curses occupy sixty-five verses (27:15–26; 28:16–68). By devoting so much attention to the curses, the impression is conveyed that they are more likely to materialise than the blessings.

Second, although the list of curses does not specifically indicate that the Israelites will fail to keep the covenant obligations, this is stated emphatically shortly afterwards in three different speeches. (a) In his final exhortation to the Israelites to keep the covenant with the LORD, Moses clearly envisages a future in which the land will be devastated (29:23) and the people exiled (30:1–4). (b) In one of the few divine speeches recorded in Deuteronomy, the LORD tells Moses:

> These people will soon prostitute themselves to the foreign gods of the land they are entering. They will forsake me and break the covenant I made with them. On that day I will become angry with them and forsake them; I will hide my face from them, and they will be destroyed (31:16–17).

To remind future generations of Israelites of this prediction the LORD instructs Moses to teach the people a special song (32:1–

43). (c) When Moses orders the Levites to place the 'Book of the Law (*tôrâ*)' beside the ark of the covenant, he comments:

> For I know how rebellious and stiff-necked you are. If you have been rebellious against the LORD while I am still alive and with you, how much more will you rebel after I die! Assemble before me all the elders of your tribes and all your officials, so that I can speak these words in their hearing and call heaven and earth to testify against them. For I know that after my death you are sure to become utterly corrupt and to turn from the way I have commanded you. In days to come, disaster will fall upon you because you will do evil in the sight of the LORD and provoke him to anger by what your hands have made (31:27–29).

Like the song in 32:1–43; the Book of the Law (*tôrâ*) will be a witness against the Israelites (31:26; cf. v. 19).

In the light of these developments towards the end of Deuteronomy, it is clear that the Israelites, due to their disobedience, will benefit little from their divine election. While they will initially enjoy God's favour in the promised land, this will be replaced in due course by divine cursing, resulting in their expulsion from the land. That Deuteronomy should envisage such a development is noteworthy. However, even in the process of being punished by the LORD, the Israelites will still be a witness to the nations regarding the righteousness of the LORD. When in the future foreigners ask why terrible disasters have come upon Israel (29:22–24), it will be stated:

> It is because this people abandoned the covenant of the LORD, the God of their fathers, the covenant he made with them when he brought them out of Egypt. They went off and worshipped other gods and bowed down to them, gods they did not know, gods he had not given them. Therefore the Lord's anger burned against this land, so that he brought on it all the curses written in this book. In furious anger and in great wrath the LORD uprooted them from their land and thrust them into another land, as it is now (29:25–28).

Thus, even when divinely punished the Israelites would be a light to the nations.

Although Israel's election gave them advantages denied to other nations, in reality due to their rebellious nature, they would forfeit these. Nevertheless, in spite of their unfaithfulness, the LORD would not abandon them completely. If in exile they showed remorse for their actions, he would be compassionate towards them (30:1–10). Significantly, in anticipating the future restoration of exiled Israelites to the promised land, Moses alludes briefly to the fact that 'the LORD your God will circumcise your hearts and the hearts of the your descendants, so that you may love him with all your heart and with all your soul, and live' (30:6). Here Moses envisages a time in the distant future when the LORD will intervene in order to overcome the inability of the Israelites to keep the covenant faithfully.

CONCLUSION

The Book of Deuteronomy highlights why the LORD chose Israel to be his people and the consequences associated with this choice. They were to be a holy nation, keeping the covenant obligations found in the Book of the Law (*tôrâ*) in order that others might know and marvel at the righteousness of God. Yet in spite of the special privileges bestowed upon them, Deuteronomy anticipates a future in which the Israelites will rebel against the LORD and break the covenant. As a result, after entering the promised land they themselves will be exiled and forced to live among other nations.

NEW TESTAMENT CONNECTIONS

Within the NT the issue of Israel's divine election is perhaps most prominent in Paul's letter to the Romans. Here Paul addresses at length how the gospel has impacted the relationship between Jews and Gentiles. In his discussion Paul highlights the belief of his Jewish contemporaries that in the 'law' they have 'the embodiment of knowledge and truth' (Rom 2:20). Such a belief is clearly derived from the way in which the Law (*tôrâ*) is presented in the book of Deuteronomy. While Paul does not dispute this view of the Law, he challenges the ability of his contemporaries to keep it. He even suggests that because of their inability to keep the law, 'God's name is blasphemed among the Gentiles' (Rom 2:24; quoting Isa 52:5; Ezek 36:22), an idea which may well have its roots in the book of Deuteronomy.

Next Paul focuses on the topic of circumcision and argues that without a circumcision of the heart, implying complete obedience to God, outward circumcision is of no benefit. Thus, although his Jewish opponents were stressing the importance of having the Law and being circumcised, Paul argues that they are mistaken in thinking that this makes them more righteous than others: 'No-one will be declared righteous in his (God's) sight by observing the law; rather, through the law we become conscious of sin' (Rom 3:20). Paul then proceeds to argue that there is a 'righteousness from God' which 'comes through faith in Christ to all who believe' (Rom 3:22). This righteousness is available to both Jews and Gentiles, to everyone who, like

Abraham, exercises faith. By focusing on this 'righteousness from God' Paul reflects the outlook of Deuteronomy that without a divinely given circumcision of the heart it would be impossible for the Israelites to keep the covenant.

Later, Paul picks up on the benefits which belong to the Israelites as God's chosen people:

> Theirs is the adoption as sons; theirs the divine glory, the covenants, the receiving of the law, the temple worship and the promises. Theirs are the patriarchs, and from them is traced the human ancestry of Christ, who is God over all, for ever praised! Amen. (Rom 9:4–5).

Yet in spite of these things, Paul willingly acknowledges that there are those Israelites who have failed to obtain the righteousness that comes by faith; rather they have sought to be righteous by keeping the law and have failed. On the other hand, Gentiles 'who did not pursue righteousness, have obtained it' (9:30). In the light of this Paul asks if the LORD has rejected his people, Israel. While he acknowledges the failure of many Jews to find salvation, he holds out the hope that 'all Israel will be saved' (11:26). Although the inclusion of the Gentiles within the people of God is a very significant development for Paul, he does not believe that this implies the complete exclusion of the Jews. Echoing Deuteronomy Paul sees the divine election of Israel as leading eventually to the salvation of the Gentiles.

NOTES

1. A similar description of Israel's unique status among the nations of the earth comes in Exodus 19:4–6.

2. In Deuteronomy, the place where the tabernacle was to be located in the promised land is referred to using either the phrase 'the place the LORD will choose' (12:5,11,14,18,21,26; 14:23–25; 15:20; 16:2,6,7,11,15,16; 17:8,10; 18:6; 26:2; 31:11) or the phrase 'to put his Name there for his dwelling' (12:5,11; 14:23; 16:2,6,11; 26:2; cf. 12:21, 14:24).

3. This is discussed more fully below.

4. The alien, the fatherless and the widow are mentioned together in the following verses: 10:18; 14:29; 16:11,14; 24:17,19–21; 26:12–13; 27:19. Elsewhere positive attitudes towards aliens are commended in 1:16; 5:14; 10:19; 14:21; 23:7; 24:14; 26:11. On occasions the Levites, who were dependent on the generosity of other Israelites for their daily needs, are mentioned alongside the alien, the fatherless and the widow (14:29; 16:11,14; 26:12–13; cf. 26:11).

5. It should be noted that Deuteronomy assumes that because these laws are divinely given, they reflect God's righteous nature. It is

therefore no surprise that Moses describes God's nature in terms which echo the regulations of the Book of the Law (*tôrâ*).

For the LORD your God is God of gods and Lord of lords, the great God, mighty and awesome, who shows no partiality and accepts no bribes. He defends the cause of the fatherless and the widow, and loves the alien, giving him food and clothing (10:17–18)

6. Apart from its occurrences in Deuteronomy, the term is used only once elsewhere in the Old Testament (Isa 44:2).

7. See below.

8. A similar view is expressed in Gen 15:16 in connection with God's promise to Abraham that his descendants will possess the land of Canaan.

9. Since Deuteronomy sees a link between religion and morality, it is more than likely that the ethical standards of the nations in Canaan were viewed as also meriting divine punishment.

10. Moses quotes the LORD as saying, 'I have given Esau the hill country of Seir as his own' (2:5). Similar statements are made concerning the Moabites (2:9) and Ammonites (2:19).

11. In passing it is interesting to observe the ban against cutting down fruit trees during the siege of a city. Implicit in this seems to be a concern to enable life, for those who survive a siege, to return to normality as a soon as possible after the conflict has ended. Even in war, the Israelites were to have a humanitarian concern.

[17]

Conclusion

From the preceding chapters it is apparent that the Pentateuch includes diverse material which has been brought together to form a narrative that is unified by a distinctive plot concerning God's special relationship with the descendants of Abraham, Isaac and Jacob. A central aspect of this plot is the creation of Israel as a nation. At the outset this is highlighted in terms of God's promise that Abraham shall have numerous descendants who will possess the land of Canaan. Later, the account of Israel's deliverance from Egypt and the making of the covenant at Sinai marks the formal establishment of Israel as God's chosen nation. The reality of this relationship is confirmed by the appearance of the divine presence at the tabernacle erected in the middle of the Israelite camp; God now dwells in the midst of his people.

Israel's privileged relationship with God, however, places special responsibilities upon the people. Most importantly of all they are to be a holy nation, abiding by moral standards superior to those adopted by others. As well as being committed to a distinctive code of ethics, Israel receives instructions regarding a wide variety of practices and rituals, all of which are designed to underline and maintain Israel's holy status. These range from instructions regarding the offering of sacrifices to prohibitions against the eating of certain foods. In various ways the Israelites are to distinguish themselves from other peoples by being holy.

Although much of the Pentateuch focuses on the special origin of the nation of Israel, the book of Genesis emphasises that the unique status of Israel must be understood against the background of God's desire to bless all the nations of the earth. From the perspective of the final narrator of the Pentateuch the destinies of Israel and all other nations are intertwined with the expectation that through the 'seed' of Abraham God's blessing will be mediated to all the families of the earth. Two aspects of this are prominent in the Pentateuch. First, the Israelites are to be an example of how people should live in harmony with both God and the rest of humanity. Second, God's blessing for all nations will be mediated through a future king descended from the tribe of Judah.

A LIGHT TO THE NATIONS

Basic to God's choice of Israel is the intention that Israel will be a light to the nations. As a result of the disobedience of Adam and Eve the whole human race is alienated from God. Furthermore, every subsequent act of disobedience merely adds to this alienation. In the light of this Israel is to provide a positive role model for others to follow; through faithful obedience they are to know God's blessing. Significantly, such blessing produces not merely a harmonious relationship between deity and humanity, but also harmony between human beings and their environment, the latter being marked by continuous human habitation in fertile and productive land. Thus, through her special relationship with God Israel is to reveal how creation may be restored to its original pristine condition. To this end Israel's life within Canaan reflects in part the situation which existed in the Garden of Eden prior to the disobedience and expulsion of Adam and Eve. Like Eden the land of Canaan will be fruitful, a land 'flowing with milk and honey', and there the Israelites will commune with God in a personal and intimate way.

The Pentateuch, however, does not envisage the Israelite occupation of the land of Canaan as heralding the total restoration of the idyllic situation which existed prior to the first act of human rebellion against God. While the Israelites are presented as having a unique association with God, their relationship with him is not completely harmonious. From the outset, following their deliverance from Egypt, they repeatedly display their reluctance to trust God fully and to obey him in everything. We see this prior to their arrival at Sinai, during their stay there and afterwards when they journey towards the promised land. Throughout the books of Exodus to Deuteronomy there are many reminders of Israel's inability to live up to her divine calling to be a holy nation. Furthermore, the concluding chapters of Deuteronomy emphasise that this failure will be evident in the future and will result in the people being expelled from the land of Canaan itself. Finally, apart from direct references to Israel's failure, the establishment of different rituals designed to deal with the consequences of human sinfulness indicates that a return to Eden is not envisaged in the immediate future. Rather God's dealings with

Israel in the land of Canaan merely anticipate that which is yet to come.

Interestingly, although God intends Israel to be a positive role model for other nations, this cannot be thwarted by her disobedience. As Deut 29:24–28 indicates, the later expulsion of the Israelites from the land, due to their disobedience, will also be a lesson for all the nations. Thus, both positively and negatively, Israel will be a witness to people everywhere regarding how each individual should live before God.

A ROYAL DESCENDANT OF JUDAH

While Israel as a nation will play an important role in the outworking of God's purposes for the whole of humanity, particular attention is focused on the establishment of a royal dynasty through whom God's blessing will be mediated to people everywhere. The importance of this royal line is indicated to Abraham in the promise that through his 'seed' all nations will be blessed. Significantly, in its present form the book of Genesis associates this 'seed' with a single descendant of royal status. Although mention of this royal 'seed' fades into the background in the books of Exodus to Deuteronomy, it is not completely forgotten. As well as the special prominence given to the tribe of Judah, the appearance of a powerful, future king dominates the fourth of Balaam's oracles (Num 24:15-19), and the establishment of an Israelite monarchy is anticipated in the book of Deuteronomy (Deut 17:14-20). However, like the promise of nationhood, the promise of a future king through whom all the nations of the earth will be blessed remains unfulfilled by the end of Deuteronomy.

BEYOND THE PENTATEUCH

As we have noted on various occasions the promises associated with Abraham, which are so important in setting the agenda for the whole of the Pentateuch, remain unfulfilled by the end of Deuteronomy and point forward to the future. Significantly, these same promises, in part at least, are important elements of the narrative in the books of Joshua to Kings. First, the subject of nationhood is particularly prominent in the books of Joshua, Judges and Samuel. Although the Israelites are slow to take full possession of the land of Canaan, by the time of the reigns of David and Solomon it is noteworthy that they possess the land as far as the boundaries defined in Genesis 15:18–21 (cf. 2 Sam 8:1–14; 1 Kgs 4:21; 9:20–21). Secondly, the books of 1 and 2 Samuel recount in detail the dramatic beginnings of the Davidic dynasty, fulfilling the expectation of the book of Genesis that this royal line will be descended from Judah. Yet, although the narrative in Joshua to Samuel advances in significant ways the fulfilment of the divine promises to Abraham, one aspect of these promises is never fully realised, the blessing of the nations.[1] Significantly, the fulfilment of this latter promise is further delayed as the book of Kings charts the demise of both the nation of Israel and the Davidic dynasty. Yet this development comes as no surprise, having already been anticipated in the book of Deuteronomy. Consequently, the expectation exists that only beyond the restoration of Israel from exile will the divine promise be fulfilled regarding the blessing of all the nations of the earth through a Davidic king. In the light of this, the NT proclamation of Jesus Christ as the saviour of the world takes on special significance.

NOTE

1. A partial fulfilment of this promise is suggested by the events surrounding Solomon's dealings with non-Israelites.

Recommended Further Reading

Many writers approach the Pentateuch from standpoints which differ from that adopted in the present works.

COMMENTARIES

Items considered to be most suitable for beginners are marked with a ***.

GENESIS

Aalders, G.C. *Genesis.* 2 vols. BSC. Grand Rapids: Zondervan, 1981.
Brueggemann, W. *Genesis.* Interpretation. Atlanta: John Knox, 1982.
Cassuto, U. *Commentary on Genesis.* 2 vols. Jerusalem: Magnes, 1964.
Coats, G.W. *Genesis with an Introduction to Narrative Literature.* FOTL 1. Grand Rapids: Eerdmans, 1983.
Gibson, J.C.L. *Genesis.* 2vols. DSB. Edinburgh: St. Andrew, 1981–1982.
Gowan, D.E. *Genesis 1–11.* ITC. Grand Rapids: Eerdmans, 1988.
Hamilton, V. *Genesis 1–17.* NICOT. Grand Rapids: Eerdmans, 1990.
Kidner, D. *Genesis.* TOTC. Leicester: IVP, 1967.***
Maher, M. *Genesis.* OTM 2; Wilmington: Michael Glazier, 1982.
Rad, G. von. *Genesis.* OTL. London: SCM, 1961.
Ross, A.P. *Creation and Blessing: A Guide to the Study and Exposition of Genesis.* Grand Rapids: Baker, 1988.
Sarna, N.M. *Genesis.* The JPS Torah Commentary. New York: Jewish Publication Society, 1989.
Skinner, J. *Genesis.* ICC. Edinburgh:T. & T. Clark, 1910.
Speiser, E.A. *Genesis.* AB 1. Garden City: Doubleday, 1964.
Vawter, B. *On Genesis: A New Reading.* Garden City: Doubleday, 1977.
Wenham, G.J. *Genesis 1–15.* WBC 1. Waco: Word, 1987.
Wenham, G.J. *Genesis 16–50.* WBC 2. Dallas: Word, 1994.
Wenham, G.J. 'Genesis'. In *New Bible Commentary (21st Century Edition),* edited by D.A. Carson (et al). Leicester: IVP, 1994.***
Westermann, C. *Genesis: A Commentary.* 3 vols. Minneapolis: Augsburg, 1984–86.
Westermann, C. *Genesis.* TI. Grand Rapids: Eerdmans, 1987.

191

EXODUS

Alexander, T.D. 'Exodus'. In *New Bible Commentary (21st Century Edition)* edited by D.A. Carson (et al). Leicester: IVP, 1994.***
Cassuto, U. *Commentary on Exodus*. Jerusalem: Magnes Press, 1967.
Childs, B.S. *The Book of Exodus*. OTL. London: SCM, 1974.
Cole, R.A. *Exodus*. TOTC. Leicester: IVP, 1973.
Durham, J.I. *Exodus*. WBC 3. Waco: Word, 1987.
Ellison, H.L. *Exodus*. DSB. Edinburgh: St. Andrew, 1982.***
Gispen, W.H. *Exodus*. BSC. Grand Rapids: Zondervan, 1987.
Hyatt, J.B. *Exodus*. NCB. Grand Rapids: Eerdmans, 1971.
Noth, M. *Exodus*. OTL. London: SCM, 1962.

LEVITICUS

Bonar, A.A. *A Commentary on Leviticus*. Edinburgh: Banner of Truth, 1966.
Harrison, R.K. *Leviticus*. TOTC. Leicester: IVP, 1980.
Hartley, J.E. *Leviticus*. WBC 4. Dallas: Word, 1992.
Knight, G.A.F. *Leviticus*. DSB. Edinburgh: St. Andrew, 1981.***
Levine, B.A. *Leviticus*. The JPS Commentary. New York: Jewish Publication Society, 1989.
Milgrom, J. *Leviticus 1–16*. AB 3. New York: Doubleday, 1991.
Noordtzij, A. *Leviticus*. BSC. Grand Rapids: Zondervan, 1982.
Snaith, N.H. *Leviticus and Numbers*. NCB. Grand Rapids. Eerdmans, 1967.
Wenham, G.J. *The Book of Leviticus*. NICOT. Grand Rapids: Eerdmans, 1979.***
Wright, C.J.H. 'Leviticus'. In *New Bible Commentary (21st Century Edition)*, edited by D.A. Carson (et al). Leicester: IVP, 1994.***

NUMBERS

Ashley, T.R. *The Book of Numbers*. NICOT. Grand Rapids: Eerdmans, 1993.
Budd, P.J. *Numbers*. WBC 5. Waco: Word, 1984.
Gray, G.B. *Numbers*. ICC. Edinburgh: T. & T. Clark, 1903.
Harrison, R.K. *Numbers*. WEC. Chicago: Moody, 1990.
Maarsingh, B. *Numbers*. TI. Grand Rapids: Eerdmans, 1987.
Milgrom, J. *Numbers*. The JPS Torah Commentary. New York: Jewish Publication Society, 1990.
Naylor, P.J. 'Numbers'. In *New Bible Commentary (21st Century Edition)* edited by D.A. Carson (et al). Leicester: IVP, 1994.***
Noordtzij, A. *Numbers*. BSC. Grand Rapids: Zondervan, 1983.
Philip, P. *Numbers*. CC. Waco: Word, 1987.
Riggans, W. *Numbers*. DSB. Edinburgh: St. Andrew, 1983.***
Snaith, N.H. *Leviticus and Numbers*. NCB. Grand Rapids: Eerdmans, 1967.
Wenham, G.J. *Numbers*. TOTC. Leicester: IVP, 1981.***

DEUTERONOMY

Christensen, D.L. *Deuteronomy 1–11*. WBC 6. Waco: Word, 1991.
Clifford, R. *Deuteronomy*. OTM 4. Wilmington: Michael Glazier, 1982.
Craigie, P.C. *The Book of Deuteronomy*. NICOT. Grand Rapids: Eerdmans, 1976.
Driver, S.R. *A Critical and Exegetical Commentary on Deuteronomy*. 3d ed. ICC. Edinburgh: T. & T. Clark, 1902.
Mayes, A.D.H. *Deuteronomy*. NCB. Grand Rapids: Eerdmans, 1979.
McConville, J.G. 'Deuteronomy'. In *New Bible Commentary (21st Century Edition)*, edited by D.A. Carson (et al). Leicester: IVP, 1994.***
Miller, P.D. *Deuteronomy*. Interpretation. Louisville: John Knox, 1990.
Munchenberg, R.H. *Deuteronomy*. Adelaide: Lutheran Publishing House, 1987.
Payne, D.F. *Deuteronomy*. DSB. Edinburgh: St Andrew, 1985.***
Rad, G. von. *Deuteronomy*. London. SCM, 1966.
Ridderbos, J. *Deuteronomy*. BSC. Grand Rapids: Zondervan, 1984.
Thompson, J.A. *Deuteronomy*. TOTC. Leicester: IVP, 1974.***
Weinfeld, M. *Deuteronomy 1–11*. AB 5. New York: Doubleday, 1991.
Wright, G.E. 'Deuteronomy', *The Interpreter's Bible*. Nashville: Abingdon, 1953.***

SPECIAL STUDIES

The following works are recommended for those who wish to explore in more detail specific topics along the lines adopted in this book. It should be noted that the works listed here vary in the extent and depth of their treatment of these topics.

THE GENEALOGICAL STRUCTURE OF GENESIS

Alexander, T.D. 'From Adam to Judah: the significance of the family tree in Genesis'. *EvQ* 61 (1989) 5–19.
——'Genealogies, Seed and the Compositional Unity of Genesis'. *TB* 44 (1993) 255–270.
Robinson, R.D. 'Literary Functions of the Genealogies of Genesis'. *CBQ* 48 (1986) 595–608.
Wilson, R.R. *Genealogy and History in the Biblical World*, New Haven: Yale University Press, 1977.
Woudstra, M.H. 'The Toledot of the Book of Genesis and Their Redemptive–historical Significance'. *CTJ* 5 (1970) 184–189.

BLESSING

Clines, D.J.A. *The Theme of the Pentateuch*. JSOTS 10; Sheffield: JSOT Press, 1978.
Muilenburg, J. 'Abraham and the Nations: Blessing and World History'. *Int* 19 (1965) 387–398.
Westermann, C. *Blessing in the Bible and in the Life of the Church*. Philadelphia: Fortress, 1978.

LAND

Brueggemann, W. *The Land*. Philadelphia: Fortress, 1977.
Frymer-Kensky, T. 'The Atrahasis Epic and its Significance for Our Understanding of Genesis 1–9'. *BA* 40 (1977) 147–155.
Wenham, G.J. 'Sanctuary Symbolism in the Garden of Eden Story'. *Proceedings of the World Congress of Jewish Studies* 9 (1986) 19–25.

ABRAHAM

Alexander, T.D. 'Abraham Re-assessed Theologically: The Abraham Narrative and the New Testament Understanding of Justification by Faith'. In *He Swore an Oath: Biblical Themes from Genesis 12–50*, edited by R.S. Hess, P.E. Satterthwaite and G.J. Wenham, pp. 7–28. 2d ed. Grand Rapids/Carlisle: Baker/Paternoster, 1994.
Gros Louis, K.R.R. 'Abraham' In *Literary Interpretations of Biblical Narratives II*, edited by K.R.R. Gros Louis and J.S. Ackerman, pp. 53–84. Nashville: Abingdon, 1982.
Hansen, G.W. *Abraham in Galatians*. JSNTS 29; Sheffield: JSOT, 1989.
Turner, L.A. *Announcement of Plot in Genesis*. JSOTS 133; Sheffield: JSOT, 1990.

PASSOVER

Alexander, T.D. 'The Passover Sacrifice'. In *Sacrifice in the Bible*, edited by Beckwith and M.J. Selman. Carlisle: Paternoster, 1995.
Bokser, B.M. *The Origins of the Seder*. Berkeley: University of California, 1984.
Segal, J.B. *The Hebrew Passover*. London: OUP, 1963.

SINAI COVENANT

Chirichigno, C.G. 'The Narrative Structure of Exodus 19–24'. *Bib* 68 (1987) 457–79.
Moberly, R.W.L. *At the Mountain of God: Story and Theology in Exodus 32–34*. JSOTS 22; Sheffield: JSOT Press, 1983.
Phillips, A. 'A Fresh Look at the Sinai Pericope: Part I'. *VT* 34 (1984) 39–52.
——'A Fresh Look at the Sinai Pericope: Part II'. *VT* 34 (1984) 282–94.
Sprinkle, J.M. 'The Book of the Covenant': A Literary Approach. JSOTS 174; Sheffield: JSOT, 1994.

TABERNACLE

Hart, I. 'Preaching on the Account of the Tabernacle'. *EvQ* 54 (1982) 111–116.

Koester, C.R. *The Dwelling of God: The Tabernacle in the Old Testament, Intertestamental Jewish Literature, and the New Testament.* CBQMS 22; Washington: Catholic Biblical Association of America, 1989.
Soltau, H.W. *The Holy Vessels and Furniture of the Tabernacle of Israel.* Grand Rapids: Kregel, 1969; first published 1865.

HOLINESS

Jensen, P.P. *Graded Holiness: A Key to the Priestly Conception of the World.* JSOTS 106; Sheffield: JSOT, 1992.
Wright, D.P. 'Holiness (OT)'. ABD 3:237–249.
——'Unclean and Clean (OT)'. ABD 6:729–741.

SACRIFICES

Anderson, G.A. 'Sarcifices and Sacrificial Offerings (OT)'. ABD 5:870–886.
Davies, D.J. 'An Interpretation of Sacrifice in Leviticus'. *ZAW* 89 (1977) 387–399.
Jenson, P.P. 'The Levitical Sacrificial System'. In *Sacrifice in the Bible*, edited by R.T Beckwith and M.J. Selman, pp. 25–40. Carlisle: Paternoster, 1995.
Kiuchi, N. *The Purification Offering in the Priestly Literature: Its Meaning and Function.* JSOTS 56; Sheffield: Sheffield Academic Press, 1987.
Milgrom, J. *Cult and Conscience: The ASHAM and the Priestly Doctrine of Repentance.* Leiden: Brill, 1976.

FOOD LAWS

Houston, W. *Purity and Monotheism: Clean and Unclean Animals in Biblical Law.* JSOTS 140; Sheffield: JSOT, 1993.
Soler, J. 'The Semiotics of Food in the Bible'. In *Food and Drink in History*, edited by R. Forster and O. Ranum, pp. 126–138. Baltimore: Johns Hopkins University, 1979.
Wenham, G.J. 'The Theology of Unclean Food'. *EvQ* 53 (1981) 6–15.

WILDERNESS WANDERINGS

Olson, D.T. *The Death of the Old and the Birth of the New: The Framework of the Book of Numbers and the Pentateuch.* Chico: Scholars, 1985.

DEUTERONOMY

McConville, J.G. *Law and Theology in Deuteronomy.* JSOTS 33; Sheffield: JSOT, 1984.
——*Grace in the End.* Carlisle: Paternoster, 1994.

Selected Bibliography

In order to restrict the size of the bibliography, only books and articles in English have been included. Fuller bibliographies on each book of the Pentateuch may be found in the commentaries of Westerman and Wenham on Genesis; Childs and Durham on Exodus; Hartley and Milgrom on Leviticus; Budd on Numbers; Christensen and Weinfeld on Deuteronomy.

Aalders, G. Ch. *A Short Introduction to the Pentateuch*, London: Tyndale, 1949.

Abela, A. *The Themes of the Abraham Narrative: Thematic Coherence Within the Abraham Literary Unit of Genesis 11,27–25,18*, Malta: Studia Editions, 1989.

Ackerman, J.S. 'The Literary Context of the Moses Birth Story'. In *Literary Interpretations of Biblical Narratives*, edited by K.R.R. Gros Louis, J.S. Ackerman and T.S. Warshaw, pp.74–119. Nashville: Abingdon, 1974.

Aitken, K.T. 'The Wooing of Rebekah: A Study in the Development of the Tradition'. *JSOT* 30 (1984) 3–23.

Albright, W.F. 'From the Patriarchs to Moses: I. From Abraham to Joseph'. *BA* 36 (1973) 5–33.

Albright, W.F. *From the Stone Age to Christianity*. 2d ed. Baltimore: Johns Hopkins, 1946.

Alexander, T.D. *A Literary Analysis of the Abraham Narrative in Genesis*, unpublished Ph.D. Thesis, The Queen's University of Belfast, 1982.

——'Genesis 22 and the Covenant of Circumcision'. *JSOT* 25 (1983) 17–22.

——'Lot's Hospitality: A Clue to His Righteousness'. *JBL* 104 (1985) 289–291.

——'From Adam to Judah: the significance of the family tree in Genesis'. *EvQ* 61 (1989) 5–19.

——'The Wife/Sister Incidents of Genesis: Oral Variants?' *IBS*, 11 (1989) 2–22.

——'The Hagar Traditions in Genesis xvi and xxi'. In *Studies in the Pentateuch*, edited by J.A. Emerton, pp.131–148. SVT 41; Leiden: Brill, 1990.

——'Are the wife/sister incidents of Genesis literary compositional variants?' *VT* 42 (1992) 145–153.

——'Genealogies, Seed and the Compositional Unity of Genesis'. *TB* 44 (1993) 255–270.

——'Abraham Re-assessed Theologically: The Abraham Narrative and the New Testament Understanding of Justification by Faith'. In *He Swore an Oath: Biblical Themes from Genesis 12–50*, edited by R.S. Hess, P.E. Satterthwaite and G.J. Wenham, pp.7–28. 2d ed. Grand Rapids/Carlisle: Baker/Paternoster, 1994.

Alter, R. *The Art of Biblical Narrative*. New York: Basic Books, 1981.

Anbar, M. 'Genesis 15: A Conflation of Two Deuteronomic Narratives'. *JBL* 101 (1982) 39–55.

Andersen, F.I. *The Hebrew Verbless Clause in the Pentateuch*. JBL Monograph Series 14. Nashville/New York: Abingdon, 1970.

——*The Sentence in Biblical Hebrew*. The Hague/Paris: Mouton, 1974.

Anderson, B.W. 'From Analysis to Synthesis: The Interpretation of Genesis 1 –11'. *JBL* 97 (1978) 23–39.

——'Unity and Diversity in God's Creation'. *CurTM* 5 (1978) 69– 81.

——*Creation in the Old Testament*. London: SPCK,1984.

Anderson, G.A. *Sacrifices and Offerings in Ancient Israel: Studies in their Social and Political Importance*. HSM 41; Atlanta: Scholars, 1987.

——'Sacrifices and Sacrificial Offerings (OT)'. ABD 5:870–886.

Andreasen, N.E. 'Genesis 14 in its Near Estern Context'. In *Scripture in Context. Essays on the Comparative Method*, edited by C.D Evans, W.W. Hallo and J.B. White, pp.59–77. Pittsburg: Pickwick, 1980.

Ashby, G.W.E.C. 'Reflections on the Language of Genesis 1 and 2'. *Semitics* 6 (1978) 58–69.

Auffret, P. 'The Literary Structure of Exodus 6. 2–8'. *JSOT* 27 (1983) 46–54.

——'Remarks on J. Magonet's Interpretation of Exodus 6. 2–8'. *JSOT* 27 (1983) 69–71.

Baker, D.W. 'Division Markers and the Structure of Lev 1–7'. In *Studia Biblica. Papers on Old Testament and Related Themes*, edited by E.A. Livingstone, pp.9–15. JSOTS 11. Sheffield: JSOT,1979.

Baker, D.W. 'Diversity and Unity in the Literary Structure of Genesis'. In *Essays on the Patriarchal Narratives*, edited by A.R. Millard and D.J. Wiseman, pp.189–205. Leicester: IVP, 1980.

Baker, J.A. 'Deuteronomy and World Problems'. *JSOT* 29 (1984) 3–17.

Baldwin, J.G. *The Message of Genesis 12–50: From Abraham to Joseph*. Leicester:IVP, 1986.

Bar–Efrat, S. 'Literary Modes and Methods in the Biblical Narrative'. *Imm* 8 (1978) 19–31.

——'Some Observations on the Analysis of Structure in Biblical Narrative'. *VT* 30 (1980) 154–173.

——*Narrative Art in the Bible*. Sheffield: Almond, 1989.

Barr, J. 'Reading the Bible as Literature'. *BJRL* 56 (1974) 10–33.

Bassett, F.W. 'Noah's Nakedness and the Curse of Canaan'. *VT* 21 (1971) 232–237.

Beattie, D.R.G. 'What is Genesis 2–3 About?' *ExpTim* 92 (1980) 8–10.

——'Peshat and Derash in the Garden of Eden'. *IBS* 7 (1985) 62–75.

Bechtel, L.M. 'What if Dinah is not raped? (Genesis 34)'. *JSOT* 62 (1994) 19–36.

Bentzen, A. *Introduction to the Old Testament*. 6th ed. Copenhagen: G.E.C. Gad, 1961.

Berlin, A. *Poetics and Interpretation of Biblical Narrative*. Sheffield: Almond, 1983.

Bird, P.A. ' "Male and Female He Created Them": Gen 1:27b in the Context of the Priestly Account of Creation'. *HTR* 74 (1981) 129–160.

Blenkinsopp, J. 'The Structure of P'. *CBQ* 38 (1976) 275–292.

——'Abraham and the Righteous of Sodom'. *JSS* 33 (1982) 119–132.

——*The Pentateuch*. London: SCM, 1992.

Blocher, H. *In the Beginning: The Opening Chapters of Genesis*. Leicester: IVP, 1984.

Blythin, J. 'The Patriarchs and the Promise'. *SJT* 21 (1968) 56–73.

Bokser, B.M. *The Origins of the Seder*. Berkeley: University of California, 1984.

——'Unleavened Bread and Passover, Feast of'. *ABD* 6:755–765.

Booif, Th. 'Mountain and Theophany in the Sinai Narrative'. *Bib* 65 (1984) 1–26.

Boomershine, T.E. 'The Structure of Narrative Rhetoric in Genesis 2–3'. *Semeia* 18 (1980) 113–129.

Brock, S. 'Genesis 22: Where was Sarah?' *ExpTim* 96 (1984) 14–17.

Brueggemann, W. 'The Kerygma of the Priestly Writers'. *ZAW* 84 (1972) 394–414.

——*The Land*. Philadelphia: Fortress, 1977.

Buck, D.W. 'Exodus 20:1–17'. *LTJ* 16 (1982) 65–75.

Butler, T.C. 'An Anti-Moses Tradition'. *JSOT* 12 (1979) 9–15.

Carmichael, C.M. *The Laws of Deuteronomy*. Ithaca: Cornell University Press, 1974.

Cassuto, U. *The Documentary Hypothesis*. Jerusalem: Magnes Press, 1961.

Cazelles, H. 'Theological Bulletin on the Pentateuch'. *BTB* 2 (1972) 3–24.

Chew, H.C. *The Theme of 'Blessing for the Nations' in the Patriarchal Narratives of Genesis*, unpublished Ph.D. Thesis, University of Sheffield, 1982.

Childs, B.S. *Introduction to the Old Testament as Scripture*. Philadelphia: Fortress, 1979.

Chirichigno, C.G. 'The Narrative Structure of Exodus 19–24'. *Bib* 68 (1987) 457–79.

Clark, W.M. 'The Flood and the Structure of the Pre-patriarchal History'. *ZAW* 83 (1971) 184–211.

——'The Righteousness of Noah'. *VT* 21 (1971) 261–280.

Clements, R.E. *Abraham and David: Genesis XV and its Meaning for Israelite Tradition*, London: SCM, 1967.

——'goy' in *TDOT* 2 (1977) 426–433.

——'Pentateuchal Problems'. In *Tradition and Interpretation*, edited by G.W. Anderson. Oxford: Clarendon, 1979.

——*Deuteronomy*. OT Guides; Sheffield: JSOT Press, 1989.

Clines, D.J.A 'Noah's Flood: 1 : The Theology of the Flood'. *Faith and Thought* 100 (1972) 128–142.

——' "Theme" in Genesis 1–11'. *CBQ* 38 (1976) 483–507.

——*The Theme of the Pentateuch.* JSOTS 10; Sheffield: JSOT Press, 1978.

——'The Significance of the "Sons of God" Episode (Genesis 6:1–4) in the Context of the "Primeval History" (Genesis 1–11)'. *JSOT* 13 (1979) 33–46.

——'What Happens in Genesis'. In *What Does Eve Do to Help? and other Readerly Questions to the Old Testament*, pp.49–66. JSOTS 94; Sheffield: JSOT, 1990.

Coats, G.W. *Rebellion in the Wilderness: The Murmuring Motif in the Wilderness Traditions of the Old Testament.* Nashville: Abingdon, 1968.

——'Abraham's Sacrifice of Faith: a Form-critical Study of Genesis 22'. *Int* 27 (1973) 389–400.

——'Redactional Unity in Genesis 37–50'. *JBL* 93 (1974) 15–21.

——*From Canaan to Egypt. Structural and Theological Context of the Joseph Story.* CBQMS 4; Washington: Catholic Biblical Association of America 1976.

——'Lot: A Foil in the Abraham Saga'. In *Understand the Word: Essays in Honor of Bernhard W. Anderson*, edited by J.T. Butler, et al, pp.113–132. JSOTS 37; Sheffield: JSOT, 1985.

——'Strife and Reconciliation: Themes of a Biblical Theology in the Book of Genesis'. *HBT* 2 (1980) 15–37.

——'Strife without Reconciliation: A Narrative Theme in the Jacob Tradition.'. In *Werden und Wirken des Alten Testament. Festschrift für Claus Westermann*, edited by R. Albertz. Göttingen: Vandenhoeck und Ruprecht, 1980.

Cody, A. 'When is a chosen people called a *goy*?' *VT*, 14 (1964) 1–6.

Cohn, R.L. 'Narrative Structure and Canonical Perspective in Genesis'. *JSOT* 25 (1983) 3–16.

Craghan, J.F. 'The Elohist in Recent Literature'. *BTB* 7 (1977) 23–35.

Crenshaw, J.L. 'Journey into Oblivion: A Structural Analysis of Gen 22:1–19'. *Soundings* 58 (1975) 243–256.

Cross, F.M. *Canaanite Myth and Hebrew Epic.* Cambridge, Mass.: Harvard University Press, 1973.

Cryer, F.H. 'The Interrelationships of Gen 5,32; 11,10–11 and the Chronology of the Flood (Gen 6–9)'. *Bib* 66 (1985) 241–261.

Culley, R.C. 'Structural Analysis: Is it done with Mirrors?' *Int* 28 (1974) 165–181.

——'Themes and Variations in Three Groups of OT Narratives'. *Semeia* 3 (1975) 3–13.

——*Studies in the Structure of Hebrew Narrative*, Philadelphia: Fortress 1976.

——'Oral Tradition and the O.T.: Some Recent Discussion'. *Semeia* 5 (1976) 1–33.

——'Action Sequences in Genesis 2–3'. *Semeia* 18 (1980) 25–33.

Dahlberg, B.T. 'On Recognizing the Unity of Genesis'. *TD* 24 (1976) 360–367.

Daly, R.J. 'The Soteriological Significance of the Sacrifice of Isaac'. *CBQ* 39 (1977) 45–75.

Damrosch, D. 'Leviticus'. In *The Literary Guide to the Bible*, edited by R. Alter and F. Kermode. Cambridge, Mass.: Harvard University Press, 1987.

Daube, D. *The Exodus Pattern in the Bible*. London: Faber and Faber, 1963.

Davidson, R. *Genesis 12–50*, Cambridge: CUP, 1979.

Davies, D.J. 'An Interpretation of Sacrifice in Leviticus'. *ZAW* 89 (1977) 387–399.

Davies, G.F. *Israel in Egypt: Reading Exodus 1–2*. JSOTS 135; Sheffield: JSOT, 1992.

Davies, G.I. *The Way of the Wilderness*. Cambridge: Cambridge University Press, 1979.

Davies, R.P. 'The Sacrifice of Isaac and Passover'. In *Studia Biblica. Papers on Old Testament and Related Themes*, edited by E.A. Livingstone, pp.127–132. JSOTS 11; Sheffield: JSOT, 1979.

Davis, D.R. 'Rebellion, Presence, and Covenant: A Study in Exodus 32–34 '. *WTJ* 44 (1982) 71–87.

DeWitt, D.S. 'The Generation of Genesis'. *EvQ*, 48 (1976) 196–221.

Dillard, R.B. and T. Longman III. *An Introduction to the Old Testament*. Sheffield: Apollos, 1995.

Douglas, M. 'The Forbidden Animals in Leviticus'. *JSOT* 59 (1993) 3–23.

——*Purity and Danger*. London: Routledge & K. Paul, 1969.

Dozeman, T.B. *God on the Mountain*. SBLMS; Missoula: Scholars, 1989.

Driver, S.R. *An Introduction to the Literature of the Old Testament*. 9th ed. Edinburgh: T. & T. Clark, 1913.

Dumbrell, W.J. 'The Covenant with Abraham'. *RefThR* 38 (1982) 42–50.

——*Covenant and Creation: An Old Testament Covenantal Theology*. Exeter: Paternoster, 1984.

——*The End of the Beginning: Revelation 21–22 and the Old Testament*. Grand Rapids: Baker, 1985.

Eakin, F.E. Jr 'The Plagues and the Crossing of the Sea'. *RevExp* 74 (1977) 473–82.

Eakins, J.K. 'Moses'. *RevExp* 74 (1977) 461–71.

Eissfeldt, W. *The Old Testament. An Introduction*. Oxford: Basil Blackwell, 1965.

Elder, W.H. 'The Passover'. *RevExp* 74 (1977) 511–22.

Ellington, J. 'Miscarriage or Premature Birth?' *BT* 37 (1986) 334–37.

Ellis, P.F. *The Yahwist. The Bible's First Theologian*, London: Chapman, 1969.

Emerton, J.A. 'Judah and Tamar'. *VT* 29 (1979) 403–415.

——'The Origin of the Promises to the Patriarchs in the Older Sources of the Book of Genesis'. *VT* 32 (1982) 14–32.

Engnell, I. 'The Pentateuch', in *Critical Essays on the Old Testament*, London: SPCK, 1970.

Enz, J.J. 'The Book of Exodus as a Literary Type for the Gospel of John'. *JBL* 76 (1957) 208–215.

Eslinger, L. 'Freedom or Knowledge? Perspectives and Purpose in the Exodus Narrative (Exodus 1–15)'. *JSOT* 52 (1991) 43–60.

Exum, J.C. ' "You Shall Let Every Daughter Live": A Study of Exodus 1:8–2:10 '. *Semeia* 28 (1983) 63–82.

Finkelstein, J.J. 'The Ox that Gored'. *Transactions of the American Philosophical Society* 71 (1981) 5–47.

Firmage, E. 'The biblical dietary laws and the concept of holiness'. In *Studies in the Pentateuch*, ed. by J.A. Emmerton, pp.122–208. *SVT* 41: Leiden: Brill, 1990.

Finn, A.H. *The Unity of the Pentateuch*. London: Marshall, n.d..

Fishbane, M.A. 'Composition and Structure in the Jacob Cycle (Gen 25:19–35:22)'. *JJS* 26 (1975) 15–38.

——'The Sacred Center: The Symbolic Structure of the Bible'. In *Texts and Responses*, edited by M.A. Fishbane and P.R. Flohr. Leiden: Brill, 1975.

——*Text and Texture. Close Readings of Selected Biblical Texts*. New York: Schocken Books, 1979.

——*Biblical Interpretation in Ancient Israel*. Oxford: Clarendon, 1985.

Fisher, E. 'Gilgamesh and Genesis: The Flood Story in Context'. *CBQ* 32 (1970) 392–403.

Fisher, L.R. 'From Chaos to Cosmos'. *Enc* 26:2 (1965) 183–197.

——'The Patriarchal Cycles'. *AOAT* 22 (1973) 59–65.

Fokkelman, J.P. Narrative Art in Genesis. Studia Semitica Neerlandica 17; Assen: van Gorcum, 1975.

——'Exodus'. In *The Literary Guide to the Bible*, edited by R. Alter and F. Kermode. . Cambridge, Mass.: Harvard University Press, 1987.

Forrest, R.W.E. 'Paradise Lost Again: Violence and Obedience in the Flood Narrative'. *JSOT* 62 (1994) 3–18.

Francisco, C.T. 'Expository Themes in the Book of Exodus'. *RevExp* 74 (1977) 549–61.

——'The Exodus in its historical setting'. *SwJT* 20 (1977) 7–20.

Fretheim, T.E. 'The Jacob Traditions. Theology and Hermeneutic'. *Int* 26 (1972) 419–436.

Friedman, R.E. 'Tabernacle'. ABD 6:292–300.

——'Torah (Pentateuch)'. ABD 6:605–622.

Frymer-Kensky, T. 'The Atrahasis Epic and its Significance for Our Understanding of Genesis 1–9'. *BA* 40 (1977) 147–155.

Garrett, D.A. *Rethinking Genesis*. Grand Rapids: Baker, 1991.

Gaston, L. 'Abraham and the Righteousness of God'. *HBT* 2 (1980) 39–68.

Geller, S.A. 'The Struggle at the Jabbok: the Uses of Enigma in a Biblical Narrative'. *JANES* 14 (1982) 37–60.

Gevirtz, S. 'Simeon and Levi in "The Blessing of Jacob" (Gen. 49:5–7)'. *HUCA* 52 (1981) 93–128.

——'*heret* in the Manufacture of the Golden Calf'. *Bib* 65 (1984) 377–381.

——'Naphtali in "The Blessing of Jacob" '. *JBL* 103 (1984) 513–521.

Gianotti, C.R. 'The Meaning of the Divine Name YHWH'. *BS* 142 (1985) 38–51.

Gibson, J.C.L. 'Light from Mari on the Patriarchs'. *JSS* 7 (1962) 44–62.

Ginsberg, H.L. 'Abram's "Damascene" Steward'. *BASOR* 200 (1970) 31–32.

Goldberg, M. 'Exodus 1:13–14'. *Int* 37 (1983) 389–391.

Goldingay, J. 'The Patriarchs in Scripture and Tradition'. In *Essays on the Patriarchal Narratives*, edited by A.R. Millard and D.J. Wiseman, pp.11–42. Leicester: IVP, 1980.

Good, E.M. *Irony in the Old Testament*. Philadelphia: Westminster, 1965.

Gooding, D.W. *The Account of the Tabernacle*. Cambridge: Cambridge U.P., 1959.

——*An Unshakeable Kingdom*. Leicester: IVP, 1989.

Gordis, D.H. 'Lies, Wives and Sisters: The Wife-Sister Motif Revisited'. *Judaism* 34 (1985) 344–359.

Gordon, C.H. 'The Patriarchal Narratives'. *JNES* 13 (1954) 217–238.

Gordon, R.P. 'Compositeness, Conflation and the Pentateuch'. *JSOT* 51 (1991) 57–69.

Gowan, D.E. *Eschatology in the Old Testament*. Philadelphia: Fortress, 1986.

Grabbe, L.L. *Leviticus*. OT Guides; Sheffield: JSOT Press, 1993.

Gray, G.B. *Sacrifice in the Old Testament*. Oxford: Clarendon, 1925.

Grayson, A.K. and Van Seters J. 'The Childless Wife in Assyria and the Stories of Genesis'. *Or* 44 (1975) 485–486.

Green, W.H. 'Primeval Chronology'. *BS* 47 (1890) 285–303.

——*The Unity of the Book of Genesis*, New York: Charles Scribner's Sons, 1895.

Greenberg, M. 'The Thematic Unity of Exodus III–XI'. *World Congress of Jewish Studies* 1 (1967) 151–154.

——'The Redaction of the Plague Narrative in Exodus'. In *Near Eastern Studies*, edited by H. Goedick. Baltimore: Johns Hopkins, 1971.

Groningen, G. van 'Interpretation of Genesis'. *JETS* 13 (1970) 199–218.

Gros Louis, K.R.R. 'Abraham: I'. In *Literary Interpretations of Biblical Narratives II*, edited by K.R.R. Gros Louis and J.S. Ackerman, pp.53–70. Nashville: Abingdon, 1982.

——'Abraham: II'. In *Literary Interpretations of Biblical Narratives II*, edited by K.R.R. Gros Louis and J.S. Ackerman, pp.71–84. Nashville: Abingdon, 1982.

Gruber, M.I. 'Was Cain Angry or Depressed? Background of a Biblical Murder'. *BARev* 6 (1980) 34–36.

Guglielmo, A. de. 'The Fertility of the Land in the Messianic Promises'. *CBQ* 19 (1957) 306–311.

Gunkel, H. *The Legends of Genesis*. Chicago: Open Court Publishing, 1901.

Gunn, D.M. 'The Hardening of Pharaoh's Heart Plot: Character and Theology in Exodus 1–14'. In *Art and Meaning: Rhetoric in Biblical Literature*, edited by D.J.A. Clines, D. M. Gunn and A.J. Hauser, pp.72–96. JSOTS 19; Sheffield: JSOT Press, 1982.

——'New Directions in the Study of Biblical Hebrew Narrative'. *JSOT* 39 (1987) 65–75.

——and D.N. Fewell, *Narrative in the Hebrew Bible*. Oxford: OUP, 1993.

Habel, N.C. 'The Gospel Promise to Abraham'. *CTM* 40 (1969) 346–355.

———*Literary Criticism of the Old Testament*. Philadelphia: Fortress Press, 1971.

Hansen, G.W. *Abraham in Galatians*. JSNTSS 29; Sheffield: JSOT, 1989.

Haran, M. 'The Religion of the Patriarchs'. *Annual of the Swedish Theological Institute* 4 (1965) 30–55.

———'Seething a Kid in its Mother's Milk'. *JJS* 30 (1979) 23–35.

———*Temples and Temple-Service in Ancient Israel*. Oxford: Clarendon, 1978.

Harrison, R.K. *Introduction to the Old Testament*. Grand Rapids: Eerdmans, 1969.

Hart, I. 'Preaching on the Account of the Tabernacle'. *EvQ* 54 (1982) 111–116.

Hasel, G.F. 'The Genealogies of Gen 5 and 11 and their Alleged Babylonian Background'. *AUSS* 16 (1978) 361–374.

———'The Meaning of the Animal Rite in Gen. 15'. *JSOT* 19 (1981) 61–78.

Hauser, A.J. 'Linguistic and Thematic Links between Genesis 4:1–16 and Genesis 2–3'. *JETS* 23 (1980) 297–305.

———'The Theme of Intimacy and Alienation'. In *Art and Meaning: Rhetoric in Biblical Literature*, edited by D.J.A. Clines, D. M. Gunn and A.J. Hauser, pp.20–36. JSOTS 19; Sheffield: JSOT Press, 1982.

Helyer, L.R. 'The Separation of Abram and Lot: Its Significance in the Patriarchal Narratives'. *JSOT* 26 (1983) 77–88.

Hendel, R.S. 'Genesis, Book of'. ABD 2:933–941.

Hillers, D.R. *Covenant: The History of a Biblical Idea*. Baltimore: Johns Hopkins, 1969.

Hoffner, H. 'Some Contributions of Hittitology to Old Testament Study'. *TB* 20 (1969) 27–55.

Honeycutt, R.L. Jr. 'Aaron, the Priesthood, and the Golden Calf'. *RevExp* 74 (1977) 523–35.

Hopkins, D.C. 'Between Promise and Fulfillment: Von Rad and the "Sacrifice of Abraham" '. *BZ* 24 (1980) 180–193.

Houston, W. *Purity and Monotheism: Clean and Unclean Animals in Biblical Law*. JSOTS 140; Sheffield: JSOT, 1993.

Houtman, C. 'Exodus 4:24–26 and its Interpretation'. *JNSL* 11 (1983) 81–105.

Hunter, A.G. 'Father Abraham: A Structural and Theological Study of the Yahwist's Presentation of the Abraham Material'. *JSOT* 35 (1986) 3–27.

Hurowitz, V.(A.) 'The Priestly Account of Building the Tabernacle'. *JAOS* 105 (1985) 21–30.

Hurvitz, A. 'The Evidence of Language in Dating the Priestly Code'. *RB* 81 (1974) 24–56.

Isbell, C. 'Exodus 1–2 in the Context of Exodus 1–14: Story Lines and Key Words'. In *Art and Meaning: Rhetoric in Biblical Literature*, edited by D.J.A. Clines, D. M. Gunn and A.J. Hauser, pp.37–61. JSOTS 19; Sheffield: JSOT Press, 1982.

Jacobsen, T. 'The Eridu Genesis'. *JBL* 100 (1981) 513–529.

Janzen, J.G. 'What's in a Name? "Yahweh" in Exodus 3 and the Wider Biblical Context'. *Int* 33 (1979) 227–239.

Jensen, P.P. *Graded Holiness: A Key to the Priestly Conception of the World*. JSOTS 106; Sheffield: JSOT, 1992.

Jobling, D. *The Sense of Biblical Narrative*. JSOTS 7; Sheffield: JSOT, 1978.

Johnson, L.T. 'The use of Leviticus 19 in the Letter of James'. *JBL* 101 (1982) 391–401.

Johnson, M.D. *The Purpose of the Biblical Genealogies with Special Reference to the Setting of the Genealogies of Jesus*. SNTSMS 8; London: CUP, 1969.

Johnston, W. *Exodus*. OT Guides; Sheffield: JSOT Press, 1990.

Kaiser, O. *Introduction to the Old Testament*. Oxford: Blackwells, 1975.

Kaufman, S.A. 'The Structure of the Deuteronomic Law'. *Maarav* 1/2 (1978–79) 105–158.

Kearney, P.J. 'Creation and Liturgy: The P Redaction of Ex 25–40'. *ZAW* 89 (1977) 375–87.

Kessler, M. 'Rhetorical Criticism of Genesis 7'. In *Rhetorical Criticism : Essays in Honor of J. Muilenburg*, edited by J. Jackson and M. Kessler. Pittsburgh: Pickwick, 1974.

Kidner, D. 'Genesis 2:5,6: Wet or Dry?' *TB* 17 (1966) 109–114.

Kiene, P. *The Tabernacle of God in the Wilderness of Sinai*. Grand Rapids: Zondervan, 1977.

Kikawada, I. 'The Shape of Genesis 11:1–9'. In *Rhetorical Criticism: Essays in Honor of James Muilenburg*, edited by J.J. Jackson and M. Kessler. Pittsburgh: Pickwick, 1974.

——'Literary Convention of the Primeval History'. *AJBI* 1 (1975) 3–22.

——'The Unity of Genesis 12:1–9'. In *Proceedings of the Sixth World Congress of Jewish Studies*, edited by A. Shinan, pp.229–235. Jerusalem, 1977.

——'Genesis on Three Levels'. *AJBI* 7 (1981) 3–15.

Kikawada, I.M. and A. Quinn. *Before Abraham Was: The Unity of Genesis 1–11*. Nashville: Abingdon, 1985.

Kilmer, A. 'The Mesopotamian Concept of Overpopulation and Its Solution as Reflected in the Mythology'. *Or* 41 (1972) 160–177.

Kirkland, J.R. 'The Incident at Salem: A Re-examination of Genesis 14:18–20 '. *StudBT* 7 (1977) 3–23.

Kitchen, K.A. *Ancient Orient and Old Testament*. Leicester: IVP, 1967.

——'Exodus, The'. ABD 2: 700–708.

——*The Bible in its World*. Exeter: Paternoster, 1978.

Kiuchi, N. *The Purification Offering in the Priestly Literature: Its Meaning and Function*. JSOTS 56; Sheffield: Sheffield Academic Press, 1987.

Klein, R.W. 'The Yahwist Looks at Abraham'. *CTM* 45 (1974) 43–49.

Kleinig, J.W. 'On Eagle's Wing: An Exegetical Study of Exodus 19:2–8'. *LTJ* 21 (1987) 18–27.

Kline, M.G. *Images of the Spirit*. Grand Rapids: Baker, 1980.

Knierim, R.P. *Text and Concept in Leviticus i,1–9*. Tubingen: J.C.B. Mohr, 1992.

Kodell, J. 'Jacob Wrestles with Esau (Gen 32:23–32)'. *BTB* 10 (1980) 65–70.

Koester, C.R. *The Dwelling of God: The Tabernacle in the Old Testament, Intertestamental Jewish Literature, and the New Testament.* CBQMS 22; Washington: Catholic Biblical Association of America, 1989.

Kselman, J.S. 'The Book of Genesis: A Decade of Scholarly Research'. *Int* 45 (1991) 380–392.

Lambert, W.G. 'A New Look at the Babylonian Background of Genesis'. *JTS* 16 (1965) 287–300.

Larsson, G. 'The Chronology of the Pentateuch: A Comparison of the MT and LXX'. *JBL* 102 (1983) 401–409.

Lawlor, J.I. 'The Test of Abraham: Genesis 22:1–19'. *GTJ* 1 (1980) 19–35.

Lawton, R. 'Irony in Early Exodus'. *ZAW* 97 (1985) 414.

Lehmann, M.R. 'Abraham's Purchase of Machpelah and Hittite Law'. *BASOR* 129 (1953) 15–18.

Lemche, N.P. 'The Chronology in the Story of the Flood'. *JSOT* 18 (1980) 52–62.

Levine, B.A. *In the Presence of the Lord.* Leiden: Brill, 1974.

———'Leviticus, Book of'. *ABD* 4:311–321.

Lewis, J.O. 'The Ark and the Tent'. *RevExp* 74 (1977) 537–48.

Lewis, J.P. *A Study of the Interpretation of Noah and the Flood in Jewish and Christian Literature.* Leiden: Brill, 1968.

Licht, J. *Storytelling in the Bible,* Jerusalem: Magnes, 1978.

Lichtenstein, M. 'Dream-Theophany and the E Document'. *JANESCU* 1/2 (1968–1969) 45–54.

Loewenstamm, S.E. 'The Divine Grants of Land to the Patriarchs'. *JAOS* 91 (1971) 509–510.

Longacre, R.E. 'The Discourse Structure of the Flood Narrative'. *JAAR* 47 (1979) 89–133.

Luke, K. 'Two Birth Narratives in Genesis'. *ITS* 17 (1980) 155–180.

———'The Nations of the World (Gen 10)'. *BibBh* 8 (1982) 61–80.

Lundbom, J.R. 'God's use of the Idem per idem to Terminate Debate'. *HTR* 71 (1978) 193–201.

———'Abraham and David in the Theology of the Yahwist'. In *The Word of the Lord Shall Go Forth: Essays in Honor of David Noel Freedman,* edited by C.L. Meyers and M. O'Connor, pp.203–209. Winona Lake: Eisenbrauns, 1983.

Maars, R. 'The Sons of God (Genesis 6:1–4)'. *ResQ* 23 (1980) 218–224.

Mabee, C. 'Jacob and Laban: The Structure of Judicial Proceedings (Genesis xxxi 25–42)'. *VT* 30 (1980) 192–207.

Magonet, J. 'The Rhetoric of God: Exodus 6. 2–8'. *JSOT* 27 (1983) 56–67.

———'A Response to P. Auffret's 'Literary Structure of Exodus 6. 2–8'. *JSOT* 27 (1983) 73–74.

Maher, M. 'The Transfer of a Birthright: Justifying the Ancestors'. *PIBA* 8 (1984) 1–24.

Malamat, A. 'Tribal Societies: Biblical Genealogies and African Lineage Systems'. *Archives Européennes de Sociologie,* 14 (1973) 126–136.

Maly, E.H. 'Genesis 12,10–20; 20,1–18; 26:7–11 and the Pentateuchal Question'. *CBQ* 18 (1956) 255–262.

Martens, E.A. *Plot and Purpose in the Old Testament*. Leicester: IVP, 1981.

Martin, W.J. ' "Dischronologized" Narrative in the Old Testament'. *SVT* 17 (1969) 179–186.

Maxwell-Mahon, W.D. ' "Jacob's Ladder": a Structural Analysis of Scripture'. *Semitics* 7 (1980) 118–130.

Mayes, A.D.H. 'On Describing the Purpose of Deuteronomy'. *JSOT* 58 (1993) 13–33.

Mazar, B. 'The Historical Background of the Book of Genesis'. *JNES* 28 (1969) 73–83.

McCarthy, D.J. 'Moses's Dealings with Pharaoh'. *CBQ* 27 (1955) 227–348.

——'Three Covenants in Genesis'. *CBQ* 26 (1964) 179–189.

——'Plagues and Sea of Reeds: Exodus 5–11'. *JBL* 85 (1966) 137–158.

——'Exodus 3:14: History, Philology and Theology'. *CBQ* 40 (1978) 311–322.

McComiskey, T.E. *The Covenants of Promise: A Theology of Old Testament Covenants*. Grand Rapids: Baker, 1985.

McConville, J.G. *Law and Theology in Deuteronomy*. JSOTS 33; Sheffield: JSOT, 1984.

——*Grace in the End*. Carlisle: Paternoster, 1994.

McCullough, J.C. 'Melchizedek's Varied Role in Early Exegetical Tradition'. *NETR* 1/2 (1978) 52–66.

McEvenue, S. 'Word and Fulfilment: A Stylistic Feature of the Priestly Writer'. *Semitics* 1 (1970) 104–110.

——*The Narrative Style of the Priestly Writer*. Analecta Biblica 50: Rome: Biblical Institute Press, 1971.

——'A Comparison of Narrative Styles in the Hagar Stories'. *Semeia* 3 (1975) 64–80.

——'The Elohist at Work'. *ZAW* 96 (1984) 315–332.

McGuire, E. 'The Joseph Story: A Tale of Son and Father'. In *Images of Man and God*, edited by B.O. Long, pp.9–25. Sheffield: Almond Press, 1981.

McKane, W. *Studies in the Patriarchal Narratives*, Edinburgh: Handsel, 1979.

McKenzie, B.A. 'Jacob's Blessing on Pharaoh: An Interpretation of Gen 46:31–47:26'. *WTJ* 45 (1983) 386–399.

McKenzie, J.L. 'The Sacrifice of Isaac (Gen 22)'. *Scripture* 9 (1957) 79–83.

McKenzie, S. ' "You Have Prevailed". The Function of Jacob's Encounter at Peniel in the Jacob Cycle'. *ResQ* 23 (1980) 225–231.

McKeown, J. *A Study of the Main Unifying Themes in the Hebrew Text of the Book of Genesis*, unpublished Ph.D. Thesis, The Queen's University of Belfast, 1991.

McKnight, E.V. *The Bible and the Reader: An Introduction to Literary Criticism*. Philadelphia: Fortress, 1985.

Mendenhall, G. 'Covenant Forms in Israelite Tradition'. *BA* 25 (1954) 66–87.

Milgrom, J. *Cult and Conscience: The ASHAM and the Priestly Doctrine of Repentance*. Leiden: Brill, 1976.

——*Studies in Cultic Theology and Terminology*. SJLA 36; Leiden: Brill, 1983.

——'Ethics and Ritual: The Foundations of the Biblical Dietary Laws'. In *Religion and Law: Biblical-judaic and Islamic Perspectives*, edited by E.D. Firmage, B. G. Weiss and J.W. Welch, pp.152–192. Winona Lake: Eisenbrauns, 1990.

——'Numbers, Book of'. ABD 4:1146–1155.

——'Priestly ("P") Source'. ABD 5:454–461.

Millard, A.R. 'The Etymology of Eden'. *VT* 34 (1984) 103–106.

Miller, P.D. *Genesis 1–11. Studies in Structure and Theme*. JSOTS 8; Sheffield: JSOT Press, 1978.

Mirsky, A. 'Stylistic Device for Conclusion in Hebrew'. *Semitics* 5 (1977) 9–23.

Miscall, P.D. 'The Jacob and Joseph Stories as Analogies'. *JSOT* 6 (1978) 28–40.

——'Literary Unity in Old Testament Narrative'. *Semeia* 15 (1979) 27–44.

——*The Workings of Old Testament Narrative*, Philadelphia: Fortress, 1983.

Mitchell, J.J. 'Abram's Understanding of the Lord's Covenant'. WTJ 32 (1969) 24–48.

Moberly, R.W.L. *At the Mountain of God: Story and Theology in Exodus 32–34*. JSOTS 22; Sheffield: JSOT Press, 1983.

——'The Earliest Commentary on the Akedah'. *VT* 38 (1988) 302–323.

——*Genesis 12–50*. OT Guides; Sheffield: JSOT Press, 1992.

Muilenburg, J. 'Abraham and the Nations: Blessing and World History'. *Int* 19 (1965) 387–398.

——'Form Criticism and Beyond'. *JBL* (1969) 1–18.

Myers, J.M. 'The Way of the Fathers'. *Int* 29 (1975) 121–140.

Neff, R.W. 'The Birth and Election of Isaac in the Priestly Tradition'. *BR* 15 (1970) 5–18.

——'The Annunciation of the Birth Narrative of Ishmael'. *BR* 17 (1972) 51–62.

Newman, R.C. 'The Ancient Exegesis of Genesis 6:2,4'. *GTJ* 5 (1984) 13–36.

Nicholson, E.W. *Deuteronomy and Tradition*. Oxford: Blackwell, 1967.

——'The Decalogue as the Direct Address of God'. *VT* 27 (1977) 422–433.

——'The Covenant Ritual in Exodus xxiv 3–8'. *VT* 32 (1982) 74–86.

Nicol, G. 'Genesis xxix.32 and xxxv.22a. Reuben's Reversal'. *JTS* 31 (1980) 536–539.

Noth, M. *A History of Pentateuchal Traditions*, Englewood Cliffs: Prentice-Hall 1972.

O'Callaghan, M. 'The Structure and Meaning of Genesis 38: Judah and Tamar'. *PIBA* 5 (1981) 72–88.

Oden, R.A. 'Transformations in Near Eastern Myths: Genesis 1–11 and the Old Babylonian Epic of Atrahasis'. *Rel* 11 (1981) 21–37.

——'Divine Aspirations in Atrahasis and in Genesis 1–11'. *ZAW* 93 (1981) 197–216.

Olbricht, T.H. 'The Theology of Genesis'. *ResQ* 23 (1980) 201–217.

Olson, D.T. *The Death of the Old and the Birth of the New: The Framework of the Book of Numbers and the Pentateuch*. Chico: Scholars, 1985.

Orlinsky, H.M. 'Enigmatic Bible Passages: The Plain Meaning of Genesis 1:1–3'. *BA* 46 (1983) 207–209.

——'The Plain Meaning of Genesis 1:1–3'. *BA* 46 (1983) 207–209.

Osborn, N.D. 'This is My Name forever: "I Am" or "Yahweh" '. *BT* 39 (1989) 410–15.

Patrick, D. 'The Covenant Code Source'. *VT* 27 (1977) 145–57.

Patte, D. and J.F. Parker 'A Structural Exegesis of Genesis 2 and 3'. *Semeia* 18 (1980) 55–75.

Petersen, D.L. 'A Thrice-told Tale: Genre, Theme and Motif'. *BR* 18 (1973) 30–43.

——'Genesis 6:1–4, Yahweh and the Organization of the Cosmos'. *JSOT* 13 (1979) 47–64.

Phillips, A. 'A Fresh Look at the Sinai Pericope: Part I'. *VT* 34 (1984) 39–52.

——'A Fresh Look at the Sinai Pericope: Part II'. *VT* 34 (1984) 282–94.

——'The Laws of Slavery: Exodus 21:2–11'. *JSOT* 30 (1984) 51–66.

Plastaras, J. *The God of Exodus*. Milwaukee: Bruce Publishing, 1966.

Polzin, R. ' "The Ancestress of Israel in Danger" in Danger'. *Semeia* 3 (1975) 81–97.

——*Moses and the Deuteronomist*, New York: Seabury, 1980.

——'Deuteronomy'. In *The Literary Guide to the Bible*, edited by R. Alter and F. Kermode. Cambridge, Mass.: Harvard University Press, 1987.

Power, W.J.A. 'The Book of Genesis'. *PSTJ* 37 (1984) 1–56.

Prewitt, T.J. 'Kinship Structures and the Genesis Genealogies'. *JNES* 40 (1981) 87–98.

Propp, W.H. 'The Skin of Moses' Face — Transfigured or Disfigured?' *CBQ* 49 (1987) 375–86.

——'Did Moses Have Horns?' *BRev* 4 (1988) 30–37.

Rad, G. von. *Old Testament Theology*. 2 vols. Edinburgh: Oliver & Boyd, 1962–65.

——*The Problem of the Hexateuch and Other Essays*, London: Oliver & Boyd, 1966.

Radday, Y.T. 'Chiasm in Tora'. *LB* 19 (1972) 12–23.

——'Chiasmus in Hebrew Biblical Narrative'. In *Chiasmus in Antiquity*, edited by J.W. Welch, pp.50–117. Hildesheim: Gerstenberg, 1981.

——'Genesis, Wellhausen and the Computer'. *ZAW* 94 (1982) 467–481.

——'The Four Rivers of Paradise'. *HS* 23 (1982) 23–31.

Redford, D.B. *A Study of the Biblical Story of Joseph (Genesis 37–50)*. SVT 20; Leiden: Brill, 1970.

Rendsburg, G.A. *The Redaction of Genesis*. Winona Lake: Eisenbrauns, 1986.

——'The Inclusio in Leviticus-xi: An Examination of a Distinctive Literary Device for Bracketing within Pentateuchal Law and Hebrew Poetry'. *VT* 43 (1993) 418–421.

Rendtorff, R. 'Traditio-Historical Method and the Documentary Hypothesis'. *Proceedings of the World Congress of Jewish Studies* 5 (1969) 5–11.
——'The "Yahwist" as Theologian? The Dilemma of Pentateuchal Criticism'. *JSOT* 3 (1977) 2–10.
——*The Old Testament: An Introduction.* London: SCM, 1986.
——*The Problem of the Process of Transmission in the Pentateuch.* JSOTS 89; Sheffield: JSOT Press, 1990.
Rice, G. 'The Curse that never was (Genesis 9:18–27)'. *JRT* 29 (1972) 5–27.
Riemann, P.A. 'Am I My Brother's Keeper?' *Int* 24 (1970) 482–499.
Robertson, O.P. *The Christ of the Covenants.* Phillipsburg, N.J.: Presbyterian and Reformed, 1980.
Robinson, B.P. 'Israel and Amalek. The Context of Exodus 17.8–16'. *JSOT* 32 (1985) 15–22.
——'Zipporah to the Rescue: A Contextual Study of Exodus iv 24–6'. *VT* (1986) 447–61.
——'Symbolism in Exod. 15:22–27 (Marah and Elim)'. *RB* 94 (1987) 376–88.
——'Acknowledging One's Dependence: the Jethro story of Exodus 18'. *TNB* 69 (1988) 139–42.
Robinson, R.D. 'Literary Functions of the Genealogies of Genesis'. *CBQ* 48 (1986) 595–608.
Rodd, C.S. 'Shall not the Judge of all the Earth do What is Just?' *ExpTim* 83 (1971) 137–139.
Rodriguez, A.M. 'Sanctuary Theology in the Book of Exodus'. *AUSS* 24 (1986) 127–45.
Rogers, C.L. 'The Covenant with Abraham and its Historical Setting'. *BS* 127 (1970) 241–256.
Rogerson, *Genesis 1–11.* OT Guides: Sheffield: JSOT Press, 1991.
Ross A.P. 'The Table of Nations in Genesis 10 — Its Structure'. *BS* 137 (1980) 340–353.
Ryken, L. 'Literary Criticism of the Bible'. In *Literary Interpretations of Biblical Narratives*, edited by K.R.R. Gros Louis, J.S. Ackerman and T.S. Warshaw, pp.24–40. Nashville: Abingdon, 1974.
Sailhamer, J. 'Exegetical Notes: Genesis 1:1–2:4a'. *TJ* 5 (1984) 73–82.
——*The Pentateuch as Narrative: a Biblical-theological commentary.* Grand Rapids: Zondervan, 1992.
Sarna, N.M. 'Abraham in History'. *BARev* 3 (1977) 5–9.
——'Genesis Chapter 23: The Cave of Machpelah'. *HS* 23 (1982) 17–21.
Sasson, J.M. 'A Genealogical "Convention" in Biblical Chronography'. *ZAW* 90 (1978) 171–185.
——'The "Tower of Babel" as a Clue to the Redactional Structuring of the Primeval History (Gen. 1–11:9)'. In *The Bible World. Essays in Honor of Cyrus H. Gordon*, edited by G. Rendsburg, R. Adler, M. Arfa and N.H. Winter, pp.211–219. New York: Ktav, 1980.
Savage, M. 'Literary Criticism and Biblical Studies: A Rhetorical Analysis of the Joseph Narrative'. In *Scripture in Context. Essays on*

the Comparative Method, edited by C.D Evans, W.W. Hallo and J.B. White, pp.78–100. Pittsburg: Pickwick, 1980.

Schierling, M.J. 'Primeval Woman: A Yahwistic View of Woman in Genesis 1–11:9'. *JTSoA* 42 (1983) 5–9.

Scullion, J.J. 'New Thinking in Creation and Sin in Genesis 1–11'. *ABR* 22 (1974) 1–10.

——'Genesis, the Narrative of'. ABD 2:941–962.

Seebass, H. 'The Joseph Story, Genesis 48 and the Canonical Process'. *JSOT* 35 (1986) 29–53.

Segal, J.B. *The Hebrew Passover*. London: OUP, 1963.

Segal, M.H. 'The Composition of the Pentateuch; A Fresh Examination'. *Scripta Hierosolymitana*, 8 (1961) 68–114.

——*The Pentateuch*, Jerusalem: Magnes, 1967.

Seybold, D.A. 'Paradox and Symmetry in the Joseph Story'. In *Literary Interpretations of Biblical Narratives*, edited by K.R.R. Gros Louis, J.S. Ackerman and T.S. Warshaw, pp.74–119. Nashville: Abingdon, 1974.

Skaist, A. 'The Authority of the Brother at Arrapha and Nuzi'. *JAOS* 89 (1969) 10–17.

Smith, F.G. 'Observations on the Use of the Names and Titles of God in Genesis and the Bearing of Exodus 6:3 on the Same'. *EvQ* 40 (1968) 103–109.

Smith, G.V. 'Structure and Purpose in Genesis 1–11'. *JETS* 20 (1977) 307–319.

Snijders, L.A. 'Genesis XV: The Covenant with Abraham'. *OTS* 12 (1958) 161–279.

Soggin, J.A. *Introduction to the Old Testament*. Philadelphia: Westminster, 1976.

Soler, J. 'The Semiotics of Food in the Bible'. In *Food and Drink in History*, edited by R. Forster and O. Ranum, pp.126–138. Baltimore: Johns Hopkins University, 1979.

Soltau, H.W. *The Holy Vessels and Furniture of the Tabernacle of Israel*. Grand Rapids: Kregel, 1969; first published 1865.

Speiser, E.A. ' "People" and "Nation" of Israel'. *JBL* 79 (1960) 157–163.

Spencer, M. 'Redemption in Exodus'. *Emmanuel* 90 (1984) 496–503.

Sprinkle, J.M. *'The Book of the Covenant': A Literary Approach*. JSOTS 174; Sheffield: JSOT, 1994.

Sternberg, M. *The Poetics of Biblical Narrative*. Indiana: Indiana University Press, 1985.

Stieglitz, R.R. 'Ancient Records and the Exodus Plagues'. *BARev* 13 (1987) 46–49.

Stitzinger, M.F. 'Genesis 1–3 and the Male/Female Role Relationship'. *GTJ* 2 (1981) 23–44.

Stock, A. *A Way in the Wilderness*. Collegeville: Liturgical Press, 1969.

Stordalen, T. 'Man, Soil, Garden: Basic Plot in Genesis 2–3 Reconsidered'. *JSOT* 53 (1992) 3–26.

Surburg, R.F. 'Wellhausenism Evaluated After a Century of Influence'. *CTQ* 43 (1979) 78–95.

Sutherland, D. 'The Organization of the Abraham Promise Narratives'. *ZAW* 95 (1983) 337–343.

Talmon, S. 'The Presentation of Synchroneity and Simultaneity in Biblical Narrative'. *Scripta Hierosolymitana*, 27 (1978) 9–26.

Tate, M.E. 'The Legal Traditions of the Book of Exodus'. *RevExp* 74 (1977) 483–509.

Terrien, S.L. *The Elusive Presence: Towards a New Biblical Theology*. San Francisco: Harper and Row, 1978.

Thompson, R.J. *Moses and the Law in a Century of Criticism since Graf*. SVT 19; Leiden: Brill, 1970.

Thompson, T.L. *The Historicity of the Patriarchal Narratives*. BZAW 133; Berlin: de Gruyter, 1974.

——'A New Attempt to Date the Patriarchal Narratives'. *JAOS* 98 (1978) 76–84.

——'Conflict Themes in the Jacob Narratives'. *Semeia* 15 (1979) 5–26.

——*The Origin Tradition of Ancient Israel: I. The Literary Formation of Genesis and Exodus 1–23*, JSOTS 55; Sheffield: JSOT, 1987.

Tsevat, M. 'Hagar and the Birth of Ishmael. *The Meaning of the Book of Job and Other Biblical Studies*, pp.53–76. New York: Ktav,1980.

Turner, L.A. *Announcement of Plot in Genesis*. JSOTS 133; Sheffield: JSOT, 1990.

Van Groningen, G. *Messianic Revelation in the Old Testament*. Grand Rapids: Baker, 1990.

Van Seters, J. *Abraham in History and Tradition*. New Haven: Yale University Press, 1975.

——'The Plagues of Egypt: Ancient Tradition or Literary Invention?' *ZAW* 98 (1986) 31–39.

——*Prologue to History: The Yahwist as Historian in Genesis*. Louisville: Westminster/John Knox, 1992.

Vater, A.M. 'A Plague on Both our Houses: Form and Rhetorical-Critical Observations on Exodus 7–11'. In *Art and Meaning: Rhetoric in Biblical Literature*, edited by D.J.A. Clines, D. M. Gunn and A.J. Hauser, pp.62–71. JSOTS 19; Sheffield: JSOT Press, 1982.

Vaux, R. de. *Ancient Israel: its Life and Institutions*. New York: McGraw-Hill, 1961.

——*Studies in Old Testament Sacrifice*. Cardiff: University of Wales Press, 1964.

Vervenne, M. 'The Protest Motif in the Sea Narrative (Ex 14,11–12): Form and Structure of a Pentateuchal Pattern'. *ETL* 63 (1987) 257–71.

Vogels, W. 'Lot in his Honor Restored: A Structural Analysis of Gen 13: 2–18'. *EgT* 10 (1979) 5–12.

Wagner, N.E. 'Abraham and David?' In *Studies on the Ancient Palestinian World*, edited by J.W. Wevers and D.B. Redford, pp.117–140. Toronto: University of Toronto Press, 1972.

Wallace, H.M. *The Eden Narrative*. HSM 32; Atlanta: Scholars, 1985.

Walsh, J.T. 'Genesis 2:4b–3:24: A Synchronic Approach'. *JBL* 96 (1977) 161–177.

Waltke, B.K. 'The Creation Account in Genesis 1,1–3'. *BS* 132 (1975) 25–36, 136–144, 216–228, 327–342.

Walton, J. 'The Antediluvian Section of the Sumerian King List and Genesis 5'. *BA* 44 (1981) 207–208.

Warner, S.M. 'Primitive Saga Men'. *VT* 29 (1979) 325–335.

Wcela, E.A. 'The Abraham Stories: History and Faith'. *BTB* 10 (1980) 176–181.

Weinfeld, M. 'The Covenant of Grant in the Old Testament and in the Ancient Near East'. *JAOS*, 90 (1970) 184–203.

——*Deuteronomy and the Deuteronomic School*. Oxford: Clarendon, 1972.

——'Deuteronomy, Book of'. ABD 2:168–183.

Weisman, Z. 'National Consciousness in the Patriarchal Promise'. *JSOT* 31 (1985) 55–73.

Wellhausen, J. *Prolegomena to the History of Israel*, Edinburgh: Adam & Charles Black, 1885.

Wenham, G.J. 'The Coherence of the Flood Narrative'. *VT* 28 (1978) 336–348.

——'The Religion of the Patriarchs'. In *Essays on the Patriarchal Narratives*, edited by A.R. Millard and D.J. Wiseman, pp.157–188. Leicester: IVP, 1980.

——'The Theology of Unclean Food'. *EvQ* 53 (1981) 6–15.

——'The Symbolism of the Animal Rite in Genesis 15: A Response to G.F. Hasel *JSOT* 19 (1981) 61–78'. *JSOT* 22 (1982) 134–137.

——'The Date of Deuteronomy: Linchpin of Old Testament Criticism'. *Them* 10 (1985) 15–20; 11 (1985) 15–18.

——'Sanctuary Symbolism in the Garden of Eden Story'. *Proceedings of the World Congress of Jewish Studies* 9 (1986) 19–25.

——'Genesis: An Authorship Study and Current Pentateuclal Criticism'. *JSOT* 42 (1988) 3–18.

Westbrook, R. 'Purchase of the Cave of Machpelah'. *Israel Law Review* 6 (1971) 29–38.

——'Lex talionis and Exodus 21,22–25'. *RB* 93 (1986) 52–69.

Westermann, C. *Blessing in the Bible and in the Life of the Church*. Philadelphia: Fortress, 1978.

——*The Promises to the Fathers*, Philadelphia: Fortress, 1980.

White, H.C. 'The Initiation Legend of Isaac'. *ZAW* 91 (1979) 1–30.

——'Direct and Third Person Discourse in the Narrative of the "Fall" '. *Semeia* 18 (1980) 92–106.

——'The Joseph Story: A Narrative Which "Consumes" Its Content'. *Semeia* 31 (1985) 49–69.

——*Narration and Discourse in the Book of Genesis*. Cambridge: CUP, 1991.

Whybray, R.N. 'The Joseph Story and Pentateuchal Criticism'. *VT* 18 (1968) 522–528.

——*The Making of the Pentateuch: A Methodological Study*. JSOTS 53; Sheffield: JSOT, 1987.

Wicke, D.W. 'The Literary Structure of Exodus 1:2–2:10'. *JSOT* 24 (1982) 99–107.

Wifall, W. 'Gen 3:15 — A Protevangelium?' *CBQ* 36 (1974) 361–365.

Wildavsky, A. 'Survival Must not be Gained through Sin: The Moral of the Joseph Stories Prefigured through Judah and Tamar'. *JSOT* 62 (1994) 37–48.

Williams, J.G. 'The Beautiful and the Barren: Conventions in Biblical Type-scenes'. *JSOT* 17 (1980) 107–119.

——'The Comedy of Jacob: A Literary Study'. *JAAR* 46 (1978) 208.

——'Genesis 3'. *Int* 35 (1981) 274–279.

Williams, J.G. *Women Recounted: Narrative Thinking and the God of Israel*. Bible and Literature Series 6; Sheffield: Almond, 1982.

Willis, J.T. 'Some Recent Studies on Genesis and the Literary-Historical Approach'. *ResQ* 23 (1980) 193–200.

Wilson, R.R. 'The Old Testament Genealogies in Recent Research'. *JBL* 94 (1975) 169–189.

——*Genealogy and History in the Biblical World*, New Haven: Yale University Press, 1977.

Winnett, F.V. *The Mosaic Tradition*, Toronto: Toronto University Press, 1949.

Wiseman, D.J. 'Abraham in History and Tradition. Part I. Abraham the Hebrew'. *BS* 134 (1977) 123–130.

Wittenberg, G. 'The Tenth Commandment in the Old Testament'. *JTSoA* 21 (1978) 3–17.

Wolff, H.W. 'The Kerygma of the Yahwist'. *Int* 20 (1966) 131–158.

Woudstra, M.H. 'The Toledot of the Book of Genesis and Their Redemptive-historical Significance'. *CTJ* 5 (1970) 184–189.

——'The Story of the Garden of Eden in Recent Study'. *VR* 34 (1980) 22–31.

Wright, D.P. *The Disposal of Impurity: Elimination Rites in the Bible and in Hittite and Mesopotamian Literature*. SBLDS 101; Atlanta: Scholars, 1987.

——'Observations on the Ethical Foundations of the Biblical Dietary Laws'. In *Religion and Law: Biblical-judaic and Islamic Perspectives*, edited by E.D. Firmage, B. G. Weiss and J.W. Welch, pp.193–198. Winona Lake: Eisenbrauns, 1990.

——'Day of Atonement'. ABD 2:72–76.

——'Holiness (OT)'. ABD 3:237–249.

——'Unclean and Clean (OT)'. ABD 6:729–741.

Wright, G.E. 'Israel in the Promised Land: History Interpreted by a Covenant Faith'. *Encounter* 35 (1974) 318–334.

Wyatt, N. 'Interpreting the Creation and Fall Story in Genesis 2–3'. *ZAW* 93 (1981) 10–21.

——'The Significance of the Burning Bush'. *VT* 36 (1986) 361–365.

Yarchin, W. 'Imperative and Promise in Genesis 12:1–3'. *StudBT* 10 (1980) 164–178.

Young, E.J. *An Introduction to the Old Testament*. Grand Rapids: Eerdmans, 1949.

Index of Biblical Texts

(References are to the English Bible)

T. Desmond Alexander is lecturer in Semitic studies at The Queen's University in Belfast, Northern Ireland. He has published articles in several scholarly journals, including *Journal of Biblical Literature, Journal for the Study of the Old Testament,* and *Vetus Testamentum.* He is the author of *Abraham in the Negev: A Source-Critical Investigation of Genesis 20:1–22:19* and the commentary on Jonah in the Tyndale Old Testament Commentary.